D0224156

193.5   Rose
H462G   Hegel Contra sociology
R796h

CHRISTIAN HERITAGE COLLEGE
2100 Greenfield Dr.
El Cajon, CA   92021

193.5
H 462G
R796h

HEGEL CONTRA SOCIOLOGY

Gillian Rose

ATHLONE · LONDON
HUMANITIES PRESS · NEW JERSEY

65111

First published in Great Britain, 1981 by The Athlone Press Ltd
90–91 Great Russell Street, London WC1B 3PY
and by Humanities Press Inc. in the USA

© Gillian Rose 1981

British Library Cataloguing in Publication Data
Rose, Gillian
Hegel contra sociology.
1. Hegel, Georg Wilhelm Friedrich
—Sociology
2. Sociology
I. Title
301′.092′4   B2949S6
UK SBN 0 485 11214 0 Cased
UK SBN 0 485 12036 4 Paperback
USA SBN 0 391 02289 –X Cased
USA SBN 0 391 02288 –1 Paperback

All rights reserved. No part of this publication may
be reproduced, stored in a retrieval system, or transmitted
in any form or by any means, electronic, mechanical,
photocopying or otherwise, without prior
permission in writing from the publisher.

Set in Monotype Bembo by
Gloucester Typesetting Co Ltd
Gloucester
Printed in Great Britain by
The University Press, Cambridge

For the Intriguer

CONTENTS

1 The Antinomies of Sociological Reason   1

Introduction, 1; Validity and Values, 2; Morality and Method, 13; The New Ontologies, 21; Neo-Kantian Marxism, 24; Canon and Organon, 39

2 Politics in the Severe Style   48

Politics in the Severe Style, 48; Absolute and Relative Ethical Life, 51; The System of Ethical Life, 59; Recognition and Misrecognition, 72; The Rational and the Real, 79

3 The Philosophy of History   92

Faith and Knowledge, 92; The Untrue as Subject, 102; Spirit at War with itself, 105; The End of Religion, 112

4 The Division of Labour and Illusion   121

The End of Art, 121; Beauty and Illusion, 123; The Classical Form of Art: Tragedy and the State, 131; The Romantic Form of Art: Poetry and Prose as Social Categories, 135; The Symbolic Form of Art: The Severe Style and the Modern, 142

5 Work and Representation   149

Self-Perficient Scepticism, 149; The Causality of Fate, 154; The Grave of Life, 159; The Barbarism of Pure Culture, 163; The End of Ethical Life, 174; The Law and the *Logic*, 181

6 Rewriting the Logic   185

Beyond the Bounds of Morality, 185; Illusion and Actuality, 192; The Unity of Theoretical and Practical Reason, 196; The Victory of Reflection, 201

7 With What Must the Science End?   204

The End of Philosophy, 204; The Repetition of Sociology, 211; The Culture and Fate of Marxism, 214

Notes   221

Select Bibliography   249

Index   259

I

The Antinomies
of Sociological Reason

Introduction

This essay is an attempt to retrieve Hegelian speculative experience for
social theory, not by means of any ingenuous and ahistorical 'return to
Hegel', but, first of all, by recognizing and discussing the intellectual
and historical barriers which stand in the way of any such rereading.

The classical origins of sociology are usually presented in terms of
two competing paradigms associated with the writings of Durkheim
and Weber and with a host of well-known dichotomies: *Erklären/
Verstehen*, holism/individualism, naturalism/anti-naturalism. Yet, the
thought of Durkheim and Weber, in spite of the divergences, rests on
an identical framework: 'the neo-Kantian paradigm.'[1]

The transcendental structure of Durkheim's and of Weber's thought
has been persistently overlooked, and this has resulted in fundamental
misunderstanding of the nature of their sociologies. The common criticisms that Durkheim's most ambitious explanations are tautological,
and that Weber's hypothesis of a rational ethic to explain rational capitalism is circular, miss the point that a transcendental account necessarily presupposes the actuality or existence of its object and seeks to
discover the conditions of its possibility. The neo-Kantian paradigm is
the source of both the strengths and weaknesses of Durkheim's and of
Weber's sociology.

Many of the subsequent radical challenges to the sociology of Durkheim and Weber were motivated by the desire to break out of the con-
strictions of the neo-Kantian paradigm. Phenomenology and the
Marxism of the Frankfurt School, for example, must be assessed in this
light. Nevertheless, I shall argue, they remain essentially within that
paradigm. More recent discussions of the significance of Marx for
social theory have also been dominated by neo-Kantian assumptions.

The very idea of a scientific sociology, whether non-Marxist or

Marxist, is only possible as a form of neo-Kantianism. This neo-Kantianism bars access to the philosophy of Hegel, and, consequently, inhibits discussion of Marxism from the standpoint of its philosophical foundations. Yet, as I shall show, Hegel's thought anticipates and criticizes the whole neo-Kantian endeavour, its methodologism and its moralism, and consists of a wholly different mode of social analysis.

Validity and Values

The 'return to Kant' which started in the second half of the nineteenth century took many different forms.[2] Among them were the critical realism of Alois Riehl (1844–1924), the metaphysical interpretations of Otto Liebmann (1840–1912) and Johannes Volkelt (1848–1930), and the neo-Friesianism[3] of Leonard Nelson (1882–1927).

The two most original developments were the logical idealism of the Marburg School, founded by Hermann Cohen (1842–1918) and Paul Natorp (1854–1924), and the logical value theory of the Heidelberg School founded by Wilhelm Windelband (1848–1915) and Heinrich Rickert (1863–1936). The Heidelberg School is also known as the Baden or South-West German School.

To call all these thinkers 'neo-Kantians' is, at best, vague, and in the case of the Marburg and of the Heidelberg School most inaccurate, because they reject Kantian critical philosophy in fundamental respects. They read the *Critique of Pure Reason* in the terms of the *Prolegomena* and transform the transcendental deduction into an exposition of objective validity. In the following paragraphs I rehearse this reading.

Kant made a rigorous distinction between the *quaestio quid facti*, the question of fact, and the *quaestio quid juris*, the question of right, that is, between the manner in which a concept is acquired through experience, and the deduction of its legal title, the manner in which concepts relate *a priori* to objects.[4] This justification of the employment of concepts would demonstrate their 'objective validity' (*objektive Gültigkeit*).[5]

Objective validity is established for what can be presented to us as an object within the limits of the constitution of our sensibility, and the functions of our understanding (*Verstand*). Objective validity is restricted to the condition of the possibility of objects of experience, of appearances, and to the conditions of all knowledge of objects.[6] The task of justification is to show how 'the subjective conditions of thought'[7] and of our sensibility possess objective validity and not merely subjective validity, and thus how experience in general is brought into existence.[8]

The exposition concerns the transcendental conditions of knowledge, that is, of the *a priori* rules which 'make possible empirical knowledge in general'. These are general rules for the synthesis of perceptions into objects of experience.[9] It is these rules, or pure, synthetic judgements which relate to the possibility of experience, and upon this alone is founded the objective validity of their synthesis.[10]

Transcendental rules thus have an empirical employment. A merely subjective perception or representation becomes experience when it is subsumed under a concept which connects the empirical consciousness of the representation within a consciousness in general (*Bewusstsein überhaupt*), and thereby provides the empirical judgement with objective validity.[11] The perception is subsumed under a concept of the understanding, and can then form part of a judgement of experience.

For example, to say 'when the sun shines, the stone is warm', is a judgement of perception. It merely conjoins the two perceptions, however often they have been perceived. 'But if I say the sun *warms* the stone the concept of cause proper to the understanding is added to the perception, and connects the concept of warmth with the concept of sunshine. The synthetic judgement becomes necessarily universally valid, consequently objective, and is converted from a perception into an experience.'[12]

The *a priori* rule for experience in general is employed empirically in relation to particular perceptions. It is an *immanent* principle whose application is confined entirely within the limits of possible experience.[13] However, a transcendental principle may be misemployed: that is, employed in a way which extends beyond the limits of experience. This is merely an erroneous use of the understanding. It is essentially different from a *transcendent* principle. A transcendent principle is not an error of judgement, the wrong use of the right principle, but an exhortation to tear down the boundaries of experience and to seize possession of an entirely new domain which recognizes no limits of demarcation.[14]

It follows from a transcendental account of experience that certain necessary features of the explanation are themselves transcendent and hence unknowable. The unity of consciousness in general which the object makes necessary is the formal unity of consciousness in the synthesis of the manifold of representation.[15] This pure, original, unchangeable consciousness of the identity of the self, 'the transcendental unity of apperception', is at the same time a consciousness of the synthesis of appearances according to rules.[16] It is distinguished from empirical consciousness which is in itself diverse and without relation to the identity of the subject, and which therefore has only subjective validity.[17] The self as transcendental unity is distinguished from the self as intuited object, and can only know itself as it appears to itself and not as it is in itself.[18] Hence pure consciousness, the source of objective validity, is unknowable.

Knowledge is the synthesis of the manifold of perception into appearances. These appearances do not exist in themselves, but only relative to the subject in which they inhere. Appearances are not things-in-themselves, but depend on our constituting them. Yet they are also 'representations of things which are *unknown* as regards what they may be in themselves'.[19]

In spite of Kant's separation of objective and subjective validity, of the question of right from the question of fact, of an empirical from a transcendental account, the critical philosophy lends itself to a psychological reading. For a transcendental account may transform the logical question of validity into the epistemological question of how we may rightly acquire knowledge. Objective validity is established by dividing the mind into faculties, and by reference to perception and representation. According to this reading, the whole project for a transcendental logic reduces validity to the synthesis of representations, to the description of processes of consciousness.

Furthermore, a transcendental account reduces knowledge to 'experience', to the synthesis of appearances. It makes the conditions of the *possibility* of experience in general likewise the conditions of the possibility of the objects of experience.[20] Objective validity pertains to the synthesis of experience, but not to any knowledge of things-in-themselves. If the idea that the mind synthesizes the objects of knowledge is accepted, then it can be argued that it makes no sense to retain 'reality' for something beyond our knowledge. The production of objects may equally well be said to be the production of their reality, not of their appearance. According to this criticism the hypothesis of things-in-themselves is otiose.

Alternatively, the restriction of legitimate empirical knowledge may be accepted, but it may be denied that this is the only kind of know-ledge possible to us. There may be other kinds of knowledge, theoretical and practical, which open up realms which are transcendent in strictly Kantian terms.

These criticisms accept the idea of a transcendental enquiry, but reject some of the conclusions which Kant drew. Other criticisms argue that the notion of the thing-in-itself is contradictory. For if the thing-in-itself is unknowable, how can it be called a 'thing'? If it is unknowable, how can its relation to appearances, which are knowable, be specified? The relation cannot be *causal*, because we could then subsume it under the concept of cause, a category of the understanding, and it would be knowable.

Thus, on the one hand, it may be argued that logical validity has nothing to do with epistemology, with questions of cognition. On the other hand, it may be argued that cognition cannot be restricted to experience, nor does it consist of the synthesis of appearances.

There have been four major generations of critics of Kant. The first generation, 1780–1790, consisted notably of K. L. Reinhold (1758–1823), S. Maimon (1753–1800) and F. H. Jacobi (1743–1819). Their disputes were concentrated on the status of the thing-in-itself.[21] The second generation, Fichte, Schelling, Hölderlin, the early Romantics and Hegel, tried to resolve these Kantian aporias by giving primacy to Kant's practical philosophy or to the *Critique of Judgement*. The third generation, in the period after Hegel's death, 1830–1870, included Bernard Bolzano (1781–1848) and Rudolf Hermann Lotze (1817–1881). They supplemented Kant's critical philosophy with Liebnizian and Platonic metaphysics. The fourth generation after 1870, known as 'the neo-Kantians', opposed the psychologism of their day which culminated in Wilhelm Wundt's (1832–1920) psychological reading of Kant. They sought to develop a non-transcendental, non-formal logic as the basis for the exact and historical sciences.[22]

This fourth generation of Kant critics flourished in the period prior to the First World War. They took their transformation of Kant's critical philosophy in crucial respects from the third generation, read it back into the *Critique of Pure Reason*, and made it serve new ends. It is this position from which the idea of a scientific sociology arose.

Who now reads Lotze? It is difficult for us to realize how great a stir he made in the world . . .[23] While Lotze is now unknown, I shall argue that his way of thinking is by no means dead. In the 1870s in England

and in America Lotze was considered to be as great a German philosopher as Kant and Hegel. His main works were translated into English; they appeared on university syllabuses, and attracted the interest and comment of major philosophers on both sides of the Atlantic: Josiah Royce and George Santayana, T. H. Green and Bernard Bosanquet.[24]

In Germany Lotze's notions of 'validity' and 'values' became the foundation of the Marburg and Heidelberg schools of neo-Kantianism and of their sociological offspring. The 'neo-Kantian paradigm' refers to those who attempted a new answer to the Kantian question of validity within the framework of validity and values first developed by Lotze. Within this framework the question of validity may be given priority over the question of values, or, the question of values may be given priority over the question of validity. Hence reconsideration of Lotze is essential for comprehending the transition from Kantian epistemology to neo-Kantian sociology.

The division of Lotze's major work, *Logic*, into three parts, the first entitled 'Of Thought (Pure Logic)' and the third entitled 'On Knowledge (Methodology)', indicates his strict separation of the logical question of validity from the epistemological question of cognition, the way knowledge is acquired on the basis of perception and representation.[25] Kant's *quaestio quid juris*, the deduction of objective validity, refers to the *a priori* preconditions of possible experience. But, for Lotze, the validity of the *a priori* elements of thought is established independently of any reference to possible experience, to representation, to the being either of appearances or of things-in-themselves. Only if validity can be established independently of cognition can the process of cognition itself be critically assessed. Both Kant's (*objektive*) *Gültigkeit* and Lotze's *Geltung* are translated into English as 'validity', but they do not have the same meaning.

'Validity' for Lotze, in opposition to Kant, pertains to propositions not to concepts.[26] Propositions can be affirmed or denied regardless of whether we are in a position actually to perceive or experience the objects to which the contents of those propositions refer. Hence a proposition which we affirm or deny has a reality which is different from the reality of events which 'occur', or of things which 'exist' or 'are'. The reality of a proposition means that it holds or is valid, and that its opposite does not hold. For example, the proposition '*x ist* [is]' is contrasted with the proposition '*x gilt* [holds or is valid]'.[27]

This kind of reality, the validity of truths, is quite distinct from the question of whether their contents can be related to any object in the external, spatio-temporal world:[28]

> This conception of validity . . . at once excludes the substance of the valid assertion from the reality of the actual being and implies its independence of human thought. As little as we can say how it happens that anything *is* or *occurs*, so little can we explain how it comes about that a truth has validity; the latter conception has to be regarded as much as the former as ultimate and underivable, a conception of which everyone may know what he means by it, but which cannot be constructed out of any constituent elements which do not already contain it.[29]

In addition to this twofold distinction between the reality of necessarily valid truths which belong to thinking, and the reality of given facts which belongs to perception and cognition, there is a third reality: the reality of determination of value.[30]

Perception of things is always accompanied by feelings of value: 'we clothe the world of values in the world of forms [nature]', although the connection between the two is not knowable, and can only be based on conviction.[31] Our way of attributing value and meaning depends on judgements which do not conform to the principles of scientific understanding (*Verstand*), but are based on a 'reason receptive to values' (*Wertempfindende Vernunft*). Reason endows values with validity by recognizing the inner value of contents in a way which cannot be justified according to the criteria of disinterested understanding.[32] We have an unshakeable faith in the validity of this value-determining reason, which is as 'genuine a revelation' as the investigations of the understanding are an instrument of experience.[33] Value-determining reason has its meaning and goal in ethical action, and thus, to a certain extent, determines the operations of the understanding.[34]

This distinction between moral or value-determining reason (*Vernunft*) and a faculty of perception and cognition (*Verstand*) is close to Kant's distinction between the legitimate role of the ideas of reason in moral philosophy, and the restriction of cognition to empirical reality in theoretical philosophy. But Lotze's distinction between validity, which he compares to Plato's Ideas, and empirical cognition is contrary to the meaning of Kant's theory which specifically denies any legitimate employment to Plato's Ideas in theoretical philosophy.[35]

In spite of the coincidence between Lotze and Kant on the relation of

Verstand and *Vernunft* in moral philosophy, Lotze's reformulation and terminology is responsible for the way in which moral philosophy became known as philosophy of value (*Wertphilosophie*), and for the emphasis on the undeniable and immediate validity of moral values.[36]

Lotze's acceptance of Kant's faculties of the mind and their restricted legitimate employment is only one aspect of a philosophical system which culminates in the personality of God, the source of validity and values, and in whose personality our own participates. God's existence cannot be proved in any logical way: it is the highest value of which we are conscious and has an immediate certainty and validity.[37]

However, it is Lotze's threefold distinction between validity, cognition of empirical reality and values which has been of importance, not the Leibnizian metaphysics which complements them.

> All our analysis of the course of the world ends in leading our thought back to a consciousness of necessarily valid truths, our perceptions to the intuition of immediately given facts of reality, our conscience to the recognition of an absolute standard of all determinations of value.[38]

In this passage 'reality' (*Wirklichkeit*) is reserved for empirical cognition, whereas in the *Logic* different kinds of reality are distinguished, such as empirical reality and the reality of validity. In this passage, too, 'validity' is reserved for 'truths', but, in the *Microcosmos* generally, values also have 'ultimate' and undeniable validity. For Lotze the reality of validity and the reality of values were ultimate, undeniable and *separate* spheres of life.

On the basis of Lotze's thought, critical, transcendental philosophy became transformed into the neo-Kantian paradigm of *Geltung* and *Werte*, validity and values. The three Kantian critical questions 'What makes judgements of experience, of morality, of beauty objectively valid?' become the questions 'What is the nature of validity in general?' and 'What is the relation between validity and its objects?' Logic is separated from cognition, validity from representation, but not from its objects. The result is a general but not a formal logic: a methodology.

A transcendental logic enquires into the conditions of the possibility of experience which is actual. A general logic enquires into how an object can and should exist or be created. Both kinds of enquiries depend on the formulation of demarcation criteria which distinguish correct from incorrect use of rules. The transcendental approach does not claim to be the *origin* of the existence of the experience whose pre-condition or possibility is uncovered. The general logic, however, is prescriptive and normative not merely in relation to rules of validity, but also in relation to the creation of the object which corresponds to those rules. The creation of this object, its objectification, becomes a 'never-ending task' for the Marburg School, a prescription (*Sollen*) for the Heidelberg School. This objectification is not the objectification of reality in general, but the objectification of the object domains of individual sciences.

Lotze's emphasis on the reality of validity in contra-distinction to the reality of empirical existence resulted in the debasement of spatio-temporal reality, and in the development of philosophies of identity: identity between pure logic and its objectifications. Lotze's distinction between validity and values proved ambiguous. On one construal, 'validity' and 'values' are equally ultimate and underivable; on another construal, 'values' or meaning are the primary bearers of validity. In this case 'values' become the origin of logical validity as well as of the moral law. In Kant and Lotze ultimate and autonomous value was the determinant of moral life, but not of theoretical validity. In the works of the Heidelberg School empirical reality or existence is subordinate to this transcendent realm of value.

The Marburg School gave the question of validity priority over the question of values; the Heidelberg School gave the question of values priority over the question of validity. But in both cases the transforma-tion of Kant's critical method into a logic of validity (*Geltungslogik*), a general method, excluded any enquiry into empirical reality. Objecti-fication became the correlate of pure logic.

Lotze's demarcation of validity set it apart from any relation either to processes of consciousness or to consciousness in general (*Bewusstsein überhaupt*). Validity was separate even from transcendental genesis, but the price of this critique of the philosophy of consciousness, of transcen-dental psychology and epistemology, was the later development of philosophies of identity. Lotze kept the examination of perception and cognition strictly separate from the logic of thinking. But, in subse-quent versions of logic of validity (*Geltungslogik*), thought, with its ultimate and underivable validity, becomes the thinking of being, or, validity emanates from a transcendent sphere of value which is both the criterion and object of knowledge.

Like Lotze, the Marburg School argued that there is a basis in Kant for a 'pure logic' (Cohen), or a 'general logic' (Natorp). This means a logic of thought which is independent of the process of cognition.[39] Since Kant's theoretical philosophy was directed against both the idea of general logic and the idea of a 'pure' reason, the Marburg notion of a pure logic heralds the end of transcendental logic.[40]

Cohen and Natorp reinterpreted Kant's transcendental *a priori* judgements as ontological principles without the reference to their necessarily empirical employment which alone guaranteed their 'objective validity' in the *Critique of Pure Reason*. They argued that Kant like Plato (*sic*) presupposes the 'factual validity' (*faktische Geltung*) of the principles of mathematics. These principles (*Grundsätze*), which Plato called Ideas, are 'hypotheses' in the sense of 'laying the base' (*Grundlegung*) of Kant's new philosophical method.[41] The principles are 'pure' because they are self-evident and underivable.

According to Cohen, Kant merely misnamed the principles when he called them 'synthetic', and he was wrong to complete their meaning by connecting their employment to sensuous perception and intuition.[42] For the idea that thought is a 'synthesis' makes its unity depend on a *given* plurality which it synthesizes. But unity and plurality are equally preconditions of any thought. Hence they cannot be 'given' to thought but must be produced or created by the act of thinking itself. There must be an 'origin' (*Ursprung*) of thought which is prior to both unifying and diversifying, prior to the distinction between thought and being. Logic is the logic of this origin.[43] Instead of calling thought a 'synthesis', with this heteronomous implication, thought should be considered a creating or producing (*Erzeugen*).[44]

The basic form of thought is the judgement. A judgement affirms or denies a state of affairs. Lotze argued that the reality of the validity which pertains to propositions is of a different kind from the reality of things which 'are' or 'exist'. For Cohen, too, the validity of judgements is independent of representation and perception, of processes of consciousness. But, for Cohen, judgements are always judgements of being. For being can only be posited by a judgement. No distinction can be made between the logic of thinking and the reality of 'being' (*Sein*). Being is the being of thinking: and thinking is the thinking of being (of being as object by being as subject: *genitivus objectivus* and *genitivus subjectivus*). Thinking in this sense is thinking of 'cognemes' (*Erkenntnisse*). Logic, which is no longer critical or transcendental, is thus not

formal, but a *doctrine* of cognemes, based on the principles of mathematical natural science.[45]

The 'unity of consciousness' does not refer to consciousness in a
realm of opposition between itself and its objects. It refers to a unity
based on the principle of pure logic, the logic of scientific consciousness.[46] Scientific thought is the unity of the creating and its creations
and its activities of unifying and diversifying are a never-ending,
infinite task.[47]

Logic investigates judgements in general, the genus character of
judgement, and the different species of judgements. Each species of
judgement creates and presupposes a corresponding unity of cognemes
and objects in its respective domain.[48]

This logic, based on the exact mathematical sciences is the ideal for
the human and cultural sciences too:[49]

> All the human sciences share the presupposition of the mathematical
> natural sciences that thought is able to give and to secure fixed, deter-
> minate and unchanging creations. The identity of Parmenides is the
> pole-star of all science and all research, of all thinking.[50]

The understanding is the faculty of rules.[51]

The Heidelberg School of neo-Kantianism was as opposed to transcendental logic as the Marburg School, and also cloaked its opposition
in Kantian terminology.

Like Lotze and the Marburg School, Windelband and Rickert believed that the origin and nature of validity cannot be ascertained by
reference to representation or to the contents of consciousness.[52] Cognition cannot be understood as the synthesis of appearances, as knowledge
of spatio-temporal objects beyond which lies the reality of things-in-
themselves.[53] Rickert argued that the twin assumptions of a knowing
subject and a reality independent of the subject, but somehow connected with it in the medium of representation, were solipsistic and
subjective.[54]

Rickert agreed with Lotze and Cohen that the primary act of consciousness is not representation or perception but judgement. Unlike
Lotze and Cohen, however, Rickert argued that a judgement is not
valid because it affirms or posits what is true, but, on the contrary, it is
the prescriptive force of the judgement which confers validity on what
we call truth.[55] This prescription which we acknowledge when we

make a judgement is 'an ought' (*ein Sollen*) or 'a value', and the moral connotations of *Sollen* and 'value' are retained in this account of judging.[56] In other terms, a judgement does not have a value because it is true, but it acquires truth by force of its value. Value confers both meaning and authority on the judgement, its validity. Rickert claimed that this explication of validity was no more circular than the one it replaced.[57]

Validity is thus in no sense derived from the relation of the judgement to empirical reality, but originates in the validity of the *Sollen*. This validity does not depend on the judging subject or consciousness. For it belongs to the very meaning of affirming a judgement that the prescription which is thereby acknowledged has a validity independent of the act of acknowledgement.[58] Rickert calls this validity of *Sollen* or values 'transcendent', by which he means both that validity is prior to any act of judging, and the more conventional meaning of 'transcendent': that validity cannot be justified within the bounds of spatio-temporal experience. Unfortunately, Rickert's insistence that values or prescriptions are *sui generis* has been hypostatized by commentators who present it as a timeless realm of eternal values, to which our access, as empirical consciousness, is limited.[59]

Like Lotze, Rickert distinguished between the reality of empirical existence and the 'irreality' of validity. By calling validity 'irreal' he meant that to say something is (*ist*), is to attribute a different mode of reality from that involved in the claim that something holds or is valid (*gilt*).[60] As in Lotze, the reality of validity is underivable, but, unlike Lotze, the force which is underivable but which confers validity is called 'value' or *Sollen*. It is value which is ultimately underivable or *sui generis*. Logical validity has a moral imprimatur.

As in the works of the Marburg School the destruction of subject/object epistemology has implications for the status of the object-domain (*Gegenständlichkeit*).[61] Rickert calls values or *Sollen* both the *criterion* of cognition and the *object* of cognition.[62] This paradox arises because, from the point of view of the judging consciousness, the *Sollen* or value is a criterion, a prescriptive force which confers validity. But judging consciousnsess is itself only possible because value or *Sollen* is valid independent of the act of judgement. In this sense value or *Sollen* is the object of knowledge.

From the point of view of the judging consciousness, a *Sollen* or value is always acknowledged in judging. It is this acknowledgement which makes cognition possible, but the acknowledgement itself is not necessarily conscious or known.[63] The unity of the object depends on the subject-predicate unity of a judgement which necessarily acknowledges a value.[64]

Rickert's *Sollen* or valid values, which make possible the unity of the object in judgement, and Cohen's 'pure cognemes', which make possible the unity of the object created by different kinds of judgement, provide a theoretical identity impossible within the terms of Kant's theoretical philosophy. The Marburg and the Heidelberg School are usually contrasted, because Cohen extended a logic based on the mathematical natural sciences to all cognition, while Rickert distinguished between the object of natural science and the object of the historical and cultural sciences. But Cohen's logic of identity, the circle of pure cognemes, judgements and objects, and Rickert's transcendental logic, the circle of value, judgements and objects, turn transcendental logic into *Geltungslogik*. They turn Kant's critical method into an autonomous logic of validity based on an original, underivable unity which is not the unity of consciousness. In both cases objectification is the correlate of the logic and can be methodically examined in any individual science. 'Validity', 'objectification' and 'method' do not have a transcendental or formal status but constitute a metaphysics of a new kind.

Morality and Method

The development of the idea of a scientific sociology was inseparable from the transformation of transcendental logic into *Geltungslogik*, the paradigm of validity and values.

Prima facie the idea of a sociological account of validity appears contradictory. For a sociological interpretation of experience, like a psychological one, might be expected to address itself to the *quaestio quid facti*, not the *quaestio quid juris*, to the history and genesis of experience, not to its justification or validity.

On the contrary, the sociology of Durkheim and of Weber endorsed the neo-Kantian critique of psychologism, the derivation of validity from processes of consciousness. Like the neo-Kantians, Durkheim and Weber treated the question of validity as pertaining to a distinct *realm* of moral facts (Durkheim) or values (Weber) which is contrasted with the realm of individual sensations or perceptions (Durkheim) or from the psychology of the individual (Weber).

Durkheim granted the question of validity priority over the question of values, and made validity into the sociological foundation of values (moral facts). Weber granted the question of values priority over the question of validity and made values into the sociological foundation of validity (legitimacy). The meaning of the paradigm of validity and values was decisively changed. It was the ambition of sociology to substitute itself for traditional theoretical and practical philosophy, as well as to secure a sociological object-domain *sui generis*.

The identification of a realm of values (*Sollen*) or moral facts, and the development of a scientific method for their investigation, a Cohen-like logic in the case of Durkheim's *Rules*, a Rickertian logic of the cultural sciences in the case of Weber, were classical neo-Kantian moves in the original project to found a scientific sociology.

But Durkheim and Weber turn a Kantian argument against neo-Kantianism. For when it is argued that it is society or culture which confers objective validity on social facts or values, then the argument acquires a metacritical or 'quasi-transcendental' structure. The social or cultural *a priori* is the precondition of the possibility of actual social facts or values (transcendental). The identified, actual, valid facts or values can be treated as the objects of a general logic (naturalistic). The status of the precondition becomes ambiguous: it is an *a priori*, that is, not empirical, for it is the basis of the possibility of experience. But a 'sociological' *a priori* is, *ex hypothesi*, external to the mind, and hence appears to acquire the status of a natural object or cause. The status of the relation between the sociological precondition and the conditioned becomes correspondingly ambiguous in all sociological quasi-transcendental arguments.

Both Durkheim and Weber were educated and worked within neo-Kantian circles. Weber's connections with the Heidelberg neo-Kantians especially Rickert, are well-known.[65] Durkheim was closely associated with the leading French representatives of German neo-Kantianism: Charles Renouvier, Emile Boutroux, Octave Hamelin and Leon Brunschwig. He was taught by Boutroux at the *Ecole Normale Supérieure*, 1879–1882, and was greatly influenced when a student by the writings of Renouvier. Hamelin was a life-long friend, and, together with Brunschwig, they were later grouped around the journal *Revue de métaphysique et de morale*, the organ of French neo-Kantianism.[66]

Durkheim claimed in several places that he was providing an alternative answer to the critical Kantian questions 'How are theoretical and moral judgements possible or objectively valid?'[67] He rejected Kant's theory of the application of the fundamental categories of thought and of faculties of the mind to explain the *a priori* preconditions of judgement, because, he said, it was tautological and uninformative, 'a purely verbal answer'.[68] Durkheim argued instead that mental capacities and the origin and employment of the categories themselves presuppose social organization: that society as a reality *sui generis* is the origin of the validity of judgements.[69] It is important to note that he did not deny that the categories are *a priori*, nor did he reject the form of the Kantian question: 'X is actual, what are the conditions of its possibility, of its objective validity?' For Durkheim, moral judgement, social facts or the categories are actual, and the task is to discover the social condition of their possibility, of their validity.[70]

The criterion for the existence of a moral or social fact is coercive force or sanction, and coercive force or moral power is also the criterion for the existence of the 'collective being' or 'personality'. This 'collective being', the origin of the moral force which confers validity on social institutions or social facts, is underivable, '*sui generis*': 'Society is a moral power . . . a *sui generis* force.'[71] It cannot be a fact, because it is the precondition of social facts and hence cannot be one of them: it is 'a transcendent objectivity'.[72]

Durkheim draws attention to the resemblance between what he calls the 'postulate' of society as 'a moral being', and Kant's postulate of God:

> The similarity between this argument and that of Kant will be noted. Kant postulates God, since without this hypothesis morality is unintelligible. We postulate a society specifically distinct from individuals, since otherwise morality has no object and duty no roots. Let us add that this postulate is easily verified by experience.[73]

Strictly speaking, in Kantian terms, a 'postulate' is introduced when it is impossible in principle for any experience to correspond to a concept. In particular, the whole critical philosophy was directed against the idea that any experience could correspond to the concept 'God'. According to Kant, the postulate or idea of 'God' can only be a *regulative* not a constitutive principle, that is, it cannot be a principle which is the basis of objective validity.[74] But, for Durkheim, society *sui generis* is *constitutive*, the basis of the validity of moral (social) experience. Since society is the transcendental precondition of the possibility of that experience, it must be *demonstrable how* it makes experience possible. By contrast a 'postulate' merely performs the function of 'making sense' of experience. Finally, neither a postulate nor a constitutive principle can be 'easily verified by experience', because they make experience possible or intelligible in the first place.

In *The Elementary Forms of the Religious Life*, Durkheim presents the relation between the conditioned (the use of the categories) and its precondition (society) in the stronger sense of constitutive, objective validity. He insists that a sociological explanation of the origin and employment of the categories must recognize their *a priori* nature and cannot reduce them to inductions from experience. For 'the mind has a certain power of transcending experience and of adding to that which is directly given to it.'[75] The real question is to know how it comes about that experience itself has 'exterior and prior' conditions, and that the categories are not fixed, but are 'unmade and remade incessantly'.[76]

Durkheim argues that an explanation is only possible if 'the social origin of the categories is admitted'.[77] If 'social origin' is the basis of the validity of the categories, then the relation between the conditioned and the precondition which confers the validity needs to be specified. In the *Critique of Pure Reason* this was achieved by an exposition of the synthesizing powers of the imagination. However, once a social origin of the categories is 'admitted', it becomes impossible to explain the relation between the origin and the categories without using the very categories (for example, the category of cause) whose possibility has yet to be justified. Durkheim tried to circumvent this problem by using non-committal phrases, such as, 'the categories . . . translate social states',[78] or 'are taken from social life',[79] or, 'are elaborated on the model of social things'.[80]

According to Durkheim, an advantage of the sociological explanation of the categories is that they are no longer 'primary and unanalysable',[81] but variations in them can be explained. However, Durkheim's very success in conforming to the structure of the Kantian argument means that the new precondition, society, becomes 'primary and unanalysable' in the place of the categories. To mitigate this consequence Durkheim affirms that a sociological explanation of the categories does not deprive them of objective value, or reason of its necessity. The 'necessity' of thought becomes moral or social necessity.[82] Thus the transcendental framework of Durkheim's sociology is precarious and elliptical.

The transcendental argument identifies a realm of natural objects, social or moral facts. This is a valid, moral realm *sui generis*, collective not individual, which may be treated naturalistically by the application of a general logic or rules of method. Durkheim was confident that his sociological transformation of the philosophical question of validity had succeeded, and that, as a result, he had isolated a realm of moral facts, defined by their 'externality' and coercive force whose transcendental possibility was established. To stress the 'natural' character of values or norms he called them 'facts'.

According to Durkheim the difference between a 'judgement of reality' and a 'judgement of value' is not the difference between theoretical and moral judgements as in Kant, but the neo-Kantian difference between a subjectively valid judgement and an objectively valid one. Durkheim calls the statement '*I like hunting*' a 'judgement of reality', which 'merely reports' individual feelings. But the statement 'This man *has* a high moral value' is a 'value judgement', objectively valid, because it is independent of individual feelings.

> Implicitly we recognize that these judgements correspond to some objective reality upon which agreement can and should be reached. These *sui generis* realities constitute values, and it is to these realities that value judgements refer.[83]

This identification of a *Sollen*, which is acknowledged by judgements and confers validity on them, sounds Rickertian. But Durkheim insists that because these moral realities are 'distinct' from individual ones, they may be treated as natural objects,[84] and can be classified, compared and explained according to the logic of any natural science sure of its object domain. He therefore prescribed a method for the collation and explanation of social facts in a way which draws on analogies from the biological, chemical and physical sciences whose validity is assumed.

Durkheim, like Cohen, gave priority to the question of validity, and the result was the same conjunction of underivable validity and a general method based on the exact natural sciences. For Durkheim, it is society which confers validity on values, and, although collective reality was defined as a moral power, its validity remains the basis of its moral effect:

I did not say that the moral authority of society derives from its role as moral legislator; that would be absurd. I said, on the contrary, that society is qualified to play the part of legislator because in our eyes it is invested with a well-founded moral authority.[85]

In contrast to Durkheim, Weber transformed the paradigm of validity and values into a sociology by giving values priority over validity. Weber's articles in the *Archiv für Sozialwissenschaft*, 1903–1917, and the first chapter of *Economy and Society*, 1921, are organized around the question of the relation between validity and values, *Geltung* and *Werte*.

Following Rickert, Weber defined culture as a value: 'The concept of culture is a value-concept. Empirical reality becomes "culture" to us because and insofar as we relate it to value ideas. It includes those segments and only those segments which have become significant to us because of this relation to value [*Wertbeziehung*].'[86] The validity of cultural values cannot be subjected to any rational or scientific assessment: 'To *judge* the *validity* of such values is a matter of *faith*.'[87] Weber thus rigorously separated values and judgements of validity and reversed their traditional status: values can be examined scientifically but not validity. *Sollen* or values are *sui generis*, and the condition of their possibility is not society, but choice, ultimately arbitrary, by the culture or by the personality: '. . . the dignity of the personality' consists in the 'existence of values to which it relates its life . . . self-realization in these interests for which it claims validity as values . . .'[88] Validity is conferred by value.

> The transcendental presupposition of every cultural science is . . . that we are cultural beings endowed with the capacity and will to take a deliberate attitude towards the world and lend it significance.[89]

Weber calls this presupposition a 'purely logical and formal condition'.[90]

How then can there be a scientific study of values, that is, one which claims validity, if validity depends on values and values cannot be justified? Quite consistently, Weber admitted that science is a value itself, the value of a particular historical culture, '. . . even the knowledge of the most certain of our theoretical sciences . . . is a product of culture'.[91] The only 'validity' science can achieve is scrupulously and continually to admit its relation to values. It must draw attention to the 'ideal-typical' nature of its concepts, which are constructs related to values, but simplified and clarified for the purpose of 'comparing' the given cultural value with the value-related ideal-type.

The role of ideal-types is thus specified in *naturalistic* terms. 'They are used as conceptual instruments for the *comparison* with and *measurement* of reality.'[92] But if reality is a value which is only properly knowable by means of ideal-types, which are accentuated values themselves, then we can have no independent access to an empirical given which might be 'measured' or 'compared' by means of the ideal-type. We cannot make the judgements of validity implied by 'measuring' and 'comparing'.

Weber conceded that what we call 'reality' or 'ideas' may already be ideal-types. 'The *practical idea* which should be *valid* or is *believed to be valid* and the heuristically intended, theoretically ideal-type approach each other very closely and constantly tend to merge with each other.'[93] The boundaries between ideal-types and the ideas or ideals, 'the empirical reality of the immediately given', under investigation is fluid, 'problematic in each individual case'.[94]

Thus Weber had to specify the function of the ideal-type in different terms. Ideal-types 'are constructs in terms of which we formulate relationships by the application of the category of objective possibility. By means of this category, the adequacy of our imagination, oriented and disciplined by reality is *judged*'.[95] 'Objective possibility' stands for the relation between ideal-type and empirical reality. A judgement of possibility is one which judges 'what would happen in the event of the exclusion or modification of certain conditions' from the construct or ideal-type.[96]

This notion of 'objective possibility' is more consistent with the basis of ideal-types in values. It prevents the social scientist from treating interpretative and historically-limited constructs as universally valid ones, as 'objective necessity' in an Hegelian or Marxist sense, because it stresses that the explanation rests on artificial, mental constructs. The notion of 'objective possibility' is, however, strange. It does not mean simply logical or formal possibility: everything is possible that is not self-contradictory. It does not mean 'real' possibility in the Kantian sense, whereby the 'objectively possible' is the precondition of the actual. Weber wished to avoid this implication. To have established the 'objective possibility' of something is simply to have devised an adequate theoretical construct, a 'heuristic' device, as Weber calls it, which helps to make the *explanandum* intelligible.

Weber's exposition of the function of ideal-types conforms to what Kant called regulative postulates in opposition to constitutive principles. An ideal-type performs the same function which Kant ascribed to an Idea. It

> is really only a heuristic, not an ostensive concept. It does not show us how an object is constituted, but how, under its guidance, we should *seek* to determine the constitution and connection of the objects of experience.[97]

Thus it is Weber, not Durkheim, who introduced postulates or regulative principles to 'make sense' of experience, and Durkheim who introduced constitutive principles, the conditions of the possibility of the actual object, its objective validity. Weber's 'objective possibility' is designed to eschew any attribution of validity in the constitutive sense. This was Weber's Kantian turn against neo-Kantiansim.

For Weber, the methodology of ideal-types can itself only have the status of a value, an infinite task, which achieves 'validity' or justification by reference to its hypothetical, contingent, corrigible status, yet which provides the sole demarcation criterion between legitimate and illegitimate relations to given values. Once validity is determined by value any subsequent attempt to establish scientific validity leads to an infinite regress. For such an attempt presupposes the very kind of judgement which can only be understood as a value.

In spite of this logical problem, Weber was able to develop a consistent and critical sociology of capitalism without making value-judgements, that is, judgements of its validity. For the very value which gives rise to the kind of science he practised, a science which limits itself to understanding values and not assessing their validity, is an exemplar of the same kind of rationality which is the defining characteristic of capitalist society. Just as the development of a Protestant ethic made possible the transition from value to instrumental (goal) rationality, science in such a society is goal-rational. It examines the relation between means and ends but does not assess the ends themselves.

For Weber, like Rickert, values are the source of validity. But Weber did not define values by *Sollen*, by prescriptive force, but by their subjective meaning, as beliefs according to which people orient their actions.[98] A legitimate or valid order is defined by the kind of belief in it, and by the possibility that action will in fact be oriented to it. The validity of social order is not defined by sanction. From a sociological point of view, according to Weber, the difference between an order enforced by external sanctions and at the same time by disinterested subjective attitude is not important. The basis of validity of a social order, that is, whether it is legal or moral, cannot be decided in general terms. Social order is defined according to its meaning, not according to its authority.

Under 'The Bases of Validity of Legitimate Order', Weber lists the different kinds of validity (*legitime Geltung*) which people acknowledge.[99] This must include an acknowledgement that the order in question is binding, but the acknowledgement and hence the order cannot be defined as conformity to prescriptions. For there may be different, even contradictory, interpretations of the same order, and deviation from it may be regarded as legitimate.[100] A valid order is identified 'in so far as it actually determines the course of action'. It cannot be defined by coercion, because there can be norms with no external coercion, and there can be sanctions which are not norms.

For Weber, subjective belief (value) constitutes validity; for Durkheim, it is the validity of a 'social being' which invests norms with a coercive power or sanction. A paradoxical result of Durkheim's granting priority to validity over values, and of Weber's granting priority to values over validity, is that Durkheim produced an 'empirical' sociology of values (moral facts) and Weber produced an 'empirical' sociology of validities (legitimate orders). In each case once the precondition had been established (validity for Durkheim, values for Weber), the object (values for Durkheim, validities for Weber) could be classified, and explained or 'understood' as a natural or given object according to the rules of a general method.

The New Ontologies

The neo-Kantian paradigm of validity and values founded two kinds of 'socio-logy', two logics of the social: a logic of constitutive principles for the sociology based on the priority of validity, and a logic of regulative postulates for the sociology based on the priority of values. The former identifies social reality by a critique of consciousness; the latter locates social reality within the realm of consciousness and its oppositions.

It is the logic which grants priority to values, which is known, strictly speaking, as 'sociology'. This tradition draws on Simmel's 'forms of sociation',[101] Weber's ideal-types, von Wiese's theory of interrelations (*Beziehungslehre*),[102] and Parsons' general theory of action. It insists on society or culture as a value, or 'orientation of action', although values may subsequently be described in a formal or systematic way. Parsons' exposition of the thought of Durkheim and Weber as a single body of convergent theory, the theory of social action, and his development of 'the action frame of reference' remain within the logic of regulative postulates.[103]

The logic which grants priority to validity was criticized for the 'positivism' inherent in it, and thus for the whole neo-Kantian paradigm itself: for the transformation of the Kantian question of validity into methodologism. The critics of methodologism sought to provide a different kind of account of validity – one which was not motivated by the search for a general logic for the exact or historical sciences, but by an historical critique of that very endeavour.

Dilthey,* Heidegger, Mannheim, Benjamin and Gadamer have this criticism in common: the neo-Kantian answers to the question of validity debase the question of being, reality, existence, life or history, by their propositional or judgmental account of truth and by the correlation between general logic and objectification. But these thinkers did not return to a transcendental logic in order to make the question of existence central again. On the contrary, they developed the kind of metacritique of Kant already attempted by Durkheim: the argument that the Kantian *a priori*, the categories, itself has a social, historical or external presupposition. This is why they are important for sociological reason.

This metacritical argument, like the neo-Kantian, rejected Kantian epistemology: the examination of the limits of discursive reason and the psychologism implicit in the reference to processes or contents of consciousness. But the critique of transcendental logic was turned against neo-Kantian logic too. Both the critical project to examine the limits of reason before employing reason itself, and the neo-Kantian

---

* The inclusion of Dilthey (1833–1911) in this list is anachronistic. Many of the neo-Kantians included Dilthey's work among the psychologism which they sought to destroy. However, Dilthey's thought can be seen to have a metacritical structure. Heidegger, Gadamer, and Benjamin rejected his use of psychology to mediate between the precondition and the conditioned but shared this underlying structure.[104]

project to establish an autonomous logic are contradictory. For how can reason be examined except rationally, and how can a general logic be established except logically? In short, both of these projects can only be accomplished by use of the very capacities whose right use is precisely to be justified. Hence it is necessary to begin in a different way: one which acknowledges the unavoidable circularity of any examination of cognition and which derives the social and historical preconditions of cognition systematically suppressed by both the Kantian and neo-Kantian approaches. Metacritique turns the neo-Kantian critique of the philosophy of consciousness against neo-Kantianism itself: it exposes the formation and deformation of both transcendental *and* methodological reason.[105]

Dilthey, Mannheim, Heidegger and Gadamer return to the Kantian question of validity, 'What are the preconditions of experience?', but judge that the Kantian reference to the categories and their application itself has a precondition: 'life' (Dilthey),[106] 'social-situation' (Mannheim),[107] '*Dasein*' (Heidegger),[108] 'history' (Gadamer).[109] These become the presupposition of the use of the categories or of meaning, the '*a priori*' of a new kind of ontology.

Husserl was the first to introduce a 'phenomenology' of meaning as a reformulation of the question of validity in the Marburg tradition. He sought to replace empirical psychology, neo-Kantian normative logic and Kantian transcendental constitution by the description of 'intentional meaning'.[110] However, Husserl's eidetic, transcendental ego remained within a philosophy of pure and solipsistic consciousness, and the phenomenological reduction bracketed out the question of existence.

Dilthey, Mannheim, Heidegger and Gadamer opened up history and culture, communal experience, to analysis by arguing that apprehension of meaning itself has historical and social presuppositions. This hermeneutic apprehension of meaning (*Verstehen*) stands squarely in the *Geltung* tradition, and has nothing in common with Rickertian and Weberian *Verstehen*, with the priority of values over validity.

However, these radical approaches to the question of validity remain within a Kantian transcendental circle: the condition of the possibility of experience (meaning) is likewise the condition of the object of experience (meaning),[111] whether the condition is 'life', 'social-situation', '*Dasein*', or 'history'. The analysis revolves within an hermeneutic or transcendental circle, that is, a circle without a result.[112]

A new identity is presupposed between the condition and the conditioned, albeit outside the discourse of consciousness and its oppositions, or of validity and its objectifications.

As in the case of Durkheim, the argument takes a quasi-transcendental form. The newly specified *a priori*, the precondition of validity, is transcendental. But the precondition is now external to the mind, and hence appears to acquire the status of a natural, contingent, empirical object. The conditioned, meaning, is isolated and defined in proper methodological fashion. Paradoxically, these approaches, which arose to combat neo-Kantian methodologism, lend themselves readily to methodological exploitation, since they can be read as sets of abstract procedural rules for cognition.

Thus metacritique, in spite of its radical intentions, remains within the paradigm of *Geltung* and cannot make the transition to a speculative position. Habermas' *obiter dictum* on Rickert is even more applicable to the generations of Rickert's critics including Habermas himself: they pose an Hegelian problem, but fail to complete 'the transition from Kant to Hegel'.[113] The Hegelian system was, of course, explicitly rejected because of its presupposition of absolute knowledge, but, except in the case of Habermas himself, not for the neo-Kantian scruple that Hegel could not justify the exact or individual sciences.

The greatest irony among the new ontologies is the success of 'phenomenological sociology'. Schutz managed to fuse or confuse the phenomenological reformulation of *validity*, the most solipsistic and asociological of the new ontologies, with Weber's *Verstehen*, the sociology based on the priority of *values*.[114] The result is a critical moment within a phenomenological sociology: that meanings or social institutions may be 'reified', that is, their intentionality may not be recognized. However, this misrecognition can only be treated as a 'fact of consciousness', a neo-Fichtean station on the road between Kant and Hegel. It is at this most unsociological station that the two branches of neo-Kantian sociology have met and ground to a halt.

Neo-Kantian Marxism

Simmel's legacy to sociology has been twofold. His early work on historical method (1892)[115] and his *Soziologie* (1908)[116] influenced Weber, and were taken up by the sociological tradition which gives priority to values. But his *Philosophy of Money* (1900) and his essays on culture contain a unique version of neo-Kantian *Geltungslogik* and had an enormous influence on the development of critical, Marxist sociology.

Simmel's sociology did not develop out of the Heidelberg philosophy of values, nor is it a sociological metacritique of Marburg methodologism. Simmel's work has been understood both as sociology of regulative postulates, and as a sociology of constitutive principles, because, like Lotze, Simmel combined a Kantian transcendental psychology with a Platonic ontology of autonomous validity and values (*Geltung* and *Werte*).

According to Simmel, the realm of validity (*Geltung*) is a 'third realm' beyond the distinction of subject and object, the realm of Platonic Forms, or Ideas. The whole value of being derives from this third realm, and it is a 'typical tragedy of spirit' to reside in the opposition between the realm of Ideas and reality. However, 'objective being' (being) and 'subjective being' (thinking), or, in other terms, 'world' and 'soul', are equally modes of realization of autonomous validity.[117]

Simmel contrasted this independent realm of logical validity and moral law with the mode of existence of psychological and physical representations. But the life of the soul, the seat of moral activity, has an inner relation to the autonomous realm. For the soul acknowledges an 'ideal demand' or *Sollen*, beyond subjectivity and beyond mere facticity. This is the Kantian moral law which is obeyed out of the pure motive of duty, and for no ulterior end, and which thus possesses an underivable value or validity.[118]

Simmel has merely recast in his peculiar terminology of 'soul', 'life', and 'forms', a typical neo-Kantian critique of Kant. The categorical validity ('forms') possessed by the moral law is extended to theoretical philosophy, but the practical realm ('the life of the soul') retains its primacy. Simmel called the realm of validity/forms/values 'objective spirit' or 'culture'. His critical philosophy of culture examines the relation between the independent realm of validities and the soul or life, which dwells partly in harmony with the realm of validities and partly in opposition.[119]

At the same time Simmel founded his sociological enquiries into the forms of sociation on the basis of an extended analogy with an extremely psychological reading of the *Critique of Pure Reason*.[120] He presented the Kantian *a priori*, 'the forms which constitute the essence of our intellect', as 'calling forth nature itself'.[121] Thus 'in the Kantian view the unity of nature emerges in the observing subject exclusively', but the unity of society is not constituted by an observing subject. 'It is directly realized by its own elements because these elements are themselves conscious and synthesizing units.'[122] Hence the consciousness of constituting with others a unity is 'actually all there is . . . to this unity.'[123] The sociological 'a priori' or 'forms of sociation' are those processes which give rise to this 'consciousness of sociation'. The forms are facts of that consciousness which is the agent of sociation itself.[124]

This location of social reality as a fact of 'theoretical' consciousness is in stark contrast to Simmel's analysis of *moral* consciousness, or of culture. Culture is defined as the content or forms of life (art, law, religion, technology) which are created in historical time, but which attain an independent validity once created which may render them inaccessible to their creators.[125] An increasing rift or conflict between subjective and objective culture, between the continuing historical process (life) and transcendent validity (forms), is analysed by Simmel as the dominant characteristic of capitalist social change in *The Philosophy of Money*.

In *The Philosophy of Money*, Simmel reaffirms that validity is underivable and exists prior to the distinction between empirical reality and values, and he also deals with the question of values as facts of consciousness.[126] Hence it is unjust to say that Simmel's theory of value is subjective, because it is the tension between objective value and subjective access to these values which provides the cutting edge of his analysis.[127] Although value is conferred on an object by a conative subject, the validity of a value is independent of the desires or acts of subjects, 'an independently valid value'.[128] 'Just as the world of being is my representation, so the world of value is my demand', but, just as truth is independent of my representation, so is value independent of my demand.[129] Simmel consistently analyses both the psychological and the ontological poles of this contrast. The transition from subjective act to objective significance or validity is a process of 'objectification' (*Objektivation*). Money is a means of objectification in the sphere of economic value.

In moral life we may become conscious that our behaviour is deviating from an ideal norm, and, similarly, we may become conscious that our subjective culture or experience is divorced from objective culture.[130] Simmel proceeds to establish a correlation between changes in the division of labour and the increasing divergence of subjective and objective culture. He places great emphasis on those features of industrial production which fragment the work process. Fragmentation of experience restricts the possibility of experience of objective culture, but it may also liberate a private realm of personality.

Simmel claimed that his theory of culture represented a generalization of Marx's theory of the contradiction between developing productive forces (life) and established relations of production (form).[131] In *The Philosophy of Money*, however, Simmel rejected all the other defining features of Marx's analysis of capitalism. *The Philosophy of Money* should be understood instead as an attempt to transform Marx's theory of value into a *Geltungslogik*, into a theory of the objectification and autonomy of validity, which has both 'liberating' and 'tragic' consequences in capitalist society.[132]

The thought of Lukács and of Adorno represent two of the most original and important attempts to break out of the neo-Kantian paradigm of validity and values. Their work has achieved renown as an Hegelian Marxism, but it constitutes a neo-Kantian Marxism. For the reception of Hegel and Marx on which it is based was determined by their neo-Kantian education. The relation of their work to neo-Kantianism is the source of both its sociological power and the peculiarity of its contribution to Marxist theory. They turned the neo-Kantian paradigm into a Marxist sociology of cultural forms by combining Simmel's philosophy of form with a selective generalization of Marx's theory of commodity fetishism.

Lukács broke out of the neo-Kantian paradigm of validity and values in the same way as Hegel transformed the meaning of Kant's philosophical method, by giving priority to the critique of aesthetic judgement.[133] In *The Heidelberg Aesthetics* (1912–1918), Lukács argued that the form of validity (*Geltungsform*) of the work of art could not be derived from theoretical or ethical validity.[134] He conceded the importance of the question of validity, but rejected both Kant's debasement of aesthetic judgement to merely 'reflective judgement',[135] and the debasement of the relation between subject and object in neo-Kantian *Geltungslogik*.[136] He developed instead a phenomenology, taken from Husserl and Lask, of 'creative and receptive behaviour', and of the subject-object relation of artist and spectator.[137] His aim was to establish 'immanent aesthetics as an autonomous science of values',[138] to rescue aesthetics from *Geltungslogik*.

Lukács' first attempts to transcend *Geltungslogik* were based on Emil

Lask's intentional account of validity, *Hingelten*. This was a phenomeno-logical account of the relation between validity and its objects. It thus presupposed a descriptive, non-constitutive identity of the phenomeno-logical kind.[139] Lukács' subsequent discussion of the 'antinomies of bourgeois thought' in *History and Class Consciousness* contains a decisive rejection of the paradigm of validity and values in particular, as well as a critique of German idealism in general.[140] While Lukács' criticism of Simmel has frequently been noted,[141] what Lukács retains from Simmel unifies his definition of culture, his generalization of Marx's theory of commodity fetishism and his studies of aesthetic form.

In the essay 'The Old Culture and the New Culture' (1920), Lukács defined culture as a 'value-in-itself' which had been destroyed by the fragmentation of capitalist production in which the economy dominates the whole society.[142] The definition of culture as a unity of subject and object or 'value-in-itself' and the analysis of fragmentation owe much to Simmel's notion of culture as autonomous validity which may or may not coincide with subjective experience.

In the essay 'Reification and the Consciousness of the Proletariat' in *History and Class Consciousness*, Lukács generalizes Marx's theory of commodity fetishism by making a distinction between the total pro-cess of production, 'real life-processes', and the resultant objectification of social forms.[143] This notion of 'objectification' has more in common with the neo-Kantian notion of the objectification of specific object-domains than with an 'Hegelian' conflating of objectification, human praxis in general, with alienation, its form in capitalist society, as Lukács later claimed.[144] By making a distinction between underlying process and resultant objectifications Lukács was able to avoid the con-ventional Marxist treatment of capitalist social forms as mere 'super-structure' or 'epiphenomena'; legal, bureaucratic and cultural forms have the same status as the commodity form. Lukács made it clear that 'reification' is the specific capitalist form of objectification. It deter-mines the structure of all the capitalist social forms.

These social forms do not have any ultimate validity, and the appearance of eternal or underivable validity is unmasked as an illusion. But the process-like essence (the mode of production) attains a validity (*unverfälscht zur Geltung gelangt*) from the standpoint of the totality.[145] Social forms are valid when viewed from the standpoint of their media-tion by the totality, but not when viewed in isolation from the total process. Lukács turned *Geltungslogik* and its objectifications, the logic of constitutive principles, away from a logic of identity in the direction of a theory of historical mediation.

The advantage of this approach was that Lukács opened up new areas of social life to Marxist analysis and critique. He used the critical aspects of Weber's sociology of rationalization as well as Simmel's philosophy of money in this extension of Marx's theory of commodity fetishism.[146] The disadvantage was that Lukács omitted many details of Marx's theory of value, and of the analysis of capitalist economies which followed on in *Capital* from the analysis of the commodity form. As a result 'reification' and 'mediation' become a kind of short-hand instead of a sustained theory.

A further disadvantage is that the sociology of reification can only be completed by a speculative sociology of the proletariat as the subject-object of history. Lukács' very success in demonstrating the prevalence of reification, of the structural factors inhibiting the formation of political, proletarian class consciousness, meant that he could only appeal to the proletariat to overcome reification by apostrophes to the unification of theory and practice, or by introducing the party as a *deus ex machina*.[147]

Thus Lukács produced a methodological Marx, a selective generalization of features of Marx's theory of value, which had great sociological force. This is not unconnected with his definition of Marxism as a method.[148] However, by 'method' Lukács did not mean a neo-Kantian general logic, nor did he intend any codification of dialectical material-ism. On the contrary, Lukács believed that the idea of Marxism as autonomous doctrine had robbed it of its revolutionary force. Lukács' injunction to take Marxism as a 'method' was, in fact, an invitation to hermeneutic anarchy, and it had an immensely liberating effect on those philosophers, such as Bloch, Horkheimer, Benjamin and Adorno, who were graduating from the schools of neo-Kantianism, but who were not satisfied with the contemporaneous phenomenological and ontological metacritiques of neo-Kantianism. Many of those who, in their youth, were taught by Lukács to regard Marxism as a form of continually-changing critical reflection, later rejected the quite different notion of dialectical method which informed, for example, *The Young Hegel*.[149] In that work, in contrast to *History and Class Consciousness*, an unanalysed and autonomous notion of dialectical materialism is opposed to an unproblematic identification and rejection of the 'idealistic' elements of Hegel's thought.

In *History and Class Consciousness*, Lukács traced 'reification', the dominant characteristic of German, bourgeois, idealist thought, back to Kant's distinction between the synthesis of appearances and the thing-in-itself. Lukács interpreted this as a distinction between the 'abstract, formal, rationalistic' faculty of cognition, and the irrational remainder, the thing-in-itself.[150] The perspective of the totality is the only one from which this dichotomy can be surpassed, and such a perspective is implied by Kant's 'Ideas' of 'God' and the 'soul', but denied by their limited function.[151]

Lukács formulates the problem of the unification of the rational and the irrational in terms of Fichte's critique of Kant:

> What is at issue, Fichte says, is 'the absolute projection of an object the origin of which no account can be given, with the result that the space between projection and the thing projected is dark and void . . . the *projectio per hiatum irrationalem*'.[152]

Fichte represents a statement and culmination of reification in philosophical thought: of an instrumental rationalism determined by the commodity form, and incapable of grasping the totality.

It is only from the 'standpoint of the proletariat' that the fetish character of objects can be dissolved 'into processes that take place among men and are objectified in concrete relations between them; by deriving the indissoluble fetishistic forms from the primary forms of human relations'.[153] In this way the 'projection' of the object (objectification) is no longer inexplicable, an 'irrational hiatus', but 'man has become the measure of all (social) things'.[154] Lukács proceeds to analyse this changed standpoint as a change in the *consciousness* of the proletariat:

> Reification . . . can be overcome only by constant and constantly renewed efforts to disrupt the reified structure of existence, by concretely relating to the concretely manifested contradictions of the total development, by becoming conscious of the immanent meanings of these contradictions for the total development.[155]

Lukács' resolution of the problem of reification in bourgeois thought, the thing-in-itself, and in social reality, the commodity form, is developed and stated in Fichtean terms. To call the 'standpoint of the proletariat' one from which 'man is the measure of all things', and to argue that this standpoint may be adopted by a change in consciousness, is to assume that 'objectification', and its specific capitalist form, 'reification', have their origin in the acts of a total social subject, and that a change in the consciousness of that subject would result in a change in the form of objectification. To put it in strictly Fichtean terms, 'objectification' is an 'act of consciousness' (*Tathandlung*), albeit the highest.[156]

It was these implications of Lukács' sociology of reification which Adorno rejected. He argued that Lukács' account of reification remained within the Fichtean assumptions in which it was couched.[157] By interpreting Marx's theory of commodity fetishism as a theory of 'objectification', Lukács was not able to transform the neo-Kantian paradigm in the way he intended. To argue that reification would be abolished by a change in consciousness, thus effecting a reconciliation between subject and object, still implies that the subject will dominate the object, 'the philosophical imperialism of annexing the alien'.[158] To call for the 'dissolution of reification' is merely to call for a change in consciousness, and to idealize pre-capitalist injustice.[159] Adorno argued that Marx did not equate reification with the capitalist division of labour or objectification, but that he had recognized the need for planning in a free society, and hence 'preserved the alien thing'.[160]

Adorno implies that Lukács remained within the neo-Kantian paradigm of validity (*Validität, Geltung*) which he proceeds to examine. To establish 'validity' as a realm of reality *sui generis* means that the act of judging is distinguished from the state of affairs which the judgement affirms. But 'judgements are retroactive treatments of already constituted facts, under the norms of their subjective intelligibility . . . and such retroactive questioning does not coincide with the judged fact itself and its objective causes'.[161] Adorno argued that the neo-Kantian separation of representation from validity was already present in Kant. Kant 'put a reflection on the cognitive subject's course in judging' in the place of 'the objective reasons for the judgement'. He made the act of judging itself into a *constituens*, although it only was appearances which were thus constituted.[162]

Adorno's criticism is an ontological one. He accuses Kant of inconsistency in his undermining of precritical ontology, and argues that this precritical ontology lived on in the neo-Kantian emphasis on validity. Thus the neo-Kantian critique of Kant's philosophy of consciousness, the critique of Kant's limiting validity to processes of discursive understanding, was not fulfilled. For to isolate 'validity' as pertaining to judgements and not to 'the judged fact itself and its objective causes' also reduces truth to processes of consciousness.[163] Kant *and* the neo-Kantians operate within a 'logical circle':

> The precedence of consciousness which is to legitimize science, as presupposed from the start of the *Critique of Pure Reason*, is then inferred from procedural standards that confirm or refute judgements in line with scientific rules.[164]

The neo-Kantians and Lukács remain within a 'phenomenology of facts of consciousness'.[165]

Adorno's criticism of Lukács' theory of reification is almost identical with Hegel's criticism of Fichte's solution of the Kantian antinomies.[166] But Adorno did not carry through this criticism, as Hegel or Marx did by developing a philosophy of history, nor by reading Marx's theory of value differently from Lukács. Adorno largely accepted Lukács' generalization of Marx's theory of commodity fetishism. Instead of understanding capitalist social, cultural and artistic forms as 'objectifications' or 'facts of consciousness', Adorno analysed them as determinants of the contradictions of consciousness.[167]

These analyses, although radically sociological, are suspended theoretically. Adorno's rejection of all philosophy of history, all teleologies of reconciliation, whether Hegelian, Marxist or Lukácsian, meant that he could not underpin his analyses of cultural forms with analysis of those economic forms on which the cogency of the theory of commodity fetishism depends. Instead of supplementing the selective generalization of Marx's theory with a speculative sociology of the proletariat, Adorno completed his critique of consciousness by a subversive 'morality of method'.

Adorno is himself famous for his critique of methodologism. In the *Positivismusstreit*, the dispute over positivism, Adorno and his antagonist, Karl Popper, never engaged with each other's position, because Adorno was attacking methodologism *per se*.[168] This refers to any neo-Kantian kind of pure logic, which grants validity to an autonomous method and its objectifications, which is 'positive' in the general sense of suppressing the social and historical preconditions of its own possibility. Methodologism or 'positivism' in this metacritical sense may be found in any approach: phenomenology, Marxism, as well as in the positivist methodology of the standard verificationalist kind. It was not surprising that Popper objected to being included in the roll-call of 'positivists', for he understood 'positivism' to mean a form of naïve verificationalism. Adorno withdrew the designation but not the charge.[169]

Paradoxically, Adorno's thought became methodological too. For he developed a Nietzschean 'morality of method' in the place of the discredited philosophies of history, and this represents a return to neo-Kantianism on his part.[170] For Nietzsche's thought, the most un-academic and sustained critique of bourgeois culture, has affinities with some versions of academic neo-Kantianism.[171]

Nietzsche launched a hyperbolic attack on the Kantian question of validity, and rejected not only the 'transcendental turn' but the very idea of disinterested, philosophical apprehension of truth or objective validity. He exposed, in his oblique and subversive manner, the 'world', and 'truth' as constructs of interested values, and, utterly consistently, he understood himself to be trying to insinuate a specific transvaluation of prevalent values. Hence Nietzsche was preoccupied with the method or logic of insinuation, 'the conscience of *method*'.[172] These twin in-terests of 'value' and 'method' were assimilated by branches of neo-Kantianism.[173]

Adorno's version of a 'morality of method' inherited all the aporias which accompany method and moralism. For, although 'method' in Nietzsche and Adorno does not mean a general logic with its attendant objectifications, it did result in a preoccupation with itself, with the mode of intervention. It thus remains in a realm of infinite striving or task, a morality (*Moralität*), in the limited sense which Hegel criticized: a general prescription not located in the social relations which underlie it, and hence incapable of providing any sustained and rigorous analysis of those relations. Adorno's references to Nietzsche disguise the neo-Fichteanism in his thought. For it was neo-Fichteanism which he had so emphatically identified and denounced in Lukács.

Adorno's sociology of illusion, like Lukács' sociology of reification, remains abstract. Both Lukács and Adorno endorsed the traditional Marxist distinction between Hegel's conservative system and his radical 'method'.[174] This very distinction, however, is a conservative, neo-Kantian one, and the effect of endorsing it is that the most radical aspects of both Hegel's and Marx's thought, which follow on from Hegel's critique of the methodological mind, are lost.

The success of Jürgen Habermas' work in both the English-speaking and the German-speaking world is testimony to the thesis that the spirit of Lotze continues to determine the structure of sociological thinking.

In *Knowledge and Human Interests*, Habermas presents his starting point as a twofold critique. On the one hand, he deplores the way in which transcendental logic *within which* the validity (*Geltung*) of science could be justified[175] has degenerated into 'an absolutism of pure methodology'.[176] This *unjustified* methodologism which disavows 'reflection', he calls 'positivism'.[177] On the other hand, he deplores with equal force the 'absolute knowledge' of Hegel, and the mono-logical structure of Marx's materialism. For these metacritiques of Kant also prevent any *justification* of science by philosophical reflection.

Habermas' aim is to restore a perspective from which the different kinds of validity (*Geltung*) pertaining to different kinds of knowledge can be recognized and justified, to restore a 'reflective consciousness' of the constitution of the different kinds of objectification, of the 'trans-cendental framework that is the precondition of the meaning of the validity' of the propositions of the individual sciences.[178] By 'reflection' Habermas means a return to a position which justifies the autonomy of validity in the neo-Kantian sense, *within* a quasi-transcendental frame-work of the sociological kind.

Therefore he sets out to establish a connection between the 'logical-methodological' rules of three different kinds of scientific enquiry and three 'knowledge-constitutive interests'. The independent validity of the procedural rules of empirical-analytic, historical-hermeneutic, and critically-oriented sciences is justified by the argument that technical, practical and emancipatory knowledge-constitutive interests are the condition of the possibility of the rules of those sciences.[179]

In the standard neo-Kantian sense, 'validity' corresponds to a domain of objectification. Habermas deplores any 'positivism' which refuses to see the connection between a domain of validity and the transcen-dental framework or interest which gives meaning to the particular form of validity.[180] He does not, however, question the connection between validity and objectification as such.

Unlike other critics of neo-Kantianism, Habermas confirms the autonomy of different kinds of validity, and justifies them by the development of the metacritical framework, which he also calls a 'quasi-transcendental system of reference'.[181] As we have seen, meta-critical or quasi-transcendental arguments are characteristic of other kinds of social theory. Habermas explains quasi-transcendental arguments by saying that the rules for the organizing of processes of enquiry are transcendental, that is, the validity of their statements is established by rules which relate *a priori* to determinate categories of experience. But this transcendental function 'arises from actual structures of human life: from structures of a species that reproduces its social life. These basic conditions of social life have an interest structure.'[182] The notion of a natural species which reproduces its social life is the 'quasi' or 'naturalistic' aspect of the argument.

Thus, unlike the other metacritiques of neo-Kantianism or of Kant, Habermas accepts the centrality of the 'logics' of 'processes of inquiry' in place of Kant's transcendental 'consciousness in general', and subjects *methodologism itself* to a metacritique.[183]

Habermas founds his notion of a quasi-transcendental argument on his reading of Marx's criticism of Hegel. His reading of Marx is a Kantian one: labour is the activity which constitutes the objectivity of possible objects of experience.[184] Labour is *the* synthesizing activity, but in a materialist sense, which Habermas contrasts with the logical accomplishment of Kant's transcendental consciousness.[185]

However, Habermas retains a Kantian moment in his insistence that nature which is synthesized also remains outside the synthesis, 'nature-in-itself'. This represents an opposition to the Hegelian position which, according to Habermas, makes nature into a mere 'other' of Spirit with which it becomes reconciled as 'absolute Spirit'.[186]

Nevertheless, Habermas concedes that a quasi-transcendental argument has a ring of Fichte's 'absolute ego' about it: nature is both created by labouring subjects and is external to them.[187] He insists that the precondition, labour as the self-constitution of a species in 'natural history', is contingent, and empirical ('quasi,' 'naturalistic') as well as transcendental; but it is not 'absolute' in a Fichtean or Hegelian sense. Habermas allows Kant and Darwin into his canon but not Fichte or Hegel.

Habermas accuses Marx of changing the meaning of his own thought by understanding it as a natural science based on instrumental action:

By equating critique with natural science, he disavowed it. Materialist scientism only reconfirms what absolute idealism had already accomplished: the elimination of epistemology in favour of unchained universal 'scientific knowledge' – but this time of scientific materialism instead of absolute knowledge.[188]

A paradoxical result of rejecting Hegel and Marx from the canon of critical sciences is that the third knowledge-constitutive framework, which gives validity to 'critical sciences' appears least justified. In order to prove the existence of the kind of validity which is justified by the framework of an emancipatory transcendental interest, Habermas uncovers an 'ideal-speech situation' in discursive rationality. This is a new-fashioned neo-Kantianism which derives normative validity from the rules of rational *discourse*, communicative competence, instead of from judgements or propositions.[189]

The result of developing a manifold metacritique of methodologies, the *three* constitutive interests, is that metacritique, *ipso facto*, becomes typological and methodological. The most radical metacritique which Habermas discusses in *Knowledge and Human Interests*, Hegel's critique of Kant, is plundered for its critique of transcendental logic, but dismissed forthwith as a 'philosophy of identity'. A corollary of this is the Kantian reading and criticism of Marx. Habermas argues that Adorno's *Negative Dialectic* is unable to deal with the individual sciences or to produce any concrete knowledge,[190] but, as in the case of Adorno, Habermas' cursory mistreatment of Hegel is one of the sources of his own preoccupation with methodology.[191]

It is a great irony that the Frankfurt School's journey away from neo-Kantianism should have culminated in a *Geltungslogik* which is as strict as any of the original models of such logic. This structure partly explains why Habermas' work has proved to be such a unifying force in the international world of sociological reason.

This examination of the attempts of Lukács, Adorno and Habermas to develop sociological transformations of the neo-Kantian paradigm suggests that Marxist sociology meets non-Marxist sociology at that Fichtean station between Kant and Hegel. The difference between these two versions of neo-Fichteanism might be expressed in the following terms. The non-Marxist versions give primacy to theoretical reason, and thus remain, illogically, at the stage of the first part of Fichte's *Wissenschaftslehre*; while the neo-Marxists give primacy to practical reason over theoretical reason, following Fichte's argument to the final part of the *Wissenschaftslehre*. This is another way of contrasting 'the cognitive paradigm'[192] and neo-Marxism.

A Note on Althusser

Althusser's notion of an 'epistemological break' between Marx's early 'humanist' writings and his later 'scientific' writings has introduced a confusion of terminology and ideas into recent debate and obscured the logical structure of Althusser's own thought. For Althusser's notion of 'science' is a *Geltungslogik* of the Marburg type, and his theory of the 'structures of social formations' is a sociological metacritique of the kind which remains within the assumptions of *Geltungslogik*. Althusser is unique in making all the classic neo-Kantian moves solely within a project of rereading Marx.

Althusser starts this reading by rejecting all 'traditional epistemology', but he defines 'epistemology' so broadly that he is able to avoid making any distinction between Kantian epistemology, that is, transcendental method, and Hegel's rejection of that notion of critical method. 'I use this term ['the empiricist conception of knowledge'] in its widest sense, since it can embrace a rationalist empiricism as well as a sensualist empiricism, and is even found at work in Hegelian thought itself. . . .'[193] By 'epistemology' or 'empiricism', Althusser appears to mean not Kantian critical philosophy or neo-Kantianism, but Hegel's philosophy of reflection which is itself founded on a *rejection* of Kantian epistemo-logy. It seems likely that what Althusser understands by 'epistemology' is not Hegel's speculative experience, but Kojève's anthropological reading of Hegel, or Sartre's decisionistic and moralistic appropriation of Nietzsche's thought, which was also based on a rejection of Kantian epistemology. In this indeterminate fashion Althusser tries to discredit philosophy in general, and thus does not acknowledge that the neo-Kantians also criticized Kant's transcendental epistemology in the name of autonomous science.

Althusser distinguishes between 'empiricism', which, in its various forms, believes that its abstractions (the categories?) apprehend the 'real',[194] and the conception of 'knowledge as a production'.[195] In the latter case 'the object' is produced in the 'operation of knowledge'. It does not exist prior to the act of cognition, but 'production itself . . . is identical with the object'.[196] This notion of the production of know-ledge, with its absence of subject-object connotations, is a crude version of Hermann Cohen's notion of cognemes and their production.[197] More basically, Althusser's distinction between the cognition of reality and the production of knowledge corresponds to the neo-Kantian distinction between epistemology as the description of processes of consciousness and logic or science as an autonomous realm of validity and its objectifications.[198] Althusser bases the realm of validity on discourse instead of on judgement.

Althusser provides a sociological metacritique of the 'traditional epistemology', according to which validity or truth is a relation between subject and object. The 'structures of the social formation' are the presupposition of the 'subject'. The priority of structures provides an account of the possibility of subjectivity, or 'acting subjects', *and* a sociological substitute for the traditional validity of subject-object epistemology.

In other places in Althusser's work 'ideology' takes the logical place of 'structures of the social formation' in the constitution of concrete individuals as subjects.[199] 'Ideology' is not the representation or misrepresentation of underlying social relations, not consciousness and its oppositions. It is the 'imaginary relationships of individuals to the real relations in which they live'.[200] Ideology is a structure which like all structure is 'ever pre-given', which precedes subjectivity.

In order to distinguish between the rejected concept of ideology meaning ideas which represent or misrepresent an essential reality in the consciousness of individuals, and the concept of ideology as the precondition of the possibility of individual consciousness, Althusser calls the latter conception 'material'. Ideology in this sense exists

> in material ideological apparatuses, prescribing material practices governed by a material ritual, which practices exist in the material actions of a subject acting in all consciousness according to his belief.[201]

Althusser explicates no further what he means by 'material', but any explanation which is not based on this distinction between ideas and material practice is itself 'ideological' (*sic*).

In his zealous attempt to develop a critique of consciousness and a metacritical account of its possibility, Althusser has completely cut off the quasi-transcendental precondition of his sociology, whether 'structures of the social formation' or 'ideology', from the object which is conditioned, 'the subject', by labelling any explanation which might connect the two as 'ideological'. The relation between them can only be conceived by reducing the subject to what is 'interpellated' by and 'subjected' to the 'subject'.[202] This is merely to rename the problem of the relation between transcendental precondition and conditioned but not to explicate it. As we have seen the problem of the status of the relation between precondition and condition is common to all meta-critical sociologies.

Althusser, however, is not as consistent as Durkheim, who was also unable to provide any account of mediation between a social structure *sui generis* and the individual for fear of compromising the structure of his argument. Durkheim kept his poles, society *sui generis* and the egoistic individual, strictly apart. But in Althusser's writings the categories for a theory of mediation are present, such as 'imaginary relation', or 'practice'. For it may be argued that an 'image' or 'representation' is determined by a social structure without reducing the reality of the social structure to the 'image' or representation', but without Althusser's dichotomy between 'imaginary' and 'real' relation in view of which the connection becomes inexplicable. Similarly, 'practices' can only mean social relations, and the notion of an 'essential object' or 'centred totality' which Althusser scorns, just means the sum of contradictory relations.

Because he splits Marx's work into a pre-scientific, transcendental philosophy of consciousness and a scientific, naturalistic critique of consciousness, Althusser is not able to understand that Marx himself provides a critique of consciousness which does not depend theoretically on transcendent and autonomous structures. Althusser's *sui generis* structures are inexplicable because the means of explication implicit in his theory are classified as 'ideology' in opposition to science. A philosophy of reflection is at the heart of Althusser's sociology, as it is in all sociological metacritiques of the neo-Kantian kind. What is regrettable is not the presence but the denial of this element of Althusser's thought.

Althusser's turning of Marx into a general logic, a 'science' with its objectifications, and his typologies of structures and ideological apparatuses with their metacritical status offer a descriptive sociology which claims to have solved once and for all the question of method and the question of the relation between the precondition and the hapless conditioned.

Canon and Organon

The distinction between 'theory' and 'method' in non-Marxist and in Marxist sociology has become systematically ambiguous. On the one hand, opposition to neo-Kantianism has meant opposition to specific kinds of methodologism. On the other hand, opposition to Marxism and to Hegel's philosophy of history has been expressed in terms of opposition to *theory*, and in the name of neutral and descriptive methodology.

Dilthey and Simmel, for example, made Hegel's notion of 'objective spirit' into a general concept of culture, and Mannheim argued that he was making Marx's particular concept of ideology into a general concept of ideology. As a result of their metacritiques of the Kantian categories, or of meaning, the categories no longer appear primary and unanalysable, but historically variable and changing. Their collective nature at different points in time may therefore be described. Hegel and Marx provided the collective and historically variable concepts. All the metacritics claimed that they had developed neutral descriptive terms which defined a distinct realm, identifiable in any society, by dropping the connections of the concepts in question with the philosophy of history associated with their original use.

In particular, the ambition to develop a 'sociology of knowledge' depended on taking concepts from Marxist theory and Hegelian philosophy of history and turning them into the *conditioned* of a quasi-transcendental metacritique. In this case, 'metacritique' and 'sociology of knowledge' mean the same thing. For the categories or knowledge are derived from a social precondition, and this produces a *sociology* of knowledge. The sociology of knowledge is one kind of metacritical argument. As a result, the sociology of knowledge has been understood as a special branch of sociological method, although it developed as a metacritique of neo-Kantian methodologism.

However, some versions of the sociology of knowledge produced critical theories of capitalism within the anti-Marxist and anti-Hegelian metacritical circle. For example, Simmel's concept of the 'tragedy of culture' can be seen to have a general metacritical structure. 'Life' is the quasi-transcendental precondition, and 'forms', 'validities', or 'objective spirit' are the conditioned. As Simmel cryptically put it, 'life is more life [precondition] and more than life [conditioned]'.[203] The precondition is connected to the conditioned, 'objective spirit' or 'validities' by the formation of 'subjective spirit' or by 'the path of the soul from itself to itself'.[204] The 'tragedy of culture' refers to the difficulty which subjective spirit experiences in bringing about the connection in any society. In *The Philosophy of Money*, Simmel analyses the new dimensions of this general difficulty under the conditions of the capitalist division of labour. As a result Simmel's notions of the 'tragedy of culture' and of 'objective spirit' become ambiguous. They are both universal and descriptive notions which can be applied to any society, and they imply a specific theory of social change in capitalist society. The point of mediation between precondition and conditioned becomes the pivot of a *theory*, a lack of identity between precondition and conditioned.

Other sociological metacritiques have taken a concept from Hegel or Marx and employed it as the *precondition* in a quasi-transcendental metacritical argument. Some of these metacritiques have also produced a *theory* of capitalism within the metacritical structure, while others have not. Thus Jürgen Habermas has 'taken' three kinds of action from Marx, and made them into the preconditions of three knowledge-constitutive interests. He has also developed a *theory* of legitimation problems of late capitalist society within the overall structure of the metacritical argument. Althusser has used Marxist concepts as the precondition of his metacritical argument, 'structures', 'apparatuses', 'ideology', but his metacritique remains non-theoretical.

Those metacritiques which had no point of encounter with Marxism, for example, some forms of phenomenology and hermeneutics, were consistently opposed to neo-Kantian methodologism. They were not interested in transforming specific theoretical terms into universal and descriptive ones. However, the paradoxical result of remaining within a transcendental circle which has no theoretical implications, that is, which has no concept of society in general, or of capitalist society in particular, is that these approaches have been read as especially 'abstract' and 'methodological' prescriptions by sociological reason.

On the whole, both non-Marxist and Marxist sociology have mystified Hegel's thought. Dilthey, Simmel and Mannheim claimed that they were 'demystifying' Hegel's notion of 'objective spirit' by detaching it from the rest of his philosophy, and demonstrating that it could have a general, descriptive use. But, by making 'objective spirit' mean the culture, thought, or 'world view' of any society, they made its relation to other spheres of social life and hence its meaning unclear. In Hegel's thought 'spirit' means the structure of recognition or mis-recognition in a society. 'Objective spirit' is inseparable from absolute spirit, the meaning of history as a whole.

Similarly, Marxist sociology has mystified Hegel by making a distinction between a 'radical method' and a 'conservative system'. As a result of this artificial distinction, the centrality of those ideas which Hegel developed in order to unify the theoretical and practical philosophy of Kant and Fichte has been obscured. These ideas, recognition and appropriation (*anerkennen* and *aneignen*), are fundamental to Hegel's notion of a system, and their importance cannot be appreciated apart from Hegel's critique of the methodologism and moralism of Kant and Fichte. Hegel demonstrated the connection between the limitations of the idea of method in Kant and Fichte and the limitations of the kind of social and political theory which they produced. Hence those critics of Hegel who divide his thought into a method and a system impose a schema on it which he fundamentally rejected. This schema mystifies instead of clarifying the connection between Hegel's systematic ambitions and his critique of Kantian critical method.

In their very different ways, both the non-Marxist and the Marxist critiques of Hegel attempt to drop the notion of the 'absolute', but, at the same time, retain the social import of Hegel's thought. In the case of non-Marxist sociology, the attempt depends on extracting a social object from Hegel's philosophy, 'objective spirit'. In the case of Marxism, the attempt depends on extracting a 'method' whose use will reveal social contradictions. But the 'absolute' is not an optional extra, as it were. As we shall see, Hegel's philosophy has *no* social import if the absolute is banished or suppressed, if the absolute cannot be thought.

The aim of Kantian critical method is to prepare a *canon* of reason, that is, a sum-total of the *a priori* principles of the *correct employment* of the faculties of knowledge.[205] The critique itself is the propaedeutic for the canon. It ascertains the necessary, *a priori* laws in relation not to particular objects, but to objects in general.[206]

A canon of reason is distinguished both from an enquiry into the empirical or psychological principles of the understanding, and from an *organon* of reason. An organon of reason does not confine itself to judging and justifying the proper use of the principles of the understanding by reference to possible experience. It produces and extends knowledge with reference to its objective content. Thus a canon of judgement which is restricted to examining the *form* of knowledge may illegitimately be turned into an organon of reason, if the pure modes or principles of knowledge are used as if they could yield by themselves the *content* of knowledge beyond the limits of experience.[207]

It follows that there can be no canon of *pure* theoretical reason, the faculty of the unconditioned. For there can be no legitimate use of principles of reason without reference to possible experience. The canon is thus the system or sum of modes of objective validity. The idea of a transcendental critique or method as a propaedeutic, that is, of the justification of objective validity, is inseparable from the limitation of valid knowledge to the employment of discursive understanding.

This division of philosophy into a legitimate canon and an illegitimate organon also has consequences for practical philosophy. 'Practical' means everything that is possible through freedom.[208] There is a canon of the pure, practical employment of reason. For there are pure, practical laws, whose end is given through reason completely *a priori* and which are prescribed to us not in an empirically conditioned but in an absolute manner.[209] The will has the power of unconditioned causation of its object denied to pure theoretical reason. But the canon of practical reason is not an organon either. For this power of the will is purely formal, and it is the universal form of the will, not its contents, which is the origin of its causal efficacy.

But does the idea of a canon of judgement deserve the propriety which it reserves to itself?

A main line of argument in the Critical Philosophy bids us pause before proceeding to inquire into God or into the true being of things, and tells us first of all to examine the faculty of cognition and see whether it is equal to such an effort. We ought, says Kant, to become acquainted with the instrument, before we undertake the work for which it is employed; for if the instrument be insufficient, all our trouble will be spent in vain. The plausibility of this suggestion has won for it general assent and admiration; the result of which has been to withdraw cognition from an interest in its objects and absorption in the study of them, and to direct it back upon itself; and so turn it to a question of form. Unless we wish to be deceived by words, it is easy to see what this amounts to. In the case of other instruments, we can try and criticize them in other ways than by setting about the special work for which they are destined. But the examination of knowledge can only be carried out by an act of knowledge. To examine this so-called instrument is the same thing as to know it. But to seek to know before we know is as absurd as the wise resolution of Scholasticus, not to venture into the water until he had learned to swim.[210]

Kant's intention to justify cognition before practising it (method) was also intended to demonstrate that justified cognition is restricted to possible objects of experience. However, if the idea of a justification of thought prior to its employment (method) is contradictory, then thought has made a mistake. It does not know itself at the very point where its self-examination commences. The demarcation of legitimate theoretical and practical knowledge turns out to be the demarcation of new areas of ignorance: God is unknowable, things-in-themselves are unknowable, the source of the causality of the will is unknowable, and the transcendental unity of apperception is unknowable. In sum, the finite only is knowable, while the infinite transcends the realm of thought.[211]

The unknowability of what Kant calls, among other names, the 'unconditioned' or the 'infinite' results in the unknowability of ourselves, both as subjects of experience, 'the transcendental unity of apperception', and as moral agents capable of freedom. *Pari passu*, the unknowability of ourselves means that the social, political and historical determinants of all knowledge and all action remain unknown and unknowable.

Hegel does not criticize transcendental method because it reduces objective validity to psychological processes, but because the restriction of knowledge to finite knowledge or discursive understanding manifestly makes even finite objects unknowable. Kant's philosophy of consciousness can only be criticized if the infinite is knowable.

Hegel does not criticize Kant's philosophy of consciousness because it grants too much importance to representation, perception or the manifold of intuition, but because it grants them too little importance. For, as long as philosophy is restricted to justifying objective validity, to the application of *a priori* forms of knowledge, the object of knowledge can only be subsumed under, or subordinated to, those forms. This holds whether the object is the empirical infinite, the unconditioned infinite, or the infinite *Sollen* of a moral will, which, out of pure reverence for the law, continually subjugates natural desire and inclination.

In the name of a neutral method which seeks solely to justify knowledge, transcendental philosophy justifies infinite ignorance not finite knowledge. It subjects the objects of both theoretical and practical knowledge to the 'domination of the discursive concept'.[212] We can only turn from our limited knowledge of the finite to an insatiable yearning for the unknowable and inaccessible infinite. But this irrational relation to the infinite makes a rational relation to the social and political conditions of our lives impossible. The limitation of 'justified' knowledge of the finite prevents us from recognizing, criticizing, and hence from changing the social and political relations which determine us. If the infinite is unknowable, we are powerless. For our concept of the infinite is our concept of ourselves and our possibilities.[213]

The idea of a canon of reason cannot earn the legitimation which it awards itself.

Hegel put a trinity of ideas in place of Kant's idea of transcendental method: the idea of phenomenology, the idea of absolute ethical life (*absolute Sittlichkeit*), and the idea of a logic. The idea of phenomenology can be seen as an alternative to Kant's theoretical *quaestio quid juris*, while the idea of absolute ethical life can be seen as an alternative to Kant's justification of moral judgements. This, however, would be to concede the Kantian dichotomy between theoretical and practical reason. The idea of all Hegel's thought is to unify theoretical and practical reason. In his *Logic*, as in all his works, the unification is achieved by a phenomenology and the idea of absolute ethical life.

As we have seen, Hegel argued that the attempt to justify theoretical and moral judgements apart from their use is contradictory. The concomitant restriction of legitimate knowledge to the application of the rules of discursive, finite understanding is equally contradictory. For it is consciousness itself which makes the distinction between the finite and the infinite, between knowable appearances and unknowable things-in-themselves. It is consciousness which posits an unconditioned infinite, a being or things-in-themselves, which exist outside any relation to consciousness, and hence at the same time are related to consciousness in a negative sense. The 'unknowable' infinite has been defined by consciousness itself.[214]

There can be no question of changing from Kant's method to a different method, for all 'method', by definition, imposes a schema on its object, by making the assumptions that it is external to its object and not defining it. The only consistent way to criticize Kant's philosophy of consciousness is to show that the contradiction which a methodological, or any natural, consciousness falls into when it considers the object to be external, can itself provide the occasion for a change in that consciousness and in its definition of its object. The new procedure and the new definition of the object may also be contradictory, in which case they, too, will change, until the two become adequate to each other.

A phenomenology thus presents the forms of knowledge according to their own methodological standards as they have occurred, or, as they appear (*erscheinendes Wissen*),[215] and it presents the realm of appearance as defined by limited forms of consciousness.

Once it is shown that the criterion of what is to count as finite and infinite has been created by consciousness itself, then a notion is implied which does not divide consciousness or reality into finite and infinite. This notion is implied by the very distinction between finite and infinite which has become uncertain. But it is not pre-judged as to what this notion, beyond the distinction between finite and infinite, might be. It is not pre-judged in two senses: no autonomous justification is given of a new object, and no statement is made before it is achieved. The infinite or absolute is present, but not yet known, neither treated methodologically from the outside as an unknowable, nor 'shot from a pistol' as an immediate certainty.[216] This 'whole' can only become known as a result of the process of the contradictory experiences of consciousness which gradually comes to realize it.

However, when the illusion of methodological consciousness, that the object is external to it, has begun to be dispelled, this may merely result in the primacy of practical reason. Kant himself taught that practical reason, which creates its object, has a primacy over theoretical understanding which synthesizes appearances. But practical reason in Kant is as contradictory as theoretical reason. It makes a distinction between morality and legality. The will is only moral if autonomous, if it imposes the law on itself out of reverence for the law, and is not motivated to conform to the law for an ulterior end, or on the basis of the external sanctions of a social order (legality). The moral law is merely formal: the will's subjective maxim is universalized in order to test whether it is contradictory or not. But it is conceivable that a maxim which is formally moral, that is, not contradictory when universalized, may be immoral in its content.

Just as the theoretical distinction between finite and infinite is contradictory, so is the practical distinction between morality and legality. Just as the theoretical dichotomy implies a unity which is present, but not pre-judged in the two senses of pre-judge, so the dichotomy of morality and legality implies a unity which is present but not pre-judged. *Sittlichkeit*, 'ethical life', refers to the unity of the realms of morality and legality, and 'the absolute' to the unity of the finite and the infinite. What *Sittlichkeit* is cannot be pre-judged, but the morality of an action cannot be 'judged' apart from the whole context of its possibility. It cannot be judged by separating its morality from its legality, by separating its meaning from the social whole.

These changes in theoretical and moral consciousness wrought by its internal contradictions, its experiences, can only take place over time, as a series of shapes of consciousness. If the absolute cannot be pre-judged but must be achieved, it must be always present *and* have a history.

It is only at the end of this history, not at the beginning, that the 'method' of its development can be discerned. It is only in the final section of the *Greater Logic*, 'The Absolute Idea', that the idea of method is discussed, at which point there can be no misapprehension that the method is a form of justification. Thus the *Logic* is a phenomenology too: it does not allow the concept of 'method' to be discussed until it can appear in a sequence of experiences. But the experiences of logic are not those of a natural consciousness progressively educating itself through its mistakes. The *Logic* presupposes that the opposition between a finite consciousness and its objects has been overcome. The experience of philosophical consciousness in the *Logic* is to *rediscover* the unity of theoretical and moral reason and natural, finite consciousness through the contradictions of the history of philosophy. The *Logic* culminates in the notion of *absolute Sittlichkeit* which is reached in the two sections of the penultimate chapter, 'The Idea of the True', and 'The Idea of the Good'.

2

Politics in the Severe Style

Politics in the Severe Style

In general religion and the foundation of the state is [*sic*] one and the same thing; they are identical in and for themselves.[1]

We may understand the proposition or judgement that religion is identical with the state in several ways. We may read it as a contingent generalization based on induction from experience. In this case we might argue, on empirical grounds, that it is wrong. We may read it as a prescription, as a recommendation that the state and religion should be identical. In this case we might disagree, and argue that such an identity is inconceivable, undesirable, or impossible. We might protest, on the basis of yet another reading, that the proposition is neither empirically wrong, nor undesirable, but unintelligible. For how can religion and the state be identical, unless 'religion' and the 'state' are so defined that the proposition becomes an uninformative tautology? If the proposition is made tautologically true, there is no point in our assent or our dissent.

All of these readings are based on the same assumptions. They divide the sentence into a grammatical subject and predicate joined by the copula 'is'. The grammatical subject is considered a fixed bearer of variable accidents, the grammatical predicates, which yield the content of the proposition.[2] Hegel knew that his thought would be misunderstood if it were read as series of ordinary propositions, which affirm an identity between a fixed subject and contingent accidents, but he also knew that, like any thinker, he had to present his thought in propositional form.

He thus proposed, in an unfortunately schematic statement, that the propositional form must be read as a 'speculative proposition'.[3] This use of 'speculative' is not the same as Kant's use of it. It does not refer to the illegitimate use of correct principles, but embraces the impossibility of Kantian justification. To read a proposition 'speculatively' means that the identity which is affirmed between subject and predicate is seen equally to affirm a lack of identity between subject and predicate. This reading implies an identity different from the merely formal one of the ordinary proposition. This different kind of identity cannot be pre-judged, that is, it cannot be justified in a transcendental sense, and it cannot be stated in a proposition of the kind to be eschewed. This different kind of identity must be understood as a result to be achieved.

From this perspective the 'subject' is not fixed, nor the predicates accidental: they acquire their meaning in a series of relations to each other. Only when the lack of identity between subject and predicate has been experienced, can their identity be grasped. 'Lack of identity' does not have the formal meaning that subject and predicate must be different from each other in order to be related. It means that the proposition which we have affirmed, or the concept we have devised of the nature of an object, fails to correspond to the state of affairs or object which we have also defined as the state of affairs or object to which it should correspond.[4] This experience of lack of identity which natural consciousness undergoes is the basis for reading propositions as speculative identities. The subject of the proposition is no longer fixed and abstract with external, contingent accidents, but, initially, an empty name, uncertain and problematic, gradually acquiring meaning as the result of a series of contradictory experiences.

Thus it cannot be said, as Marx, for example, said, that the speculative proposition turns the predicate into the subject and therefore hypostatizes predicates, just like the ordinary proposition hypostatizes the subject. 'The important thing is that Hegel at all times makes the Idea the subject and makes the proper and actual subject, like "political sentiment", the predicate. But the development proceeds at all times on the side of the predicate.'[5] But the speculative proposition is fundamentally opposed to the kind of formal identity which would still be affirmed by such a reversal of subject and predicate.

The identity of religion and the state is the fundamental speculative proposition of Hegel's thought, or, and this is to say the same thing, the *speculative experience of the lack of identity* between religion and the state is the basic object of Hegel's exposition. Speculative experience of lack of identity informs propositions such as 'the real is the rational', which have so often been misread as ordinary propositions.

Some of Hegel's works[6] present experiences of both religion and the state, or, in other terms, which Hegel uses, of subjective disposition (*die Gesinnung*)[7] and absolute ethical life. *The Philosophy of History* and the *Phenomenology of Spirit* present experiences of both religion and the state. *The Philosophy of Religion* is mostly concerned with the meaning of religion and has important sections on the relations between religion and the state. *The Philosophy of Right* and the earlier political writings from the Jena period refer least of all to religion and to history. These writings concentrate on ethical life and less on forms of subjective disposition, although it is the relation between the two which makes up the whole of ethical life. Thus in these political writings the presupposition of absolute ethical life is more explicit than it is in those works where the relation between the different illusions of natural consciousness (religious, aesthetic, moral) and absolute ethical life is presented.

This is not to say that the earlier works consist of 'regional ontologies', as Habermas has argued,[8] that is, of examinations of distinct realms of social life, not unified by any absolute identity. On the contrary, I am arguing that the unifying presupposition is more explicit in the earlier works, and hence the lack of unity in political life is more explicit too.

However, the earlier political writings and the *Philosophy of Right* are not 'shot from a pistol'. They are phenomenologies: the illusions and experiences of moral and political consciousness are presented in an order designed to show how consciousness may progress through them to comprehension of the determination of ethical life. Hegel starts from what appears to ordinary consciousness as the most 'natural' and 'immediate' ethical relations, the family, or the sphere of needs, civil society. The order of exposition is therefore not necessarily the order in history. The family and the sphere of needs are not autonomous realms antecedent to the state, and to see them as such would be to produce an anthropological reading. But it is even less correct to understand the family or civil society as emanations of an hypostatized state, and to see them as such would be to produce a panlogical reading. Hegel is stressing, in opposition to liberal natural law, that the institutions which appear most 'natural' and 'immediate' in any society, such as the family or the sphere of needs, presuppose an overall economic and political organization which may not be immediately intelligible.[9] Unfortunately, the mistakes of natural consciousness which Hegel was exposing have frequently been attributed to him.

Absolute ethical life is more explicit in the political writings than in other writings. In the *Philosophy of Right* this is because the other illusions which made Hegel despair of any reunification of political and religious life are not prominent.[10] Yet, he could not 'justify' in the Kantian sense the idea of absolute ethical life; he could not provide any abstract statement of it apart from the presentations of the contradictions which imply it. For an abstract statement would make manifest that this ethical life does not exist in the modern world. This would be to turn ethical life into an abstract ideal, an autonomous prescription, a *Sollen*, which would be completely 'unjustified' because not implied by the contradictions between political consciousness and its social and historical bases. Hegel's solution to this dilemma was to emphasize the presence of ethical life, not the task of achieving it. Ironically, as a result, the *Philosophy of Right* has been read as the justification (*sic*) of a *status quo*, instead of the attempt in speculative (dis)guise to commend the unity of theory and practice.

It may therefore be said that Hegel's political theory is written in the 'severe' style (*der strenge Stil*) according to his definition of such style in the *Aesthetics*.[11] The severe style is concerned to give a true representation of its object and makes little concession to the spectator. It is designed solely to do justice to the integrity of the object. It is distinguished from a 'lofty' or 'ideal' style which maintains the integrity of the object, but is concerned, too, that the representation should harmonize with the meaning.[12] An object in the lofty or ideal style receives a more 'complete exposition' than an object presented in the severe style.[13]

It is in the severe style that Hegel wrote what is sometimes called his 'first system', the early Jena writings. In these writings the idea of absolute ethical life emerges from a political critique of Kant and Fichte's 'subjective idealism', as Hegel called it. He always saw Kant and Fichte's thought as illusion which needed to be exposed and acknowledged, but the gradual discovery of the other illusions of natural consciousness made it clear that the political problem could not be solved in the severe style.

Absolute and Relative Ethical Life

In his essay on natural law (1802–3), Hegel explains and criticizes the view of the state and social relations found in both empirical and idealist natural law.[14] He shows how a distinction between 'absolute' and 'relative' ethical life can both account for the contradictions in natural law theory, and give a different account of the relation between society and the state. The essay offers a 'statement' of the position which the phenomenologies of the later Jena period and after develop without the bald terminology of 'absolute' and 'relative'.

Hegel does not name any specific theories of empirical natural law, whereas his discussion of formal or idealist natural law concentrates specifically on the theories of Kant and Fichte. He argues that the claim that any of these modes of treating natural law is scientific is 'spurious'.[15]

It is the relation between what counts as 'empirical' and the organizing principle which he contests in the case of both empirical and formal natural law. In both cases the organizing principle is shown to be an arbitrary, imposed schema, and not a 'scientific' presentation of the underlying structure of law. As a result, natural law theory cannot comprehend the relation between society and the state, or between society and the individual. The unity can only be presented as negative, as an ideal which *should* dominate real relations. In empirical natural law, an organizing principle is essential, but it cannot itself be justified on empirical grounds, and hence can only be arbitrarily chosen. In formal or idealist natural law, the organizing principle is justified in the wrong way, and hence arbitrarily imposed.

Pure and scientific empirical natural law, which are discussed only in very general terms, depend on abstractions, especially the idea of the multiplicity of atomized individuals in a chaotic state of nature.[16] The idea of the mass of individuals in a state of nature is an abstraction disguised as an empirical observation. The abstraction is constructed on the strength of the argument that all known social relations, customs and historical institutions are contingent and transitory. What remains after these historical residues have been subtracted, the chaos of individuals, is then said to be both 'the basic truth of men's condition', and merely a 'fiction' which has to be imagined. This position is 'the harshest contradiction'.[17]

Once this multitude of particular and opposed individuals is posited as a 'state of nature', the kind of law which will abolish the evils of such a state is derived either from 'capacities' or 'faculties' which these atoms are said to possess, or from the destruction which would otherwise prevail. Thus to be in a state of law is 'alien to individuals', and it can *unite* them only abstractly and externally.[18] It cannot *unify* them, because, *ab initio*, they are presupposed as a multitude of non-social beings, and because on empirical principles no unifying principle can be *justified*.

This theory is 'empirical' in a sense which it does not acknowledge. It has taken *a posteriori* a specific sphere from existing society and made it into the *a priori*, the condition, of the limited, external, political cohesion which results from the conflicting interests of the members of that sphere.[19] This sphere is the 'sphere of needs' organized by the private property relations of the entrepreneurial class.[20] Instead of deriving the political unity of society from an imagined state of nature as it claims, empirical natural law 'derives' the real, observed, superficial lack of unity in bourgeois society from an observation of particular fragments of social life which are analysed as if they constituted the fundamental elements of the whole.[21]

This idea of the whole is thus a pre-judice (*Vorurteil*), a part elevated into the whole, and an absolute for which empiricism, which knows no absolutes, can provide no justification.[22]

Kant and Fichte were opposed to empirical natural law, but, in Hegel's eyes, they represent its culmination. They make their unifying principle explicit, whereas empiricism presented its unifying principle in a confused and unacknowledged manner. But they also rigorously separate the empirical realm of necessity from the moral realm of freedom. The freedom of rational beings is defined in opposition to the necessity of the natural, spatio-temporal world. Thus natural law, the science of the rights and duties of rational beings, can no longer be confused with empirical nature. Finally, idealist natural law, like empirical natural law, assumes 'the being of the individual as the primary and supreme thing'.[23]

Hegel's discussion of Kant's justification of moral freedom and of Fichte's justification of legal freedom is prefaced by a devastating attack on the separation of theoretical and practical reason on which their accounts of freedom are based. 'Pure reason' or 'the infinite' is understood by Kant as the unifying idea of reason, which, although it has no legitimate constitutive status in theoretical philosophy does have a legitimate rôle as practical reason. The 'infinite' or 'ego' in Fichte is understood as the primacy of practical reason whose original act posits the non-ego.[24]

In both theoretical and practical philosophy, 'reason' (or, the 'infinite', 'unity', 'the concept') exists in relation to objects of the natural world. For if there were no natural objects (or, the 'finite', 'multiplicity', 'intuition'), there would be no reason. In the case of theoretical reason the relation (*Verhältnis*) between reason and the natural world is one of equality. The 'multiplicity of beings' which stand opposed to reason have an equal status with reason. In the case of practical reason, the 'multiplicity', or natural objects, is 'cancelled' or 'destroyed' in the quest for autonomy.

But the equal status between reason and nature in the one case and the destruction between reason and nature in the other can only be *relative*. For, if the equality or destruction were absolute, *ex hypothesi*, the two poles would not be *related*, and hence reason, with nothing in opposition to it, would not exist at all.

Practical reason (freedom) subordinates what is opposed to it. Hence it cannot be a principle of unification, because it presupposes an opposition between itself and the 'real' or the 'many'. Theoretical reason, on the other hand, grants primacy to what is opposed to it and hence to the relation in which it stands to its objects.[25]

In other terms, critical philosophy divides reason in two: theoretical and practical. In both cases reason is a compound of *unity*, the domination of reason over its object, and *relation*, the relation to what is opposed to it, to what is not identical with it. In moral or practical reason, the unity or domination is given primacy over the relation, over the non-identical. In theoretical philosophy, the relation of reason to its objects, the lack of identity, is given priority over the unity of reason.

In both cases 'unity' does not unify. For the different kinds of unity in theoretical and moral philosophy are only intended to *justify* the validity of judgements in that realm. 'Unity' or 'infinity' are merely formal, to be understood as the *contraries* of 'multiplicity' or the 'finite', but not as the basis of the unification of the finite, of the multiplicity of beings.

Transcendental or critical philosophy cannot conceive of the *content* of freedom but only of the *form* of freedom because it limits itself to justification of the kind of judgements made by a reason which is divided in two. Kant's notion of moral autonomy is formal, not only because it excludes natural desire and inclination from freedom, but because it classifies legality, the social realm, with the heteronomous hindrances to the formation of a free will. Fichte endorses Kant's distinction between morality and legality, but he argues, in his doctrine of natural law, that a community of free, rational beings is conceivable without any reference to the good will.[26] Hence Fichte's natural law is also abstract and formal.

Freedom cannot be concretely conceived by Kant and Fichte because it depends for them on an absolute difference between the realm of necessity (theoretical reason) and the realm of freedom (practical reason). Freedom can therefore only be conceived in a negative sense, as freedom from necessity.[27]

Hegel acquired the practice of reading Kant in terms of these crude dichotomies between reason/nature, infinite/finite, concept/intuition, unity/multiplicity, identity (indifference)/non-identity, from Fichte, whose own reading was indebted to Reinhold's influential interpretation of Kant.[28] Reinhold simplified and perverted Kant's thought in this egregious way.[29] For example, it is incorrect to say that nature is the 'object' of pure practical reason in Kant, although it is true that desire and natural inclination cannot motivate a good will. However, Reinhold's dichotomizing of Kant's philosophy had the positive effect of making it possible to compare the operations of theoretical and practical reason in the same terms, and Reinhold was the first to posit an original act which unified the two spheres of reason.[30]

Hegel argued, however, that Fichte's original act, *Tathandlung*, unified theoretical and practical reason in a merely formal way, and in effect reinforced the separation between theoretical and practical reason.[31] Fichte had not understood what the separation of theoretical and practical reason represented in Kant's transcendental justifications. Thus, on the one hand, Hegel remorselessly indicts Kant and Fichte for their inability to conceive of concrete freedom by a crude assimilation of their different positions. On the other hand, he treats the dichotomies which he attributes to them with great seriousness. For, he argues, only if the dichotomies within each realm of reason (or unity, or identity) are also understood as *relations* or lack of identity can a qualitatively different identity be conceived.

> There is no question of denying this standpoint; on the contrary, it has been characterized above as the aspect of the relative identity of the being of the infinite in the finite. But this at least must be maintained, that it is not the absolute standpoint in which the relation has been demonstrated and proved to be only one aspect, and the isolation of the relation is likewise thus proved to be something one-sided.[32]

An idea of freedom which is not based on a separation of theoretical and practical reason, of necessity and freedom, must recognize the lack of identity or *relation* in Kant and Fichte's theoretical and practical philosophy. These relations (*Verhältnisse*) between reason and its objects presuppose a lack of identity between what is related.

In the second half of the essay on natural law, Hegel demonstrates that this epistemological lack of identity or *relation* must be understood as re-presenting a real social relation, which he calls 'relative ethical life' or 'the system of reality'.[33] The system of reality is the system of the political economy of bourgeois property relations in which law is separated from the rest of social life.

This ethical life is relative in two senses. In the first place, this sphere of life, the practical sphere of enjoyment, work and possession, is only a part of the whole. It is a relative aspect of absolute ethical life, which natural law elevates into the unity of the whole, into the negative principle of the whole society. In the second place, bourgeois property relations are based on a lack of identity (relation). For they make people into competing, isolated, 'moral', individuals who can only relate externally to one another, and are thus subjected to a real lack of identity. Bourgeois private property presupposes real inequality, for the law which guarantees abstract, formal property rights presupposes concrete inequality (lack of identity).

This connection between the relations, the lack of identity, which arise in Kant and in Fichte's philosophy and the real social relations to which the philosophical dichotomies correspond is the most important and difficult point in this essay on natural law.

> This is the reflex which morality in the usual meaning, would more or less fit – the *formal* positing, in mutual indifference, of the specific terms of the relation, i.e. the ethical life of the *bourgeois* or private individual for whom the difference of relations is fixed and who depends on them and is in them.[34]

Kant and Fichte's philosophy assumes individuals in this relation to each other, relative ethical life, and fixes them in it. Like empirical natural law, Kant and Fichte abstract from all specific, historical aspects of social life, and thus reaffirm an abstracted, 'moral' individual who only represents one part of it. Relative ethical life is the life of isolated individuals who exist in a relation to each other which excludes any real unity.[35]

However, in order to achieve and maintain a different viewpoint, absolute ethical life must be understood in a way that is not itself abstract and negative as in Kant and Fichte. It must be realized that to the prevailing system of reality, any other principle of unity will itself appear formal, relative and abstract, because relative ethical life takes itself to be the whole, the absolute.[36] Thus the idea of absolute ethical life must be developed so that it is not abstract and negative, reigning supreme over the reality it suppresses.

Hegel shows in detail that Kant and Fichte's 'formal' notions of freedom, which depend on a relation between reason and its object, presuppose and 'fix' specific, bourgeois, property relations. Kant's justification of moral judgement is based on universalizing the subjective maxims of the will. With reference to Kant's examples, Hegel demonstrates that specific social institutions, above all, private property, are 'smuggled in' (*untergeschoben*) and affirmed by means of this 'formal' criterion.[37]

For example, Kant asks whether we should increase our fortune by appropriating a deposit entrusted to us. Translated into the assertive mood, this becomes the subjective maxim of the will. When it is universalized, that is, when it is considered what would happen if everyone appropriated deposits entrusted to them, the maxim is judged immoral, because a contradiction arises: if everyone appropriated deposits, deposits would not exist.[38] Hegel points out that this is an odd use of 'contradiction'. It is not a *logical* contradiction for no deposits to exist. In effect, reason has legislated a tautology: 'Property is property.' It has presupposed that the maintenance of a specific form of property is desirable. Hegel objects that the contradiction lies instead in the very conceit of 'universalizing' a maxim concerning private property. For private property, by definition, is not universal: if it were universal, it would, *ipso facto*, be abolished as private property. Hegel argues that to 'universalize' property is itself immoral, because it involves taking something *conditioned*, that is, determined by specific social relations, and transforming it into a spurious absolute.[39] The example shows how a formal criterion for the legislation of the will depends on specific, material assumptions. The *relation* between the will and the world reproduces a real social *relation*, a lack of identity.

Hegel criticizes Fichte for the converse fault, for concentration on legality, a free society, without any reference to morality, to the good will.[40] Fichte devised a blueprint for law in a 'free' society apart from any consideration of the subjective disposition of the individual. As a result the blueprint can only be realized by enforcing it on individuals. Hence it is a negative principle of abstract unity. The relation or lack of identity between ego and non-ego becomes the means of conceiving individuals in this social *relation* to each other, a merely external relation. The 'ideal' relation between the individual and the community is achieved by suppressing all aspects of the non-ego, of social life and of the individual, which do not confirm to the ideal. The ideal relation therefore reproduces the lack of identity first assumed.[41]

In Kant and Fichte actions are judged on the basis of an opposition between freedom and necessity. The realm of freedom corresponds to a specific relation or lack of identity, to a real social relation which is only part of social life. But 'freedom' cannot be conceived if it is thus opposed to necessity. Hegel refers this illusion of freedom to the relations or lack of identity which it reveals.

> Thus there is posited a relation of absolute ethical life which would reside entirely within individuals and be their essence, to relative ethical life which is equally real in individuals. Ethical organization can remain pure in the real world only if the negative is prevented from spreading all through it, and is kept to one side. We have shown above how indifference appears in prevailing reality and is formal ethical life. The concept of this sphere is the *practical* realm, on the subjective side, feeling or physical necessity and enjoyment; on the objective side, work and possessions. And this practical realm, as it can occur according to its concept, taken up into indifference, is the formal unity or *law* possible in it. Above these two is the third, the absolute or *ethical*. But the reality of the sphere of relative unity, or of the practical and legal, is constituted in the system of its totality as a class. Thus two classes are formed. . . .[42]

At the beginning of this passage Hegel claims that absolute ethical life is as real in all individuals as relative ethical life, the practical and legal spheres. But, at the end of the passage, he says that absolute ethical life is present as a distinct class with a different property relation. Absolute ethical life does not mean simply the sum of social relations. It means a unity which includes all the real property relations, all the lack of identities, in social life. It is only by acknowledging the lack of identity as the historical *fate* (*Bestimmung*) of a different property structure that absolute ethical life can be conceived. This ethical life includes relations (lack of identity), but these relations do not give rise to the illusion that they afford the immediate and absolute basis for the 'moral' freedom of the individual.

The task of specifying this different kind of unity, this different kind of property relation, is the most complex issue in Hegel's thought. In this text, the idea of absolute ethical life is filled in in a number of tentative ways: the negative unity of the 'system of reality' is contrasted with the real unity of war;[43] the entrepreneurial class is contrasted with a class of politicians, of courageous men, who are released from the sphere of needs and devote themselves to the universal interest;[44] the private property relations of ancient Roman society are contrasted with the absence of any distinction between private and public life in ancient Greece;[45] individuals are contrasted with nations or peoples;[46] and the separation of law and custom is contrasted with the unity of law and custom.[47]

This essay on natural law is important precisely because the distinction between absolute and relative ethical life *is* 'shot from a pistol'. The advantage is that the connection between Hegel's critique of Kant and Fichte's epistemology and the analysis of property relations is particularly clear. The disadvantage is that the text is not a phenomenology: the lack of identity, or relations, is not presented as the experience of a natural consciousness which gradually comes to appropriate and recognize a political relation and unity which is different from that of relative ethical life.[48] As a result of the non-phenomenological structure, the question of the different property relations of absolute ethical life can only be dealt with in an external manner, in the severe style. This explains the wealth of different notions of absolute ethical life.

A phenomenology is, nevertheless, intimated: 'A reality is reality because it is totality and itself the system of stages or elements.'[49]

The System of Ethical Life

The short text, *System der Sittlichkeit*, the system of ethical life, was found in Hegel's *Nachlass*. It was first published in a shortened version in 1893, and the first complete publication did not occur until 1913. Hegel did not give the manuscript any title, but the phrase 'System der Sittlichkeit' is used in the text.[50]

The manuscript is usually dated 1802, and said to have been written slightly before the essay on natural law.[51] It is often said to be philosophically more primitive than the essay on natural law; first, because the former does not refer to different historical periods, and secondly, because it is, putatively, organized on principles taken from Schelling, indicated by the use of the term *Potenz* (stage). The *System der Sittlichkeit* is simply attributed to the period when Hegel is said to have been under the influence of Schelling. Further discussion of the work tends to ignore the so-called 'Schellingesque' structure, and to treat the difference aspects of social life solely in terms of their content, without any reference to the structure within which the concepts appear.[52]

This text is, in certain respects, unlike anything else Hegel wrote. However, there is internal evidence that, philosophically speaking, it comes after the essay on natural law. The *System der Sittlichkeit* consists of a detailed vindication of the radical challenge which Hegel made to Kant and Fichte in the essay on natural law. The structure of the text is designed to demonstrate that the lack of identity, the relations, in the theoretical and practical philosophy of Kant and Fichte correspond to real social relations. In the essay on natural law, the first part of this proposition is discussed in the second section, while the second part of the proposition is addressed in the third section. In the *System der Sittlichkeit*, the discussion of the two parts of the proposition is integrated. It is thus the first 'phenomenology'.

The *System der Sittlichkeit* is informed by the same dichotomies which were attributed to Kant and Fichte in the earlier work, especially the dichotomy or relation (*Verhältnis*) between concept and intuition (*Begriff* and *Anschauung*). In the course of the *System der Sittlichkeit*, the dichotomy between concept and intuition, the dualistic structure of critical philosophy, is replaced by the triune structure of recognition in both the *form* and the *content*. The transition from *Anschauen*, seeing-into, to *Anerkennen*, re-cognizing, is also the transition from propositions of identity to speculative propositions. The emergence of 'recognition' as the central notion depends on the analysis of social and historical forms of misrecognition, or lack of identity. Recognition is, by definition, re-cognizing of non-identity.

First, I will explain the overall structure of the *System der Sittlichkeit*, before discussing the items covered under each head with reference to that structure.

The System of Ethical Life

Editor's Contents	Corresponding Topics	Concept and Intuition
Introduction		
1 Absolute Ethical Life according to its Relation		
A First Potency of Nature. Concept subsumed under Intuition	(a) need/enjoyment	I/C
	(b) work	C/I
	(c) child	I/C
	tool ⎬ *Mitte*	C/I
	speech	Totality of Mitte
B Second Potency of Infinity, Ideality in its Form or in its Relation		
(a) Concept subsumed under Intuition	Machine Property	I/C
(b) Intuition subsumed under Concept	Exchange Contract	C/I
(c) The Potency of the Indifference of (a) and (b)	Master/Slave Family	Totality of (a) and (b)
2 The Negative or Freedom or Crime	(a) devastation	I/C
	(b) robbery	C/I
	(c) suppression	Totality of
	revenge	(a) and (b)
	war	
3 Ethical Life		
First Section: The Constitution	(a) Absolute Ethical Life	
	(b) Relative Ethical Life	
I Ethical Life as a system, tranquil	(a) absolute class	
	(b) class of law	

Editor's Contents	Corresponding Topics	Concept and Intuition
II Government		
A The absolute government		
B Universal government		
A System of Needs		
B System of Justice		
C System of Breeding		
C The free government		

In the essay on natural law, Hegel compared theoretical and practical reason by contrasting the unity and lack of unity or relation which existed in each case between the concept and the object – 'nature' or the 'finite' or 'multiplicity'. In both theoretical and practical reason, the two terms in the relation are united and also distinct from each other or related, not united. In the case of theoretical reason, the terms have an equal status and therefore the sense in which they are related predominates over the sense in which they are united. In the case of practical reason the concept or the unity predominates and therefore the relation is less apparent. However, the relation, or lack of identity persists in the latter case even more strongly, because the concept 'cancels' or 'destroys' multiplicity; it imposes itself, and does not genuinely unify the two poles of the relation.

It was suggested in the essay on natural law that the relations or lack of identity evident in Kant and Fichte's formal epistemology correspond to specific social relations or lack of identity. The *relations* (*Verhältnisse*) re-presented a *relative* part of ethical life which had been presented by Kant and Fichte as the whole, and that part corresponds to the relations (inequalities) of bourgeois private property.

Hence the first part of the *System der Sittlichkeit*, 'Absolute ethical life according to its Relation [*Verhältnis*]' means *relative* ethical life. This relative ethical life is ethical life from the perspective of the social relations which make absolute ethical life invisible. Hence relative ethical life can at first only be presented 'according to its relation'. To be able to see that the relation (*Verhältnis*) is relative (*relative*) implies a change in perspective. The organization of the first part follows from the point

made in the essay on natural law, namely, if relative ethical life predominates in a society, then absolute ethical life cannot simply be
asserted as its truth, for this would make absolute ethical life into an
equally arbitrary and negative absolute.

The second part, 'The Negative or Freedom or Crime', demonstrates how in a society where relations (lack of identity) are made into
the principle of unity, the absolute, the result is a negative, external
notion of freedom, which justifies equally the lack of freedom or crime
which arises out of the property relations it presupposes.

The third part reaches absolute ethical life. The previous parts are
then retraversed according to the perspective from which they can now
be seen, not as relations (*Verhältnisse*), but as relative ethical life. The
previous stages are re-cognized as specific class and property relations.
A different property relation designed to counterbalance bourgeois
private property is outlined in order to fill in the notion of absolute
ethical life. Absolute ethical life is substantially not merely formally
free.

The stages are called *Potenzen*. *Potenz* means 'stage' in the sense of a
part which must be re-cognized as an active and real part of a whole,
but which mistakes itself for the whole. A stage constitutes one of a
series of lack of identities and anticipates a different kind of identity
which will acknowledge it.[53]

In the *System der Sittlichkeit*, Hegel's basic dichotomy, his shorthand
for critical philosophy, is the dichotomy between concept and intuition,
instead of the dichotomies between reason and nature, infinite and
finite, unity and multiplicity, which abound in the essay on natural law.
Intuition becomes increasingly central because Hegel is critical of the
way both Fichte and Schelling, in the latter's transcendental works,[54]
endorse the idea of intellectual intuition, but, nevertheless, remain
within the dichotomies and antinomies of critical philosophy. It is
Kant, Fichte and Schelling's (intellectual) intuition which is transmuted
into recognition (*Anerkennen*) and hence into the concept or absolute,
and not their notion of the infinite or concept which Hegel adapted.
Hegel was combating not endorsing the primacy of practical reason in
Kant, Fichte and Schelling. This primacy is developed by Fichte and
Schelling into an original positing of the ego and non-ego, or into an
act of intellectual intuition, which precedes the processes of empirical
consciousness.

The text of the *System der Sittlichkeit* is set out in a way designed to derive one by one the social institutions re-presented by the philosophical dichotomies between concept and intuition. These derivations continue up to the point where it becomes possible to leave the sphere of individualistic misunderstanding, of relations (*Verhältnisse*), and to reconsider them as relative ethical life.

The first part, 'Absolute ethical life according to its Relation', is divided into two sections. The first section, A, is called the 'First Potency of Nature. Concept subsumed under Intuition'. The second section is called 'Second Potency of Infinity, Ideality in its Form or in its Relation'. The title of the first section refers to the way theoretical reason gives primacy to nature or intuition, but only by subsuming its opposite, the concept, not by unifying the *relata*. The title of the second section refers to the way practical reason, or infinity, or ideality, achieves a unity by dominating nature or what is opposed to it. Under the second section, there are three subsections. Each subsection examines the relations, lack of identity, which infinity cannot avoid as long as it imposes itself. The first subsection looks at the relations from the point of view of the intuition (nature) which infinity attempts to suppress, the second subsection looks at the relations from the point of view of the concept which attempts to suppress the intuition. The third subsection demonstrates that the social relations which correspond to the previous two subsections must be acknowledged as parts of a totality (indifference).

This pattern of deriving the social relations and institutions which correspond to the domination of concept over intuition and of intuition over concept, and of demonstrating the relativity of those institutions by further deriving the totality of that sphere of institutions, is repeated many times within A and within the subsections of B. Thus Hegel establishes a logical order for comprehending the connections and lack of identity of the social totality. It is irrelevant to describe this procedure as non-historical, for even in Hegel's 'historical' works the logical order is prior to the historical material. All Hegel's works roam backwards and forwards over history to establish the connections between property forms and political relations.

The *System der Sittlichkeit* is an attack on the primacy of the concept, and on the predominance of social relations to which such philosophical primacy corresponds. At the same time the exposition of absolute ethical life starts from these relations, lack of identity or difference, from their own (mis)understanding of themselves.[55] The absolute identity cannot be starkly opposed to these relative identities, for the absolute identity would then also be only negative and abstract, another imposed concept. Hence this different kind of identity must be evolved out of intuition, the nature which is subsumed. To put it in different terms, the idea of a just society where pure and empirical consciousness coincide cannot be merely legislated, for then it would be as unjust as the one imposed by the concept. The idea of a just society can only be achieved by a transformation not of the concept but of intuition (*Anschauung*). Intuition, *an-schauen*, means a 'seeing-into'. Instead of nature being subordinated, the manifold of intuition, which is seen into or intuited, must be able, in its turn, to look back, *without*, in its turn, subsuming or denying the difference of that at which it looks back.

The relations or lack of identities do not consider themselves to be in a state of relation, for they do not see that their unity has been achieved by subsumption. The 'first potency' is overall 'natural ethical life'. It refers to the most simple, objective, general relations; but the manifold has subsumed the concept, and hence these relations are arbitrary not universal.[56] Strictly speaking, nature or intuition can predominate but not subsume, and hence the institutions are 'natural', not aware of any opposition to the universal.

The potency of feeling (intuition) is considered in two ways. When it subsumes the concept, it is sheer need or desire; when it is subsumed by the concept, it is work, productive labour. In other terms, the simplest feeling which determines human agency is the feeling of need, lack of identity or difference from the world; while the simplest form in which human agency dominates or controls its most basic needs is productive labour. Labour presupposes the difference or lack of identity of need, but changes it into a relation, equal and different, by imposing itself on and transforming the material world to satisfy the need. Labour makes the object 'ideal' in a transformation which acknowledges the difference in this relation.[57]

The subsequent potencies presuppose these two. Once the relation of desire or need is transformed into work, other relations in which either the concept or intuition dominate can be derived which presuppose the previous relations. In this way the more complex relations are the summation or totality of the old ones. Love and education represent relative identities between lack of identities in which intuition dominates the concept (love), and the concept dominates intuition (education).[58]

The first two 'relative identities' of feeling and labour are themselves brought into relation or *mediated* by *Mitte* – means.[59] The introduction of the term '*Mitte*' is new, but the idea that more complex relations develop out of simpler ones is not. The *Mitte* are also derived from the relative predominance or identity of concept over intuition and of intuition over concept.

In this way the child, the tool and speech are introduced. The child is a *Mitte*, the difference which is acknowledged when the concept is subsumed by intuition. For the child is natural and also different. It presupposes the difference and unity of the sexes. This corresponds to the earlier stage of feeling.[60]

The tool corresponds to the earlier stage of labour: intuition subsumed under the concept. As a 'means' it connects human agency and nature. It is 'rational', because it can be used by anyone and hence connects people; but it is domination because the tool subordinates and dominates the object. The child on the other hand 'is a means as pure, simple intuition,' which does not dominate, but which, for example, will be dominated in its education.[61]

Speech is the *Mitte* which connects the two others, the child and the tool.[62]

In the second part, 'Infinity, Ideality in its Form or in its Relation', the dominance of the concept corresponds to those social institutions or relations where the universal interest is acknowledged. This universal is conceived as external domination, as the suppression of some by others. The first section of this part derives property from the point of view of the isolated individual; the second section derives exchange and contract from the same point of view. The third section derives the relation between individuals which the institutions of the first two sections presuppose. This relation is the domination of some individuals by other individuals. Domination of some people by other people implies non-domination, and thus the family, the simplest natural form of non-domination, is derived.

These forms of domination are derived from the relations which arise between people when they define themselves as 'persons', the term for bearers of legal property rights according to Roman and modern bourgeois property law.

In the first section, the concept is subsumed by intuition. The interest of particular individuals and the division of labour is derived from this. Each individual produces according to his particular interests with the result that the labour and the products become increasingly diverse and fragmented. This division of labour gives rise to surpluses which cannot be used by the individual who produced them, but can be used to satisfy the needs of others. In this limited sense, individual activity achieves a universal reference.[63]

The possessor of surpluses, who is recognized by others merely in this negative sense – by virtue of what he does not need or cannot use – is a possessor of property. Property as abstract property in this sense is recognized by law. The possessor is recognized in law as a person. 'Personality' is an abstraction of the law, and the claim to possess is the basis of the right to be recognized by law: '*Recht an Eigentum ist Recht an Recht* [Right to property is right to right [law]].'[64]

In the second section, the concept subordinates intuition. The institutions of exchange and contract are derived. Exchange and contract depend on making things which are particular and different formally comparable or abstract, turning them into value or price.[65] Exchange and contract depend on the recognition of formal equalities which presuppose lack of identity or inequality.

The third section is the potency of indifference, or the unity of property (first section) and exchange (second section) so far considered solely from the individual's point of view. In this potency the recognition between people or the totality which the institutions of property and exchange presuppose is derived. People are relatively identical, or exist in relation to each other as persons. They are 'identical' in the same formal way that things exchanged are identical. One property is abstracted and made definitive and commensurable. This kind of identity is relative, and it presupposes a real relation or lack of identity. The concept of equal persons, meaning equal right to own property, presupposes people without property. It presupposes people in all those relations which have not been taken up into the legal concept of 'person'. People who are not persons, who do not have even the right to property, are, in Roman property law, things, '*res*'. The formal recognition of private property right presupposes this relation or subordination of others. One 'person' behaves as the 'cause', 'concept', or 'unity' of the other. If this identity has no means (*Mitte*) to mitigate it and transform it, it is the relation of master to slave.[66]

The family is the relation which restores a real totality, an identity of needs, sexual difference and relation of parents to children, which cannot be considered a formal property relation. Hegel was opposed in general to deriving social cohesion and political unity from any of the concepts of bourgeois private property, such as the idea of the state as a 'contract'. He was therefore opposed to the particular idea in Kant of marriage as a contract. This was to view the family as the concept subsuming intuition, while for Hegel it represents intuition subsuming the concept, natural ethical life.[67]

The second part of the *System der Sittlichkeit* concerns the way this society acknowledges an ideal unity, its idea of itself as a whole or identity.[68] This unity is negative, for while it recognizes the relations or lack of identity, it only does so in order to dominate and suppress them. It is a moral ideal which subsumes and cancels nature, and hence it reconfirms the unjust property relations on which it is based. Hegel's argument is that any notion of freedom, whether Kant's moral autonomy or Fichte's legal freedom, which is opposed to necessity or the realm of nature, *justifies* the crimes which arise out of the real inequality presupposed by the formal equality of private property relations.

This ideal of freedom or unity denies real relations and hence fixes them. It cannot transform real relations, it can only injure them: '*das Leben ist in ihr nur verletzt* [in it life is only injured].'[69] For the ideal of law or social unity implies revenge. All aspects of social life which do not conform to the abstract ideal are injured, punished, suppressed. The abstract notion of freedom creates crime, because all the aspects of social life which are unacknowledged become criminal.

It is the crimes against 'persons' and property which Hegel lists: rape, robbery and so on. These crimes are inversions of the master-slave relation. The master-slave relation is a limiting case which occurs when one of two persons is so dominated that he ceases to be a person, he is enslaved. No crime is possible in this case, for to commit a crime presupposes that one is not totally suppressed. It is the ambiguity or the gradations of relations of suppression implied by the definition of people as 'persons' which correspondingly classifies acts as crimes. Death is an extreme case of master-slave relation, honour of the personality the opposite extreme.[70]

By the third part, 'Ethical life', the potencies have been considered both in their particularity (intuition, *Anschauung*) and their universality (concept). This universality is so far only abstract universality, and hence always in an unacknowledged relation (*Verhältnis*) to intuition. The family was the most universal relation, when intuition is not suppressed or subsumed by the concept. Each member of the family sees him or herself in the others and acknowledges the difference. However, the family is a form of natural cohesion, and is not a model for social and political cohesion.[71]

There must be an identity, a real freedom or unity which is not a negative ideal, not opposed to empirical consciousness, according to which the individual, beyond natural determinations, but without suppressing them, can achieve 'a seeing of himself in the alien'.[72]

> Through ethical life and in it alone, intellectual intuition is real intuition, the eye of spirit and the loving eye coincide: according to nature man sees the flesh of his flesh in woman, according to ethical life he sees the spirit of his spirit in the ethical being and through the same.[73]

In this way, a seeing into (*An-schauen*) which does not dominate or suppress but recognizes the difference and sameness of the other is conceived. Hegel calls this real intuition, 'absolute intuition' (*absolute Anschauung*), and it means the same as what he also calls 'spirit' and later calls the 'concept'.[74] In other terms, when the other is seen as different and as the same as oneself, as spirit not as a person, as a living totality not as a formal unity, then empirical consciousness will coincide with absolute consciousness, freedom with necessity. This can only be achieved in a just society. To say that absolute and empirical consciousness coincide is to say that society, in its complexity, is transparent. It is not dominated by an imposed unity which makes real relations invisible, and which prevents empirical consciousness of the isolated individual from coinciding with universal consciousness (everyone's consciousness and consciousness of everyone) because so many others and so many aspects of oneself are suppressed.[75]

From the absolute point of view the starting point is not individual action, but the universal spirit, reciprocal recognition, which acts in the individual. This identity is not the identity of bourgeois relations, but bourgeois relations are recognized in their limited place.[76]

The rest of the *System der Sittlichkeit* retraverses the institutions already derived 'in their relation', but from the perspective of absolute intuition. Bourgeois society is now seen as relative ethical life in which the opposition between relative and absolute ethical life is hidden. The notion of absolute ethical life is filled in by counterbalancing bourgeois private property on the one side by a virtuous class, and on the other side by a class of peasants or farmers which also does not partake of the 'freedom' of bourgeois private property relations. By acknowledging the contradictions of bourgeois enterprise and private property, Hegel hoped to surmount and contain them. He developed a notion of absolute ethical life which does not deny and suppress, nor reproduce, real relations, lack of identity.[77]

The great achievement of the *System der Sittlichkeit* is the demonstration that Fichte and Schelling's 'intellectual intuition' is 'real intuition'.

Kant argues that there could be no legitimate application of a concept without reference to the forms of empirical intuition, time and space. There can be no justification of intellectual intuition in the pre-critical sense of deriving existence from a concept. Fichte and Schelling, without any return to the pre-critical position, argue that the primacy of practical reason, which Kant established, presupposes pre-conscious, original, free acts *prior* to the empirical or discursive operations of consciousness. These acts of positing the ego and the non-ego make possible the distinctions between the legitimate operations of theoretical understanding and the legitimate operations of practical reason on which Kant's critical philosophy depends. The original acts explain Kant's unexplicated and inexplicable transcendental unity of apperception and the causal efficacy of the will. The operations of a discursive, empirical understanding which must connect intuitions to concepts presuppose these acts. Hence Fichte calls the original act, 'intellectual intuition',[78] while Schelling calls it 'productive intuition'.[79]

Hegel argues that Fichte's and Schelling's intuition justifies and does not resolve the oppositions and *aporias* of Kant's theoretical and practical reason. Intellectual intuition does not resurrect the intuition which is dominated and suppressed in Kant, but establishes even more strictly the primacy of the concept of practical reason.[80] 'Intellectual' and 'productive intuition' are new ways of justifying the domination of the concept.

In the *System der Sittlichkeit*, Hegel shows that 'intellectual intuition' must be understood as 'real intuition', not as an opposition or relation between two poles, concept and intuition, but as a triune recognition. This recognition assumes a relationship (*Beziehung*) in which the *relata* are able to see each other without suppressing each other. Hegel initially kept the word 'intuition', 'seeing into', to express this, because it had the advantage, once the 'intellectual' is dropped, of avoiding the dichotomies of the philosophies of reflection. 'Reflection' as applied to philosophies based on the dichotomy of concept and intuition means that 'a' sees itself directly in what is opposed to it, 'b', but the seeing is one-sided. 'A' sees itself in 'b', but 'b' does not see itself in 'a'. Hence 'a' sees only a distorted view of itself, the reflection of individual domination. Absolute intuition or absolute reflection means that 'a' in seeing 'b' also sees 'b' looking back at 'a', and hence 'a' sees itself fully as both 'a' and 'b'. 'A' sees that 'b' is not 'a', and that 'b', too, can see 'a' either one-sidedly or reciprocally. It was the impossibility of stating this adequately in terms of 'images', or 'mirrors' implied by the terminology of 'reflection', that led Hegel to abandon the term intuition, and to distinguish sharply between thought (philosophy) and media of images or representation (*Vorstelling*), art and religion.

In the Jena lectures of 1803–4 and 1805–6 Hegel gradually changed intuition, *An-schauen*, into re-cognizing, *An-erkennen*. 'Re-cognizing' emphasizes the lack of identity or difference which is seen. *Anschauen*, to intuit or to perceive, has the semantic disadvantage of sounding too immediate, too pre-critical, too successful. The 'an', 'into', becomes 're', 'again' in *An-erkennen*. *Anerkennen* thus implies an initial experience which is misunderstood, and which has to be re-experienced. It does not imply an immediate, successful vision, but that the immediate vision or experience is incomplete, '*Das Bekannte überhaupt ist darum, weil es bekannt ist, nicht erkannt* [The well-known is such because it is well-known, not known].'[81] The familiar or well-known, the immediate experience (*das Bekannte*), is a partial experience which has to be re-experienced or known again (*anerkannt*) in order to be fully known (*erkannt*). Hence 're-cognition' implies initial mis(re)cognition, not an immediate 'seeing into'.

'Recognition' refers to the lack of identity or relation which the initial dichotomy between concept and intuition, or consciousness and its objects, represents. But it also implies a unity which includes the relation or lack of identity. This unity mediates between the poles of the opposition and is hence triune. 'Recognition', 'concept' and 'spirit' all have this triune structure. They all refer initially to lack of identity, relation, or domination. They all yield speculative propositions, and eschew the propositions of identity based on the primacy of the concept of pure practical reason. Miscognition implies, but does not pre-judge, real recognition.

In the two series of Jena lectures 'recognition' is introduced as formal recognition and hence as miscognition.[82] In the *System der Sittlichkeit* and the lectures of 1803–4, property and possession precede formal recognition. In the lectures of 1805–6, taking and holding possession presupposes formal recognition.[83]

In the *System der Sittlichkeit*, the simplest, triune unity or mediation was expressed in terms of a discrete means (*Mitte*), something which mediated between, or united, concept and intuition. The simplest mediation is one in which the relation or lack of identity predominates, when the concept subsumed intuition, in work. Work was accomplished by using a tool, and the product of labour belonged to the individual as his possession. By working, using a tool, or possessing the product, the individual sees himself, but in a formal way. He does not see the activity of others in his own activity, nor does he see other aspects of his own activity.

By making the world, the tool, the product, his own, by appropriating them (*an-eignen*), the individual recognizes himself in a formal and partial sense. Appropriation, making someone or something into one's own ('an' means 'into', 'eignen' means 'own'), is the simplest but formal way of re-cognizing oneself. It does not see what is excluded, the relation or non-identity. Hence this recognition is a new form of misrecognition and remains so as long as it occurs within bourgeois property relations.

Only in the *Phenomenology of Spirit*, but not in the master-slave section, did Hegel connect re-cognition and appropriation within the context of absolute ethical life in an exposition of a different property and work relation.[84] In the 'phenomenologies' of the earlier Jena period, recognition and appropriation occur only in the potencies of relation (*Verhältnis*), of bourgeois private property, which is later seen to be relative ethical life, the sphere of society called 'the state of nature' in natural law.

Recognition and Misrecognition

Recognition as a form of misrecognition arises out of the contradiction of bourgeois private property. What is the contradiction of bourgeois private property?

In the essay on natural law, Hegel argued that it was 'immoral' for Kant to 'universalize' any subjective maxim of the will which presupposes the institution of private property, since private property cannot, by definition, be universal: '. . . property itself is directly opposed to universality; equated with it, it is abolished.'[85]

Private property is a contradiction, because an individual's private or particular possession (*Besitz*) can only be guaranteed by the whole society, the universal.[86] The universal (*das All-gemeine*) is the community (*die Gemeine*).[87] This guarantee makes possession into property (*Eigentum*). Property means the right to exclude others, and the exclusion of other individuals (particular) is made possible by the communal will (universal). But, if everyone has an equal right to possess, to exclude others, then no-one can have any guaranteed possession, or, anyone's possession belongs equally to everyone else.

The idea of possession thus contains a contradiction. For things are, in themselves, universal, and are made into the possession of the particular individual. This contradiction appears to be removed by the communal recognition of possession as property. The security of my property is the security of the property of others: I recognize their right to exclude me from their property in return for my right to exclude them. But the contradiction remains that no-one can have any secure property. The only alternative is for my possession, *qua* possession, to remain in my possession, but, *qua* property, for it no longer to refer solely to me, but to be universal. *Qua* property, my possession belongs to everyone, and is hence no longer individual private property. This would remove the contradiction of private property by abolishing private property as such.[88]

However, Hegel starts from the actuality of individual private property. The universal notion of property has not been maintained and the private form predominates. Each private possessor or owner exists abstractly, for himself, outside the universal, the society as a whole.[89]

Although the totality of individuals, the community, is the whole of the people, as individuals they live in an extension of their existence, private property. In this way they are complete masters. They are only conscious of their own individuality, their personality, and their external possessions, things. Individuals isolated in this fashion have no honour and no respect for each other. They take their isolated possessions to be the totality, the universal.[90]

How can there be any reference to absolute ethical life in a society based on bourgeois private property, on lack of identity, on relative ethical life, where the real totality can only appear to these isolated individuals as abstract and unreal?

In a two-page fragment placed by the editors at the end of the Jena lectures of 1803–4, Hegel starts to expound the other forms of recognition which correspond to the recognition of private property relations.[91] When in private property the concept subsumes intuition and relations predominate, then in art intuition subsumes the concept and unity or the universal predominates. Hence absolute ethical life is represented or intuited by art. But in a society based on private property relations, art, too, becomes a form of misrecognition. For if intuition predominates over the concept, art can only re-present a real social relation not a real unity. Art (and religion) is 'absolute' in the sense that it presents absolute ethical life, but it is also imagination (*Vorstellung*) or intuition, a form of misrecognition, because configuration (*Gestaltung*) or image (*Bild*) or intuition predominate.

In the later works this condensed analysis of the connection between bourgeois private property relations and art is developed into an historical typology of different property relations, division of labour and art forms. The analysis of different historical types is a way of extending the analysis of the contradictions of modern, post-revolutionary, bourgeois society.

In a society which can only represent absolute ethical life to itself as the relations of private property, as isolated individuals, corresponding illusions of the absolute appear in the form of art. In art, too, individuals are seen or misrepresented as isolated. Their only way of appearing universal is represented, at its simplest, by the inner emotion of love. 'Love', however, remains particular, without any universal achievement (*werklos*).[92] If the individual is represented as active, he acts not on behalf of the universal, but appears engrossed in individual, romantic adventures. The appearance of these individuals is not beautiful, for the intuition or configuration of isolated individuals dominates and is in *relation* not harmony with the universal.[93]

In a society in which the idea of universality or unity is not an existing reality but a concept imposed on reality, the concept of pure practical reason, which subsumes nature or intuition, that unity can only be misrepresented by art. The unity is represented as dwelling in a realm distinct from real social relations.[94] It has no *presence* as the communal achievement (*Werk*) of existing individuals, and can only be represented as *beyond* real existence. This unity or absolute is thus in opposition to the real life of individuals who do not live in it. The art form which represents this is the divine comedy. Divine comedy

represents an absolute beyond which annihilates individual consciousness, in contrast to the epic which presents a present in which individuals live. Divine comedy represents a humanity which has absolute
certainly only in its negation, whose acts are immediately destroyed.
The spectator of a divine comedy can only burst into tears. As a witness
he is powerless, because human character is represented as eternally
past and unchangeable.[95]

Art in bourgeois society, whether it represents love, romantic
adventures or divine comedy, denies the present and is an absolute,
impotent longing (*Sehnsucht*) for the past or the future.[96]

This beautiful fragment ends with an enigmatic allusion to the
alternative:

Der Innhalt in dem das absolute Bewusstseyn erscheint, muss sich
von seiner Sehnsucht, von seiner Einzelnheit die ein Jenseits der
Vergangenheit und der Zukunft hat befreyen, und der Weltgeist
nach der Form der Allgemeinheit ringen; der blosse Begriff des
absoluten Selbstgenusses muss aus der Realität in die er sich als
Begriff versenkt hat, erhoben [werden], und inden er sich selbst *die
Form* des Begriffs, reconstruirt er die Realität seiner Existenz und
wird absolute Allgemeinheit. Nachdem . . .

(The content in which the absolute consciousness appears must free
itself from its yearnings, from its singularity that has a beyond in the
past and the future, and wrest the world-spirit forth in the form of
universality; the mere concept of absolute self-enjoyment must [be]
elevated out of the reality in which it has submerged itself as concept,
and as it [gives] itself *the form* of concept, it reconstructs the reality of
its existence and becomes absolute universality. After . . .)[97]

The imperative, commendatory note of this apostrophe is unmistakable.

The Jena lectures of 1805–6 conclude with a section, not a fragment,
on 'Art, Religion and Science'.[98]

Art is now considered as the simplest of two forms which misrepresent absolute ethical life in a society based on the relations of bourgeois
private property.

Art is the predominance of intuition over the concept. But in
bourgeois society absolute ethical life is misconceived as the primacy of
the concept of pure practical reason, of the predominance of concept
over intuition. Recognition is therefore formal, and the concept

dominates so much that the intuition subsumed becomes fragmented and arbitrary.[99]

Art is the re-presentation of the kind of recognition or misrecognition prevalent in a society, of its spirit, in the 'medium of intuition'.[100] But in bourgeois society intuition is displaced and distorted. As a consequence art fluctuates between representing the extremely isolated individuals, the formal recognition of the concept or pure ego, and representing the arbitrary, debased intuition in its mass of disconnected and random details. Art in such a society is unable to unify concept and intuition, or meaning and form (*Gestaltung*), but emphasizes one or the other. Art is thus not art, not the representation of recognition in the medium of intuition.[101] It falls into a contradiction. This contradiction reproduces the contradiction between real social relations and an imagined unity in a society of private property relations. The divorce between the real relations and imposed unity is reinforced by the oscillation of art between representation of the isolated ego and representation of autonomous detail.

Art thus becomes a screen, which hides truth (absolute ethical life) and does not present it (in the medium of intuition).[102]

Religion represents absolute ethical life more adequately than art. But it projects its image into a realm beyond real social relations.[103] Religion is a second 'medium of intuition', which is more successful than art in presenting extreme individuality as universal.[104] It is better able to unite the concept (individuality) with intuition, and thus to transform the meaning of relations between isolated individuals into universality, into an ideal of recognition between them which is not formal, into spirit or 'God'.[105] Religion raises each individual to an intuition, to a seeing of himself as universal.

The absolute religion (*die absolute Religion*) is that religion which unifies concept and intuition, intuition and concept, and thus transforms the dichotomy into recognition, into the knowledge that the isolated individual (concept) is God (intuition), and that God (concept) is finite man (intuition).

If concept and intuition were thus fully transformed the copulae in the propositions 'God is man' and 'Man is God' would be taken as speculative not identical. But in a society based on bourgeois private property relations, the 'is' can only be misrepresented as an ordinary identity in which intuition dominates. Hence the propositions 'God is man', and 'Man is God' are represented or imagined by religion as referring to an event in the past or in the future. God as man and man as God are represented in the medium of intuition, and hence intuition predominates over the concept and remains in the realm of relation (*Verhältnis*).

Thus religion, too, is a form of misrecognition. Instead of presenting absolute ethical life as real recognition, recognition is misrepresented as occurring in a world distinct from the world of real social and political relations, as occurring in heaven. It is the real domination of these social and political relations which determines the displacement of religious intuition. This displacement is not a *divorce* between concept and intuition as it is in art, but a unity which is removed from the real world. This displacement of intuition encourages dreams and delusions. Everyone believes himself to be a prince or God.[106]

Instead of uniting concept and intuition religion debases real social relations even more than art. For art remains in the contradiction between intuition and concept. Religion, however, reconciles concept and intuition in another world, and thus makes our relation to both the world beyond and real existence one of impotent longing. Religion, unlike art, maintains the image or intuition, the promise of a real transformation, but at the same time, prevents its actual development.

Religion represents the recognition or spirit prevalent in the community, but in the medium of imagination (*Vorstellung*) or faith (*Glauben*).[107] Intuition, seeing into, which is immediate, and hence not a re-cognition, predominates. Hegel calls this the opposition of church and state: '*Die Kirche hat ihren Gegensatz am Staate.*'[108] This proposition appears to controvert the proposition with which this chapter commenced, that religion is identical with the state. However, it does not refer to the constitutional history of church and state, but to religion in general (the church) as a form of intuition, which re-presents absolute ethical life, the unity of concept and intuition, in a realm beyond real social relations (the state) but which is determined by those relations.

A result of this separation is that the church and state, as distinct sets of social institutions, become 'fanatical'. Each seeks to impose itself on the other. The church, which represents the predominance of intuition over the concept, of unity over relation, wants to bring about the rule of heaven on earth with no reference to real social and political relations. The state, which represents the predominance of concept over intuition, of bourgeois property relations, wants to rule without any respect for people's conscience or beliefs.[109]

Nevertheless, both religion and the state in this condition of mis-recognition refer to real recognition, and thus they can, in principle, guarantee and secure each other.[110] In many of his later works Hegel relates misrecognition and recognition in these spheres to each other. As long as bourgeois property relations and hence formal recognition prevail religion can only be a form of misrepresentation.

Since relative ethical life and its corresponding media of misrepresentation do prevail, the initial question of how absolute ethical life can appear in a society based on specific property relations without itself appearing abstract and unreal remains unanswered. For art and religion merely re-present absolute ethical life in the medium of mis-representation, intuition, and thus present only relative ethical life.

However, absolute ethical life has been alluded to as an unspecific unity of concept and intuition, intuition and concept, as a universal (*allgemeine*) in the communality (*die Gemeine*),[111] and as a reform of religious thought. Real recognition requires different property relations. It is philosophy (science) which has been intimating this real unification.

What is the status of this *unjustified* philosophy, which is briefly discussed by way of conclusion?[112]

On the one hand, philosophy, as the *exposition* of real recognition between concept and intuition, intuition and concept, does not fall into the dichotomy itself. It does not present the unity as past or future, as beyond the real world. The unity of spirit, of reason and nature, of concept and intuition, is presented as eternal and in time. For the eternal is in time, not beyond it.

On the other hand, philosophy is the *concept* of real recognition. It cannot be intuition, because then it would be a medium of misrepresentation like art and religion. It is the concept of real recognition, that is, abstract, because it arises in a society where real recognition has not been achieved. Philosophy, in this sense, reinforces the primacy of the concept, and falls into the terms of the dichotomy which it seeks to transform. It thus contains an abstract imperative, a moment of *Sollen*.

It is important to understand this paradox in Hegel's philosophy of philosophy, because it accounts for the unjustifiable and unacknowledged *Sollen* in his thought. It shows that an element of *Sollen* must be present, and that this element is consistent with his critique of *Sollen* in Kant and Fichte.

The Rational and the Real

On the second page of the 'Preface' to the *Philosophy of Right* (1821, 1827) Hegel stresses that the exposition presupposes 'the nature of speculative knowledge' as set out in the (Greater) *Logic*.[113] Notoriously, however, the fundamental propositions of the *Philosophy of Right* have been read as propositions of identity. 'The real to the rational' has been read as a justification of the *status quo*, and the famous statements about philosophy have been read as justifying quietism, as retrospective reconstruction.

In the 'Introduction' to the *Philosophy of Right*, Hegel defines the will as

> the *self*-determination of the ego, which means at one and the same time the ego posits itself as its own negative, i.e. as determinate and limited, and remains by itself, in its identity with itself and universality, and in its determination binds itself to itself.[114]

This is an abstract statement of the prevalent philosophical concept of the will couched in Fichtean terms of an initial discrepancy between ego and non-ego which is resolved by the ego's realization that it itself has posited the non-ego and is united with it. The freedom of the will is this 'self-relating negativity of the ego'.[115] Hegel is restating this abstraction, not endorsing it; it is the beginning not the result of the exposition of ethical life: 'It is the will in its concept, or for an external observer.'[116]

The *Philosophy of Right* continues the critique of the philosophical account of an ego which posits a non-ego which began in the *Differenzschrift* and which culminates in the *Logic*. Fichte's basic notion of 'positing' is shown in the *Philosophy of Right* to presuppose a specific social institution. What is posited (*gesetzt*) is bourgeois law (*Gesetz*).

The *Philosophy of Right* develops the critique of idealist natural law. It transposes the categories of idealist natural law into social relations, and presents absolute ethical life on the basis of the analysis of relative ethical life in modern, bourgeois society. The contrast between relative and absolute ethical life is no longer presented in those stark terms. Instead the text traces the illusions of natural consciousness, and therefore has a phenomenological form.

Nevertheless, the *Philosophy of Right* is written in the 'severe style'. Like the earlier 'political' writings, it is not historical: it concentrates on the contradictions and possibilities of modern society. It has little to say about religion, even though the contradictions of modern religious consciousness are elsewhere deplored for preventing the development of a rational social and political life. In the *Philosophy of Right* disunion in religion is briefly said to work to the benefit of rational political relations.[117]

The advantage of the 'severe style' is that it reveals unequivocally Hegel's preoccupation with the contradictions of bourgeois society. Hegel explains how Plato's *Republic* has been misread. It has been understood as an utopian work, 'a dream of abstract thinking', because Plato 'displayed only the substance of ethical life (absolute ethical life)', and excluded 'particularity' or 'difference', that is, private property relations.[118] Instead the *Republic* should be read as a one-sided analysis of a society which presupposes the relations which Plato sought to exclude. Hegel sought to avoid such one-sidedness, to show that ethical life is not a utopia but inseparable from relative ethical life.

In all the 'political' writings Hegel tries to turn the weakness of modern society, the subjective will or ego, the property relations of isolated individuals, into its strength. Institutions designed to counteract and contain the inequity and inequality of bourgeois property relations are presented in the attempt to acknowledge injustice, but not to recreate it by imposing an equally abstract ideal, a new form of injustice.

As the recently published lecture series from the 1820s on philosophy of right have shown, crucial aspects of the exposition of ethical life are systematically ambiguous.[119] For example, the role of the monarch varies from merely 'crossing the i's and dotting the t's', to that of being far more than a figurehead. This inconsistency, minor in itself, is an instance of a fundamental ambiguity in Hegel's exposition of ethical life.

Throughout all Hegel's writings reference is made to a series of property forms. Out of these distinct historical 'types', Hegel tried, time and time again, to compound an alternative: absolute ethical life. The forms are: Oriental property, Greek property, Roman property, feudal property, abolition of property (French Revolution), and modern, post-revolutionary, bourgeois property. These property forms, communal and private, are juxtaposed, criticized and plundered for an idea of an alternative property relation. This alternative is never definitively explicated. The fundamental paradox of Hegel's thought is that he was a critic of *all* property forms, but his central notion of a free and equal political relationship is inexplicable without concepts of property (*eigen, Aneignen, Eigentum, Anerkennen*), and hence incomplete without the elaboration of an alternative property relation.[120]

The two basic speculative propositions of the *Philosophy of Right* are, 'What is rational is actual and what is actual is rational',[121] and 'To comprehend *what is*, this is the task of philosophy, because *what is*, is reason.'[122] The copulae in these propositions have been misread as affirming identity between the terms related.

In the case of the proposition that the actual is rational, what has been overlooked is the explanatory coda that the truth of this proposition must be sought – 'in dem *Schiene* des Zeitlichen',[123] in the illusion of the temporal, of history. The proposition has been misread as if it equated natural law with positive law, as if it *justifies* existing law,[124] when it summarizes Hegel's critique of natural law. For it is natural law theory which takes the illusions or relations of bourgeois private property as the rational principle of the whole society. It is natural law theory which *justifies* bourgeois positive law which it 'derives' from the fictional state of nature. Hegel is precisely drawing attention to the illusions (relations, difference) of bourgeois society. He is warning against an approach which would see illusion as rational, which makes illusion into the absolute principle of the whole. The proposition that the actual is rational is speculative. It refers to the experience of illusion, to the way bourgeois relations, or lack of identity are mistaken for rationality. This illusion must be acknowledged as real, but not made into the principle of rationality, nor can another principle of rationality be abstractly opposed to the prevailing illusion.

The proposition 'To comprehend *what is*, this is the task of philosophy, because *what is*, is reason',[125] has also been misread without reference to *Schein*, illusion. 'What is, is reason.' Social relations contain illusion, and thus 'what is' contains illusion, but this is not an ordinary definition. It refers to the experience of lack of the identity between 'what is' in the condition of illusion, and philosophy, which has a task. Philosophy, by acknowledging the illusion, may attain truth and become reason or absolute ethical life. Hegel calls this the unity of 'form', philosophy as 'speculative knowing', and 'content', or 'reason as the substantial essence of actuality'.[126]

'Philosophy is its time apprehended in thoughts'[127] and 'Philosophy . . . always comes on the scene too late to give instruction as to what the world ought to be [*wie die Welt sein soll*].'[128] First, to say that philosophy is its time apprehended in thoughts is not a generalization about all philosophy. It makes a contrast between Hegel's philosophy and practical philosophy based on abstract prescriptions, *Sollen*. Secondly, if philosophy was not thought but projected abstract ideals or images beyond real social relations, it would no longer be philosophy but a medium of intuition, religion or art. In both cases philosophy would be powerless. Thus Hegel does not mean that philosophy is a form of reconstruction which cannot contribute to social and political change. On the contrary, these propositions, read speculatively, indicate the conditions under which philosophy becomes effective.

The penultimate paragraph of the 'Preface' where Hegel says that philosophy appears *after* the formation of actuality, and as the ideal apprehends the real world in its ideal terms,[129] should not be read as a contemplative, passive account of philosophy. For it announces that the time of a different philosophy has arrived, the first time when philosophical apprehension may coincide with subjective freedom, when theory and practice may be united. Philosophy will no longer be esoteric,[130] the concept of rationality, but exoteric,[131] no longer the position of the external observer, but the unfolding of consciousness itself: the unity of form, philosophy as speculative knowing, and content, reason as the substantial essence of actuality.

Hegel presents here not a quiescent justification of the *status quo*, but a speculative proposition: that it is the time, after the time of art and religion, for the owl of Roman Minerva, the esoteric *concept* of philosophy, to *spread* its wings and to turn back or rather forwards into Greek Athena, the goddess of the unity of the *polis* and philosophy, absolute ethical life, the exoteric unity of theory and practice, of concept and intuition. Thus this reading of the task of philosophy runs contrary to the common reading which contrasts the active role proclaimed for philosophy in the 'Preface' to the *Phenomenology of Spirit* with the passive role delineated in the 'Preface' to the *Philosophy of Right*.[132]

The abstract Fichtean statement of the free will is set aside in the Introduction for the experience of the 'natural will' (natural consciousness). In the essay on natural law the illusions of empirical natural law and of idealist law and the social institutions which correspond to them were discussed separately, but in *The Philosophy of Right*, the illusions of the immediate experiences of the natural or ordinary will and the social institutions which correspond to the assumptions of natural law are presented simultaneously.[133]

An introduction to a phenomenology, to the *Philosophy of Right* and to the *Phenomenology of Spirit*, is contradictory. For if it is the experiences of natural consciousness or natural will which are to be presented, there can be no preliminary, abstract statement of that presentation or of its result. Such a statement would be an external justification of a procedure, a method, and it would prejudice the result by providing a concept of what the result should be.

In the 'Introduction' to the *Philosophy of Right*, Hegel introduces the concept of the free will in Fichtean terms of ego and posited non-ego, and in non-Fichtean terms of the connection between intuition and concept. The will which subordinates or subjugates what is opposed to it, whether other people or parts of itself, is in the condition of relation (*Verhältnis*), but the will which is free, whose existence or determinations or whatever stands opposed to it is not subordinated, is the equal of its concept. The concept of the will then 'has the intuition of itself for its goal and reality'.[134] This will is called 'pure'; it refers to itself (*bezieht*), that is, it recognizes difference or determinations, and is hence not in a condition of relation (*Verhältnis*), that is, of subordination. This distinction between *Beziehung* and *Verhältnis* is crucial, but both are usually translated into English as 'relation'. Both the references and the relations of the will imply social institutions. Kant, according to Hegel, could only understand the will in the relations (*Verhältnisse*) of abstract right and morality, Fichte could only understand the will as posited (*gesetzt*) as the law of civil society.

The *Philosophy of Right* has the same overall structure as the *System der Sittlichkeit*. First, the relations (*Verhältnisse*) of the will are considered outside the perspective of ethical life. They are then retraversed as relative ethical life within the perspective of absolute ethical life. However, in the *System der Sittlichkeit* the social relations and institutions were derived from the philosophical relations, from the primacy either of the concept or of intuition. But in the *Philosophy of Right*, the experiences and relations of the natural will, which reappear in Kant and Fichte's thought, are directly presented. It is the contradictions between the will's definition of those institutions and its experience of them which transformed both the institutions and the definition. Hence Marx was quite wrong to accuse Hegel of deriving reality from the concept in the *Philosophy of Right*,[135] and it would be an equally incorrect accusation in relation to the *System der Sittlichkeit*, because the derivations in that text undermine the dominance of the concept.

The first two parts of the *Philosophy of Right*, 'Abstract Right' and 'Morality', correspond to the two parts of Kant's *Metaphysic of Morals*, the doctrine of law and the doctrine of virtue.[136] Kant's *Metaphysic of Morals* is a post-critical work, that is, it presupposes that the principles of practical reason have been justified, and proceeds to examine the concepts which can be derived from those principles. Hegel's presentation of 'Abstract Right' follows Kant's order of exposition closely.

Kant deduces the law or rights of possession and the property rights of persons in relation to things and in relation to other persons from the 'juridical postulate' of practical reason.[137] Hegel demonstrates the origin and nature of the social and political relations which Kant's postulate presupposes. Kant's juridical postulate of practical reason asserts that

It is possible to have any and every object of my will as my property. In other words, a maxim according to which, if it were made into a law, an object of will would have to be in itself ownerless [*herrenlos*] (*res nullius*) conflicts with law and justice.[138]

In the *Metaphysics of Morals* all Kant's deductions are accompanied in parentheses by the point of Roman civil law which has been deduced. The categories of Roman law are deduced by Kant as the law of modern, private property relations. Kant calls these private property relations the 'state of nature'. He emphasizes that the state of nature is a state of society, but one which does not stand under the principles of distributive justice.[139] The state of nature is contrasted with civil society, the state of distributive, legal justice. [140] According to Kant, this corresponds to the difference between 'provisional' private property, and property under the laws of justice, the right to acquisition.[141]

Hegel provides a 'commentary' on the details of these deductions by presenting the contradiction between the natural will's definition of these Roman rights or laws with its experience of them. Thus the definition of a legal person as the bearer of property rights is stated in its abstract definition because this is what the natural will immediately takes itself to be. The experience of the specific forms of subordination or subjugation which the distinction between persons and things presupposes is then presented.

The discrepancy between the legal definition and the social reality is traced through possession, use, and alienation of property, and culminates in the complex property relation of contract. The contradiction between the universal and formal recognition of the contract, the will's definition, and the fact that the contract depends on the interests of the particular individuals involved is seen to be the origin of fraud, crime and coercion in a society based on the specific property relations previously described. Thus by the end of the first part of the *Philosophy of Right* that natural will has come to acknowledge the connection between its immediate definition of itself as a 'person', and the social reality of crime.

For example, 'personality' is the first, still wholly abstract definition of the will. The 'person' considers the sphere distinct from him to be immediately different from him, not free, not personal, without rights.[142] It may therefore be appropriated or possessed on an arbitrary and capricious basis. I become the master of what I possess, and it is the embodiment of my 'personality'.[143] I treat the thing as a mere natural object, whether it is an inanimate object or another human being.[144] In the latter case I have enslaved the other.

Hegel does not condemn this. To do so would be to stop outside the phenomenology and to impose another abstract definition of what the experience should be on the will. The discrepancy between the natural will's definition and its experience, the social reality presupposed by the definition, itself transforms the inequity. Appropriation which subordinates the object anticipates a form of appropriation which does not subordinate it. When the first experience or appropriation is recognized as misappropriation, a more universal form of appropriation is recognized. Hence the experience is formative not deforming. The appropriation of objects, or the abstract relation between 'persons' and 'things', or concept and intuition, is an elementary form of misrecognition which becomes part of a transition to real recognition.[145]

The subordination of one to another in possession and appropriation is dualistic. It is a simple encounter with another as subordinated to one's own ends, as a means (*Mitte*). When the contradiction between the definition and the reality becomes apparent, the means, *qua* instrument, is re-cognized as a mediation, a formative experience, in which a third was involved, although suppressed, in the transition to a new definition of oneself. For if the notion of 'person', the bearer of the right to suppress others, is abstract, then it also implies the suppression of all the other characteristics and relations of the 'person' except those pertaining to property rights. But if an experience is re-cognized as one of misappropriation, then not only is the relation to the suppressed object transformed but so is the definition of the 'person' by the natural will or consciousness. The means, *qua* instrument, has become the means, *qua* mediation, in the transition to a different stage of (mis)-recognition.

> . . . so ist der moralische Standpunkt der Standpunkt des *Verhältnisses* und des *Sollens* oder der Forderung.

> (. . . therefore the moral standpoint is the standpoint of *relation* and of the *ought*, or of demand.)[146]

If the individual defines himself as a 'person', the bearer of property rights, he has abstracted from all his other characteristics and social relations. A corollary of defining part of oneself as a legal 'person' in contradistinction to other legal 'persons' is that a further dimension of oneself is isolated: subjectivity, the substratum in which the accident of being a bearer of property rights inheres. 'Subjectivity' is thus even more cut off from the totality of social relations which determine it:

> Diese Reflexion des Willens in sich und seine für sich seiende Identität gegen das Ansichsein und die Unmittelbarkeit und die darin sich entwickelnden Bestimmtheiten bestimmt die *Person* zum *Subjekt*.

> (This reflection of the will into itself and its identity for itself – in opposition to its in itself and immediacy and the determinations developed within it – determines the person as a subject.)[147]

The second part of the *Philosophy of Right*, 'Morality', is divided into three sections: 'Purpose and Responsibility'; 'Intention and Welfare'; 'Good and Conscience'. The subject, the corollary of the legal person, defines itself as responsible for the motives and intentions of its actions but not for their consequences. For the consequences occur in the realm of private property relations, and the moral standpoint precisely understands itself as not implicated in that realm. Morality is defined as the autonomous realm of what ought to be, of a concept of good intention which the individual should continually impose on himself, of a relation which suppresses part of himself, and is not unified with the realm of the deed itself. Hence a bad deed may be obviated by a good intention, and the good intention should be repeatedly espoused.

As in the *System der Sittlichkeit* and in the *Phenomenology of Spirit*, Hegel shows that, on the one hand, the standpoint of subjective morality arises out of bourgeois private property relations, and on the other hand, that the standpoint can equally justify immoral as well as moral acts. It is utterly self-contradictory. The natural will defines itself in a number of ways, as 'good intention' or in relation to the 'welfare' of others. These definitions separate the motive from the deed, and, as a result, responsibility for the consequences of any deed can be avoided on the grounds that it was intended to serve the welfare of others, and hence had a good intention. In this way acting in one's own interests and any crime can be morally justified.[148]

The moral standpoint is thus a blatant casuistry. The discrepancy between the moral definition of the will as 'good intention' or 'serving the interests of others', and the licence these definitions bestow is exposed; the contradiction between definition and experience is particularly stark.

The epitome of the moral standpoint, 'Good and Conscience', separates the definition of the morally good will more decisively from abstract property relations, from the 'welfare' of others and from 'good intentions', in order to escape the casuistry. The will is now defined as 'absolute right in contrast with the abstract right of property and the particular aims of welfare'.[149]

This definition of the will is even more abstracted from real relations than the previous ones. The 'good' is defined as doing one's duty, but 'duty' is defined only formally as submission to a command in the case of every subjective maxim of action. Duty therefore depends on the individual's contingent insight into his duty, and is thus mere intuition not recognition.

Furthermore, the good is defined as absolute opposition to the world of real relations including the other relations of the moral subject to himself. Duty becomes 'a bitter, unending struggle against self-satisfaction, as the command: "Do with abhorrence what duty enjoins." '[150] The formal definition of duty – not to fall into contradiction – hides the real institutions which have determined that duty: the maintenance of specific property relations.

This definition of the good thus cuts subjectivity off from the institutions which have determined it even more than the definition of the abstract legal person. In its isolation the subject can only be certain of itself (*Gewissheit*), but this arbitrary certainty has been made into the determining and decisive element in him, his conscience (*Gewissen*).[151] But if conscience is defined as the ultimate authority in moral acts, it is even freer to justify evil, hypocrisy and irony, because it is even more removed from the consequences of its deeds, even more 'liberated' from the private property relations which have determined it and in the context of which it acts.

The sphere of abstract right and morality are re-presented within the perspective of ethical life as civil society. The stage of ethical life is attained when the natural will or particular individual defines itself in reference to (*in Beziehung auf*) other natural wills and hence defines itself as universal, as mutual recognition.[152] However, this is a formal universal. The individual only recognizes the other because he is dependent on it.[153] This is the stage of the law of civil society, the *form* of universality, the concept of a common interest which is imposed on intuition, on the mass of individuals in relations of private property.[154]

The particular individual (intuition) *refers* to the universal (concept). He is no longer merely at the standpoint of *relation*, where he has no reference to the universal, but is thoroughly particular. If the particular individual refers to the universal then he is not dominating it. Instead the universal is present in the particular as illusion, *Schein*. The universal is seen, intuited by the particular and not subordinated. But the particular is still not identical with the universal. It is still in a state of difference. Hence the universal can be seen or intuited, it shines (*scheint*) in the particular, but is not fully recognized by the particular. The particular mistakes what can be seen, what shines (*scheint*) for the rational principle of the totality, and thus what can be seen or shines (*scheint*) is an illusion (*Schein*), not identical with what it presents, the universal.[155]

This is a restatement of Hegel's critique of natural law, for the natural will takes the law of civil society, private property relations, to be a rational principle which unifies the whole, when it merely reproduces the contradictions and inequity of bourgeois private property. The natural or particular will defines the law as rational, but this is an illusion because the law is only the *form* of rationality. Law which guarantees private property relations cannot, *ex hypothesi*, be rational in content.

The institution which natural law theory justifies in opposition to a state of nature are real institutions which reproduce specific property relations. Right or civil law (*Gesetz*) is posited (*gesetzt*) and becomes *positive* law. The formal recognition of civil society is made into a law which is recognized as universally applicable:

Was *an sich* Recht ist, ist in seinen objektiven Dasein *gesetzt*, d.i.
durch den Gedanken für das Bewusstsein bestimmt und als das was
Recht ist und gilt, *bekannt*, das Gesetz; und das Recht ist durch diese
Bestimmung *positives* Recht überhaupt.

(What is right *in itself* is *posited* in its objective existence, that is,
determined by thinking for consciousness, and is *well-known* as that
which is right, as the law; and right thus determined is *positive* right
in general.)[156]

Hegel is not saying that positive law is *ipso facto* right and imprescript-
ible. On the contrary, he is criticizing the idea that what is posited
(*gesetzt*), specifically, law (*das Gesetz*), is really universal in bourgeois
society. He is saying that positive law, law which is posited and
recognized as right (justified by natural law theory), bears only the
form of universality in a society based on bourgeois private property.[157]

Similarly, for example, civil society as a whole considers individuals
as universal, as 'man', without reference to class, religion or nationality.
But the designation 'man' in a society based on private property relations is only the *form* of universality, not the content or actuality.[158]

The idea that a society is rational and free when individuals have
posited right as law and recognized the law as their positing is an illusion of universality, freedom and rationality which presupposes
specific, inequitable property relations. Similarly the standpoint of
morality was seen to reinforce the lack of freedom of these property
relations. Law (*Gesetz*) which is right posited (*gesetzt*) and hence positive, recognized in such a society, is a form of misrecognition. For the
very idea of positing law presupposes that the law is separable from
other social institutions. It presupposes a specific kind of law.[159]

In an ethical community law would not be set apart from the totality
of social institutions. It would not be private property law.[160] In a
simple, just, ethical community real recognition would be enshrined in
custom, *Sitte*. Hence ethical life, *Sittlichkeit*, would be natural, the concept and intuition equal, and the life of the community would be 'a
natural history of spirit' [*wird hiermit eine geistige Naturgeschichte sein*].[161]
This life would consist of mutual recognition in all social institutions.

Der Staat ist die Wirklichkeit der sittlichen Idee – der sittliche Geist
als *offenbart*, sich selbst deutliche, substantielle Wille, der sich denkt
und weiss und das, was er weiss und insofern er es weiss, vollführt.
An der *Sitte* hat er seine unmittelbare und an dem *Selbstbewusstsein* des

Einzelnen, den Wesen und Tätigkeit desselben, seine vermittlelte Existenz, so wie dieses durch die Gesinnung in ihm, als seinem Wesen, Zweck und Produkte seine Tätigkeit, seine *substantielle Freiheit* hat.

(The state is the actuality of the ethical idea – the ethical spirit as *manifest*, self-transparent, substantial will, which thinks and knows itself and brings about what it knows as far as it knows. In *custom* it has its immediate existence and in the *self-consciousness* of the individual, in his being and activity, it has its mediated existence just as the individual through his conviction of the state as the essence, goal and the product of his activity, has his *substantial* freedom.)[162]

It should be noted, first that the state in this exposition does not mean civil law, the modern state, but all the institutions and relations discussed in the *Philosophy of Right* and others not discussed, namely, custom and disposition. Secondly, this is not a glorification of the state, for in the Greek state, and, *a fortiori*, in the modern state, difference persists and leads to tragic collision.[163] In a just society and, *a fortiori*, in an unjust, modern society, the state is tragic. Conflict occurs even in a transparent society. This will be discussed in the following chapters.

Hegel's presentation of the institutions which effect the transformation of bourgeois subjectivity, of bourgeois property relations into concrete universality, into freedom, is incomplete, for it excludes reference to '*Gesinnung*', disposition, as expounded in the passage quoted above. The question of disposition will be discussed in the following chapters.

The phenomenology of the *Philosophy of Right* is *incomplete* because it is presented in the 'severe' style. The *Philosophy of Right* culminates in the experience of ethical life presented as the will's definition of a series of institutions which are concretely universal. These institutions of the state are normally read as the reconciliation of the contradictions traced, and are thus taken in isolation from subjective disposition and the other contradictions of a society based on bourgeois private property relations which make the analysis of modern society and of absolute ethical life even more complex than the *Philosophy of Right* implies. In the following chapters discussion of the state will be related to these other aspects of ethical life.

Hegel's consistent opposition to the primacy of the concept of pure practical reason emerges clearly from the writings discussed in this chapter. The social institutions which give rise to that primacy are first derived and analysed from the dichotomies of philosophy and later presented as the definitions and experiences of the natural will itself.

The speculative reading of these texts developed here suggests that Marx hypostatized Hegel's 'concept' of the state in a way utterly at odds with Hegel's thinking.[164] For Hegel, the whole aim of absolute ethical life was to eschew the domination of the *concept* of pure practical reason. Absolute ethical life is a critique of bourgeois property relations. It may be elusive, but it is never dominant or pre-judged. Minerva cannot impose herself. Her owl can only spread its wings at dusk and herald the return of Athena, freedom without domination.

3

The Philosophy of History

Faith and Knowledge

Hegel's philosophy has no social import if the absolute cannot be thought.[1] How can the absolute be thought, and how does the thinking of it have social import?

> The idea which a man has of God corresponds with that which he has of himself, of his freedom.[2]

If 'God' is unknowable, we are unknowable, and hence powerless. If the absolute is misrepresented, we are misrepresenting ourselves, and are correspondingly unfree. But the absolute has always been mis-represented by societies and peoples, for these societies have not been free, and they have re-presented their lack of freedom to themselves in the form of religion.

Religion is the medium of *Vorstellung*. *Vorstellung* means re-presentation (*Vor-stellung*) and 'pictorial' or 'imaginative' thinking. It is also translated as 'ordinary idea' or 'conception'. Religion is not the concept or thought of the absolute, but some form of its misrepresenta-tion. As long as the absolute is *represented* as 'God', it is *inconceivable* as the absolute.

> A nation which has a false or bad conception of God, has also a bad state, bad government, bad laws.[3]

According to Hegel, European societies have a bad conception of God and a bad state. For the conception of God is one which makes him unknowable, and this unknowable God is the re-presentation of the extreme subjectivity, the lack of freedom, in social and political relations. 'Subjectivity' is the correlate of the legal definition of persons as bearers of private property rights. Misrepresentation of the absolute is the correlate of subjectivity.

On the one hand, the absolute is misconceived as the principle of political unity, as discussed in the previous chapter, and, on the other hand, the absolute is misrepresented as a conception of 'God'. This divorce in the idea of the absolute, as the state and as religion, itself indicates the real lack of freedom. The absolute can only be re-presented in terms of the prevailing dualisms, in terms of the domination between concept and intuition, between legal person (master) and thing (slave).

The *speculative* proposition that religion and the state are identical implies the *experience* of a bad religion and a bad state, where the state and religion are in opposition, not identical. The experience of the disunion of the state and religion reoccurs in the realm of religion, in the medium of representation.

Natural or ordinary consciousness defines and understands the absolute as otherworldly, in opposition to social and political relations (the state), and, correspondingly, defines and understands itself in its relation to the absolute as otherworldly, thereby excluding its social and political relations. The absolute and natural consciousness are misrepresented, abstracted from real social relations. But natural consciousness' definition of the absolute contradicts its experience, its definition of itself which excludes its real social relations. As a result of this contradiction natural consciousness changes its definition of the absolute and thus of itself, perhaps by trying to exclude real relations even more, or by acknowledging real relations as they appear exclusively. In both cases, further misrepresentation of both the real relations and of the absolute ensues.

If religion, by definition cannot think the absolute, how can it be thought? By a speculative reading of the propositions of religion, or, to say the same thing, by the philosophical completion of the meaning of religion, by the uncovering of the truth and untruth of religious representation, of the social relations to which such representation corresponds, and of the different relations to which it refers.

The fundamental religious representation or proposition asserts that 'God exists.' Natural consciousness understands the proposition that 'God exists' as an ordinary proposition. Thus to ordinary consciousness 'God' is unknowable. For only something which has characteristics, determinations, can be known. To say merely that 'God exists' is to ascribe bare, characterless existence to a meaningless name.[4]

However, if natural consciousness attributes predicates to 'God', such as, God is 'perfect', 'essential', or 'love', 'God' still remains unknown. For the predicates in such ordinary propositions can only denote external accidents. They cannot be added up to tell us what the empty name 'God' means.[5]

The proposition that the state and religion are identical, read speculatively, refers to our experience of their disunion. Similarly, the proposition 'God exists', read speculatively, implies that we, finite beings, are not free. 'God' is a pictorial, imaginative name for something which ordinary consciousness finds impossible to conceive: a species (universal) in which the individual member of the species (the particular with its specific determinations) is identical with the species and hence infinite. By contrast, in any finite species, the individual member of the species is not identical with the universal: the individual dies, but the species continues.[6] This is still an analogical, abstract statement of the opposition between infinite and finite.

'God exists', read speculatively, implies an individual whose particularity (characteristics, determinations) is universal. It does not predicate bare existence of an empty name. Hence 'God exists' refers to our experience that, as particular individuals, we are not immediately universal, we are not species, not God, not infinite, that we live in societies where our experience as individuals does not correspond to the experience of all, where our empirical consciousness is not pure or universal consciousness, where we are not substantially free.

> God alone is the thorough harmony of concept and reality. All finite
> things involve an untruth: they have a concept and an existence, but
> their existence does not meet the requirements of the concept.[7]

'God exists' implies that we live in (or experience) the 'contradiction between the determination or concept and the existence of the object',[8] in the contradiction between pure and empirical consciousness, or, between our definition of ourselves and our experience of real social relations. We are finite, but, unlike other finite species, we are capable of *experience*, of awareness of the contradiction between species and existence, between our definition of ourselves and real social relations, between infinite and finite. We are limited, but can become aware of the determinations of the limit. Thus 'infinite' implies 'finite' and 'finite' implies 'infinite'. They are not an exclusive, abstract opposition, as long as the infinite is not pre-judged.

The speculative reading of religious representation explicates the contradiction between consciousness' definition of the absolute and its real existence. It is thus a phenomenology, a presentation and critique of the contradictions of the 'standpoint of consciousness'.[9] Only in the *Logic* can the absolute be thought.

In the present age an opposition between 'faith' and 'knowledge' has developed in philosophical and in ordinary consciousness. 'God' cannot be an object of knowledge but only of faith.

> The possibility of knowing God [is] a prominent question of the day . . . or rather – since public opinion has ceased to allow it to be a matter of *question* – the *doctrine* that it is impossible to know God.[10]

In the *Differenzschrift* and the early political writings, Hegel demonstrated how the division between theoretical and practical philosophy in Kant and Fichte prevented them from conceiving of substantial freedom. Starting from a critique of their theories of natural law, Hegel showed how the fundamental structure of their thought reproduced the lack of freedom of real social relations. In *Faith and Knowledge* he demonstrates how the distinction between faith and knowledge made by Kant and Fichte, their accounts of the unknowability of God, prevents them from conceiving of substantial freedom. He shows how the fundamental structure of Kant and Fichte's thought, the division between theoretical and practical philosophy, which was designed to destroy deductive metaphysics, also destroys the meaning of religion and the meaning of freedom. He shows how the formal notion of God corresponds to the formal notion of freedom.

Kant and Fichte would have agreed with Hegel that our concept of God is our concept of ourselves, of our freedom. For Kant and Fichte the command to act morally, as we ought, is an inexplicable fact of ordinary consciousness: 'The consciousness of this fundamental law may be called a fact of reason.'[11] Our moral duties constitute a realm of freedom where the will is the cause of action. This realm is distinguished from the world of appearances which is governed by natural necessity.

Kant introduces the postulate of God only after he has justified the possibility, the objective validity, of moral judgements. A postulate is 'a theoretical proposition which is not as such demonstrable, but which is an inseparable corollary of an *a priori* unconditionally valid practical law.'[12] God is not the *condition* of the possibility of moral freedom, but an 'idea' which is 'necessarily connected with the moral legislation of pure reason'.[13] The ideas of an infinite Being and of the immortality of the soul are 'of great use' in maintaining the holiness of the inexorable moral law.[14]

For Fichte, too, moral volition

> is demanded of us absolutely for its own sake alone – a truth which I
> discover only as a fact in my inward consciousness, and to the know-
> ledge of which I cannot attain in any other way.[15]

Fichte introduces the idea of an infinite will, not as a postulate, but as
the *law* of the moral realm which he calls the 'supersensuous world'.[16]
It is through the infinite will that we recognize the freedom of others,
but how this occurs is a 'mystery', 'absolutely inconceivable'.[17]

In both Kant and Fichte, the fact of the moral law, of freedom, precedes the postulate of God, or the idea of the infinite will. In this way
moral autonomy is distinguished in principle from mere obedience to
the will of another, from heteronomy – whether the other is God or
finite beings or any end other than the pure law itself. Religion is thus
kept 'within the bounds of reason alone', and all 'revelation' is beyond
these bounds. As a result both Kant and Fichte were, at different times,
accused of atheism by the authorities.[18]

However, the cost of keeping religion 'within the bounds of reason'
is that rationality becomes inexplicable, and God or the infinite will
unknowable. For Kant, justification of moral judgement involves no
reference to God, although it leads to 'a subjective moral necessity to
assure the existence of God'.[19] Kant calls this a 'rational faith',[20] because
it 'springs from reason' but cannot be justified.[21] But a 'rational faith'
is a contradiction *in adjecto*.

Fichte gives the primacy of the interest of practical reason over
speculative reason established by Kant[22] an overall unifying rôle in his
thought in a way which destroys the meaning of Kantian critique,
justification and validity. Fichte argues that if the will, which he defines
as 'the impulse to absolute, independent self-activity',[23] has primacy
over the understanding (*Verstand*), over knowledge of the empirical,
finite world, then it cannot be justified. For justification itself depends
on the will, and the will depends on immediate 'conviction', 'feeling',
or 'faith'.[24]

> It is not knowledge, but a decision of the will to allow the validity
> of knowledge.[25]

Faith becomes the fountain of the validity of both moral action and
theoretical understanding.

Not inferences of reason, for there are none such. It is our *interest* in a reality which we desire to produce: in the good absolutely for its own sake, and the common and sensuous for the sake of the enjoyment they afford. No one who lives can divest himself of this interest, and just as little can he cast off the faith which this interest brings with it. We are all born in faith.[26]

Thus, for both Kant and Fichte, our concept of God is our concept of ourselves, of our freedom. For Kant the *limited* legitimacy of the idea of God was necessary for his conception of moral autonomy. Fichte took the inexplicable fact of moral freedom from Kant, and replaced the deduction of the validity of moral judgement by unjustifiable faith in the moral law. The realm of freedom and its law, the infinite will, are therefore 'invisible and absolutely incomprehensible',[27] for only the world of sense is comprehensible. The command to do our duty, to will morally, is the source of rationality. Thus we can only have faith in it, we cannot justify it, for it is the precondition of justification.[28] 'It is the commandment to act that of itself assigns an end to my action'.[29] Whatever the consequences of our will in the sensuous, visible world, we must continue to obey the law of the supersensuous, invisible world.[30] Thus to our present life, the other 'future' life which we must blindly will, is not 'present to sight':[31]

> The present life is, therefore, in relation to the future, a life in faith.[32]

Fichte's *Vocation of Man* (1800) is divided into three sections, entitled, 'Doubt', 'Knowledge' and 'Faith'. Hegel took over the titles of the last two sections for the title of his essay 'Faith and Knowledge' (1802). Fichte represented to Hegel a clear and extreme example of the connection between the unknowability of God and the unknowability of ourselves, of religion within the bounds not of reason, but of the irrational, within the bounds not of freedom, but of bondage:

> In sighs and prayers he [the individual] seeks for the God whom he denies to himself in intuition, because of the risk that the understanding [*Verstand*] will cognize what is intuited as a mere thing, reducing the sacred grove to mere timber.[33]

It is Fichte who denies that the understanding can know or see God. Instead the heart and feeling have a conviction of the infinite will, the intelligibility of whose commands is not 'present to sight', that is, cannot be intuited or seen.

Hegel argues that this relation to God destroys and cannot justify the freedom of individuals. For Kant and Fichte, freedom means freedom from the sensuous world, from the necessity of nature. To Hegel this notion of freedom is 'a flight from the finite'.[34] The rigid dichotomy between the sensuous world (the finite, nature) and the supersensuous world (the infinite, freedom) prevents the comprehension of either. By degrading empirical existence in order to emphasize that the infinite is utterly different, the infinite is itself debased. For it is deprived of all characterization, and hence turned into an empty abstraction, an idol, made of mere timber:

> It is precisely through its flight from the finite and through its rigidity that subjectivity turns the beautiful into things – the grove into timber, the images into things that have eyes and do not see, ears and do not hear.[35]

By separating freedom from cognition of the finite and sanctifying it – for it cannot be 'justified' – solely on the basis of the heart and the yearning for God, rational action is made impossible. Rationality or moral judgement cannot be justified or objective for it is the precondition of justification, and it cannot comprehend reality, for it has split reality in two, and left the creation and comprehension of the sensuous world to enjoyment: 'We desire . . . the common and sensuous for the sake of the enjoyment they afford.'[36] The sensuous world is either debased in opposition to the supersensuous, or embraced as the realm of sheer enjoyment:

> Hence this reconciliation did not itself lose the character of absolute opposition implicit in beautiful longing. Rather, it flung itself upon the other pole of the antithesis, the empirical world.[37]

In both cases the rigid opposition between freedom and necessity, infinite and finite, means that the only *relation* possible between the two is one of domination, '[*die*] *Beziehung des Beherrschens*'.[38] Either the infinite dominates the finite in an incomprehensible way (God), or the finite dominates the infinite as sensuous enjoyment. In the former case, God is incalculable and inconceivable, in the latter case, reason, devoted to enjoyment, is limited to calculation, to subordinating the concept to finitude.[39] The relative identity of domination is the correlate of the absolute antithesis of infinite and finite.

If the identity of infinite and finite is 'posited affirmatively', it can only be 'a relative identity', the domination of the concept 'over what appears as real and finite – everything beautiful and ethical here included'. If the concept is 'posited negatively', that is, if the finite dominates the infinite, or, intuition dominates the concept, this refers to the real domination of the 'natural strength and weakness of the subjectivities opposed to one another'.[40] The 'affirmative' concept is completely ineffective in relation to this real domination. For the concept reigns above finitude as 'an emptiness of Reason', a characterless God of faith, who has no influence in the sensuous world, and whose commands are incomprehensible in the supersensuous world. This powerless God is the obverse of the power of the finite, 'it is devoid of rationality', but 'called rational because the reason which is restricted to its absolute opposite recognizes something higher than itself from which it is exluded.'[41]

The effect of these abstract oppositions between finite and infinite, freedom and necessity, is 'the hallowing of a finitude that remains as it is'.[42] The real relations of domination are legitimized and reproduced in these conceptions of freedom and of God.

As, for example, in *System der Sittlichkeit*, Hegel is developing here a speculative reading of Kant's formal rule, 'Thoughts without content are empty, intuitions without concepts are blind'.[43] He has demonstrated that this is not an ordinary proposition or general rule, but represents a real lack of identity between concept and intuition, or the domination of relative identity. This applies to religious representation as much as it did to natural law. In religion the concept dominates intuition and is empty, a characterless and unknowable God; while the abstract command to subjugate natural impulse confirms the domination of enjoyment, of the finite, of intuition, and is thus blind, the *status quo* uncritically reaffirmed.

Fichte undermines Kantian justification and subordinates cognition even of finite reality to the will. But this unconditioned will produces not greater freedom, but a worse bondage. Hegel sought to demonstrate that Fichtean freedom was no freedom at all, and that to 'derive' freedom from faith was to destroy both freedom and faith.

In Fichte's thought the place of the Kantian concept and intuition are reversed. Intellectual intuition of the ego, and empirical intuition of the non-ego take the place of Kant's discursive understanding which connects concept and intuition. But intellectual intuition is blind. It cannot see because it abstracts 'from everything alien in consciousness', and hence leaves nothing to be seen.[44] Everything which is alien to the pure, characterless ego becomes the empirical, the non-ego.

Fichte's pure ego is no longer the Kantian ego which submits to a deduction of objective validity and is hence conditioned. The Fichtean ego is unconditioned and its cognition immediate. But it cannot be unconditioned, because it has to abstract from what is alien to it in order to intuit itself.[45] Fichte acknowledges this incompleteness of the pure ego by the idea of the infinite will. This idea of the infinite will, however, 'signifies here nothing but the negativity of something that is needed'.[46] But anything which is defined negatively in opposition to something else, takes on, *ipso facto*, a characteristic, a definition, and is hence partial or finite. Fichte admits he can give no character to his 'infinite will', for 'all characteristics are limitations and imperfections and hence inadequate'.[47] He thereby confers a character on the infinite, the character of opposition to characteristic as such, to the sensuous world. This leaves the ordinary world just as it is, 'but with a negative sign',[48] in all its relations of domination. Thus to be 'free' from the empirical world is to be 'imprisoned' in the dualism between inconsequential 'freedom' and the sensuous world.[49]

Fichte's opposition between the two worlds, empirical and moral, finite and infinite rests on 'faith' and 'makes faith in the beyond necessary'.[50] 'Beyond' means both beyond the sensuous world, and beyond the present, for 'the ought is perennial'.[51] To live for the unattainable future as well as to live for an incomprehensible moral law is to live without freedom.

Thus in Fichte's system the absolute cannot be thought, it can only be an ought, an infinite task.[52] The divorce between faith and knowledge in Fichte is different from their divorce in Kant. The object of faith in Fichte is not a postulate, for to call it a 'postulate' would still smack of justification. It is thus even less determinate than a postulate, derived from the heart and feeling. 'Faith' becomes Fichte's *a priori*, his way of connecting impulse (reality) and freedom (ideality).[53] Fichte says

All our thought is founded on our impulses . . . These impulses compel us to a certain mode of thought only so long as we do not perceive the constraint; the constraint vanishes the moment it is perceived.[54]

But this 'perceiving' merely means accepting the unjustifiable faith to which we are born. Hence the integration of real and ideal is merely formal and excludes the 'sensuous world'.

Fichte's glorification of the primacy of practical reason, of absolute freedom justified by faith alone and by action, by the will 'positing itself',[55] is bought at the terrible cost of subjugating everything from which it is necessary to abstract in order to arrive at this empty notion of freedom. The will has even less content in Fichte than in Kant, 'it soars above the wreckage of the world',[56] and hence reaffirms that world more than Kant's moral law 'smuggled' it in.

Fichte's destruction of Kantian objective validity means that he is caught entirely within the subjective standpoint. The ego posits the no-ego, but 'The ego is not posited, no being pertains to it',[57] for all being is to be negated in the act of the will, since it is 'absolutely bad'. Fichte's view of nature is unremittingly negative, whereas Kant at least found beauty and a *telos* in nature in the *Critique of Judgement*.[58]

Hegel accuses Fichte of merely restating a hackneyed moral sentimentalism in his obsession with the eternal evils of the world which we are utterly powerless to change.[59] Fichte can only imagine an infinite number of singular, rational beings because he has no concept of ethical life.[60] Political life in Fichte is therefore presented as an absolute tyranny. The state and law, like the ego, abstract from the rest of life, from custom (*Sitte*) and then impose themselves on the alien life.[61] This concept of the legal, abstract state which Hegel abhorred in Fichte has been wrongly attributed to Hegel himself.

Fichte cannot conceive of the infinite nor of freedom,

> For the infinite is posited as originally un-unified [*unvereint*] and un-unifiable [*unvereinbar*] with the finite, the ideal cannot be united with the real or pure reason with existence.[62]

For the absolute to be thought, for the infinite to be unifiable with the finite and not torn apart, the relative identity or domination would have to be disintegrated and reconstructed:

> This reconstruction must disclose . . . how the essence of nature in the form of possibility as spirit has enjoyment of itself as a living ideal in visible and active reality; and how it has its actuality as ethical nature in which the ethical infinite, that is, the concept, and the ethical finite, that is, the individual, are one without qualification.[63]

The Untrue as Subject

Ordinary or natural consciousness represents the absolute to itself as utterly and completely unique, different 'in nature' not merely 'in degree' from the rest of reality.[65]

When we say, for example, 'I absolutely refuse . . .', or 'I absolutely cannot . . .', we mean to exclude completely any alternative. We affirm a position which brooks no compromise with all that it rejects. This connotation is carried over into the ordinary idea of an absolute being or God which is defined in opposition to everything which is not absolute. The absolute in this sense differs in nature not in degree from what is not absolute, but the only thing we know about this different 'nature' is that it has none of the characteristics of what is not absolute, of nature. It is thus 'infected by its opposition to finitude'.[66] This is a merely negative notion of the absolute, 'the negative side of the absolute', for the absolute is defined solely in terms of what it is not.[67] Hegel is himself using this negative notion of the absolute when he says, for example, that Kant and Fichte have made infinity into an 'absolute principle' by excluding finitude.

The 'positive side' of the absolute cannot be pre-judged or justified, but it is a notion of the absolute which *includes* the finite; a notion which therefore goes against the grain of ordinary consciousness, of our ordinary idea of an 'absolute'. This 'positive' notion cannot be abstractly stated or justified, it can only be shown to be contained implicitly in the 'negative' notion of the absolute.

The philosophies of reflection, especially Kant and Fichte, have turned the absolute 'into subjectivity',[68] and remain within the abstract dichotomy of infinite and finite. Nevertheless 'the philosophy of infinity is closer to the philosophy of the absolute than the philosophy of the finite is.'[69] Philosophies which make the absolute into the subject are preferable to those which make the absolute into empirical reality or intuition, because 'the inner character of infinity is negation or indifference'.[70]

For the abstract opposition of infinite and finite in the philosophies of reflection implicitly acknowledges that the finite is different from the infinite, or, that the finite is negative in relation to the infinite. The infinite acknowledges that this negative is in a *relation* to the finite. Infinity can only achieve a *relative* identity with the finite as long as it is in opposition to it, a unity achieved by imposition or domination.

This is the speculative reading of Kant's formal rule that concepts without intuitions are empty and intuitions without concepts are blind. The concept (the infinite) which suppresses intuition (the finite) is empty, but it is a form which could be filled. Intuition without a concept is simply blind. It is a seeing which sees nothing because it has nothing 'present to sight'. Fichte's intellectual intuition is both blind and empty. The pure ego is empty, because it has abstracted itself from everything alien to itself, and it is also blind, because it has nothing left to see, and because it is born and lives in an incomprehensible faith in an invisible world.

The unity or identity which presupposes the fixed opposition between infinite and finite can only produce a relative identity. This unity is therefore a conditioned *unity* which cannot *unify* the infinite and the finite. But this relative identity, or, to say the same thing, relative difference, is the basis for an identity or unity which re-cognizes the difference or negativity of the finite, not as the opposite of the infinite but as part of it. This kind of unity would be *unconditioned*, not *relative*, because it includes the relative identity. Thus the 'inner character' of both formal and substantial identity is negation.

This is itself a *formal* statement of *Aufhebung*, the term which is usually translated into English as 'sublation', and said to contain the three meanings of 'preserve', 'abolish', and 'transcend'. *Aufhebung* is usually understood to refer to a consecutive and higher stage in a developmental sequence. But *Aufhebung* is another term for speculative experience, for the experience of difference or negation, of relative identity, of a contradiction between consciousness' definition of itself and its real existence which is miscognized and re-cognized at the same time.

> All we mean by reconciliation, truth, freedom, represents a universal process, and cannot therefore be expressed in a single proposition without becoming one-sided.[71]

How can Hegel make good his charge that Kant and Fichte have destroyed the meaning of both religion and freedom? He re-cognizes their formal philosophies as refining and presenting the oppositions which are to be speculatively and substantially reunited.[72] He thus does not deny that ordinary experience is lived in these oppositions.

The abstract, pure concept or infinity in Kant and Fichte is 'the abyss of nothingness in which all being is engulfed'.[73] The infinite is opposed to being, that is, to the finite, to all determination, and hence is nothing itself ('nothingness'). This nothingness is imposed on all being ('the abyss . . . in which all being is engulfed'). This 'signifies' the 'infinite grief' of the finite: the individual feels abandoned by a characterless, omnipotent and hence impotent God.[74] This experience of 'infinite grief' is re-cognized as the historical meaning of Christianity *in the present*. The feeling that God is dead or absent has always been central to Christian religious experience, because in the Christian religion the absolute is misrepresented as beyond human life, not present in it.

Kant and Fichte have expressed this religious experience for their own age. As in the past, so in the present, it is this experience of loss and opposition which makes possible the re-cognition of substantial freedom, to put it in philosophical terms, or, which makes possible the revelation of reconciliation between God and man, to put it in Christian terms, or, to put it in terms which are both philosophical and religious, which makes possible the knowledge that substance is subject. Hegel uses the following terms at this point:

> Thereby the pure concept . . . must recreate for philosophy the Idea of absolute freedom and along with it the absolute passion, the speculative Good Friday in the place of the historic Good Friday, and in the whole truth and harshness of its Godforsakenness. Since the happier, ungrounded idiosyncracies of the dogmatic philosophies and of natural religion must vanish, the highest totality can and must achieve its resurrection solely from this harshness, encompassing everything, and ascending in all its earnestness and out of its deepest ground to the most happy freedom of its shape.[75]

How is the speculative Good Friday to take the place of the historic Good Friday? How can rationality encompass revelation? Philosophy is to take the place of the older dogmatic metaphysics, of the critical philosophy and of religion in the task of creating an *idea* of absolute freedom. It can only do so by completing the meaning of these philosophies and religions, by revealing their social and political foundations. To reveal their social and political foundations means to show that religious misrepresentation has been the *fate* of absolute freedom, of absolute ethical life. It has been the 'fate' in the sense of *Bestimmung* which means both destiny and determination. Substantial ethical life (the absolute) became subjectivity in a specific historical society and this subjectivity has continued through history to misrepresent the absolute to itself as religion.

Philosophy may recognize religion and the 'faith' of critical philosophy as the absolute, by re-cognizing this subjectivity as substance, as the historical fate of absolute ethical life. The historic Good Friday is replaced by the speculative Good Friday, by the philosophy of history.

The speculative Good Friday will remain speculative. It will recreate the idea of freedom 'for philosophy'. It will not become a new negative absolute in the sense of an imposed or relative identity. It re-cognizes the lack of identity between subject and substance. The truth must be known not only as substance but equally as subject.[76] But religious representation when it takes the form of pure knowledge as in Kant and Fichte 'does not know itself as spirit, and is consequently not substantial but subjective knowledge'.[77] The speculative proposition that substance is subject refers to a reality in which subject does not know itself as substance but is, nevertheless, a determination of substance.

Philosophy establishes its 'idea' of freedom by a speculative reading of the history of religion. From Rome to the present day the exoteric terms have been religious ones. Misrepresentation has occurred in the form of religion, and religious representation is a form of ordinary thinking. Philosophy thus transcribes a terminology which is already understood.

The philosophy of history is thus the speculative reading of how substance became subject, or, how absolute ethical life became religious representation, or, how the state and religion became divorced. It is especially concerned with the religion which forced that divorce on representation, and which, read speculatively, is the idea of absolute freedom, the speculative Good Friday. Christianity is this religion, 'the absolute religion'. It is the religion in which the absolute is represented as a subject.

Spirit at War with itself

The standpoint of consciousness is therefore not the only standpoint.[79]

It is the great advance of our time that subjectivity is known as absolute moment; it is thus essentially determination. However, everything depends on how it is determined.[80]

The necessity of the religious standpoint . . . is objective necessity, not a merely subjective business; it is not we who posit this necessity in movement, but it is the act of the object itself, or, the object produces itself.[81]

The lectures on the philosophy of religion present 'divine history', the history of religious doctrine read speculatively. The lectures on the philosophy of history present 'the history of the religious relation [*Verhältnis*]', the speculative reading of the connection and divorce between the state and religion.[82] Although the texts of both of these lecture series are corrupt, composed from the notes of students by successive editors, they are, philosophically speaking, companion texts.

In both lecture series there is no sustained phenomenology. Instead the 'standpoint of the absolute' is abstractly and repeatedly stated and contrasted with the standpoint of religious relation, difference, representation or consciousness. The two texts reveal the *aporia* of subjectivity: the subjective standpoint is criticized by means of the exposition of its formation; but the absolute is thought as subject. The lectures on the philosophy of religion concentrate on the second proposition of this chiasmus, that the absolute is determined as subject; the lectures on the philosophy of history concentrate on the first proposition, that the subject does not know that it is a determination of the absolute.

These two notions of the subject are determined differently, '. . . everything depends on how it is determined'.[83] The 'subjective standpoint' as evidenced in Kant or Fichte knows itself as pure ego by excluding all determination, all difference, all nature, and relates to its objects by imposing itself, by domination, by relative identity. Its inner character is negative, and this subjectivity is 'contingent or fortuitousness'.[84] The 'absolute standpoint' is one from which determination is acknowledged and not excluded or suppressed. It 'mediates itself in the totality of its determinations'.[85] This standpoint is that of a subject which stands opposed or in relation to its objects, but does not dominate them: it 'mediates itself'. It knows the finite, the determinate, as a means of its own determination. Thus the inner character of the absolute is negative. It is a subject, because to be a subject means to be conscious of existing in a relation of opposition and to be conscious that what stands opposed, the finite, determination, may be excluded or suppressed. It is substance because the determination is re-cognized and not suppressed or excluded. This subjectivity means 'self-determination'.[86]

Since the subjective standpoint prevails, philosophy *qua* philosophy, 'for us', and not *qua* phenomenology, can show how the absolute has been misrepresented by subjective consciousness, how substance is not subject, not the absolute standpoint which knows itself as subject, but is subjective, the subjective standpoint which does not know itself as substance. Religious misrepresentation is thus derived from the fate, the determination, of the absolute, or,

> The necessity of the religious standpoint . . . is objective necessity, not a merely subjective business . . .[87]

> The necessity of the progression has, however, to present, explicate, prove itself in the development itself.[88]

There is no question of justifying or deducing this necessity. 'Presentation' takes the place of Kantian justification and Fichtean faith. A phenomenology is the presentation of the contradiction between natural consciousness' definition of itself and its experience. In these texts, however, there is a simply historical and chronological presentation of religious representation and its speculative completion.[89]

Ordinary consciousness' conception of the Christian religion is transcribed into speculative terms, into terms of freedom. Christianity is the 'absolute' religion, because in it God is understood as spirit:[90] 'Spirit bears witness to spirit.'[91]

> Spirit is not something having a singular existence but is spirit only in being objective to itself and intuits itself in the other as itself. The highest determination of spirit is self-consciousness, which includes this objectivity in itself.[92]

This speculative statement refers to the contrary experience, to the way in which the 'subjective side' defines itself as finite, and makes 'God' into an object towards which it does not stand as self-consciousness, but in a dualistic relation in which the subject debases itself. It also refers to the possibility of a mediation in which subjectivity is restored to itself by re-cognizing the object as itself and itself as the object.[93]

The means (*Mitte*), the mediation which may make the experience of unity possible is Christ. In the revelation Christ is God become man, the infinite and finite unified without suppression. This reconciliation is not a dualistic suppression but a triune re-cognition or trinity. Hence it represents freedom not domination.

The Christian act of worship and the Christian idea of love are unique experiences, not only because in them ordinary consciousness recognizes or acknowledges differences or determination as itself, but because it knows itself to be the difference or determination which is re-cognized by the absolute as its own determination.

> In yielding myself up to God, I am at the same time only as it were a reflection out of God into myself.[94]

The finite is therefore an essential moment in the nature of God, and 'thus it may be said it is God himself who renders himself finite, who produces determinations within himself.'[95] In Christian worship and in Christian love, 'the finite is a moment of divine life.'[96]

This is a speculative reading of Christianity which transcribes religious into philosophical terms in order to expound the *concept* of the absolute religion, of substantial freedom. This reading does not refer to the *history* of religion, to the history of Christianity. It tells us how the absolute is subject, and this is 'the rational way of looking at finiteness'.[97]

The discussion of the Christian religion is rational, speculative. It is balanced by explication of the way speculative truth is translated into popular religious ideas of good and evil, into the narratives and histories found in the Bible. The connection between social and political change in religious representation is not central to the exposition of Christianity although this connection is the focus of the exposition of the pre-Christian 'determinate religions'. The two groups of earlier religions, the religions of nature and the religions of spiritual individuality, are shown to re-present the different relations between individual and society, and the relation between individual and society is shown to be re-presented in each religion. But the discussion of Christianity, the absolute religion, is almost entirely speculative or rational: 'It is the speculative way of regarding things which rules here.'[98] The first and third, final part of the lectures on the philosophy of religion end with a brief discussion of the relation between the Christian religion and the state. This has led commentators to undervalue the importance of this aspect of the account of Christianity.[99]

The presentation of the absolute religion is divided into three sections. The first section, the kingdom of the father, the abstract universal idea of the Christian God, contains a speculative but abstract exposition of the trinity. The second section, the kingdom of the son, concerns the trinity as it is known, as Christ. It concerns the 'positing of the difference' or relation and accounts for ordinary consciousness' misunderstanding of Christ.

The third section is the kingdom of the spirit. It covers, first, the ideal but one-sided unifying of the first two sections in worship and in the spiritual community. It covers, secondly, the contradiction between the speculative reading of Christian worship or the spiritual community as substantial freedom and the real lack of freedom which Christian worship and the spiritual community represent when considered in their social and historical context.

Thus divine history, the speculative account of Christian doctrine and ritual, is fundamentally different from the real history of Christianity in time and space. This begins with the very events of Christ's life,

> The divine history is thus regarded as something past, as representing the historical proper so called.[100]

If the absolute is eternal, then once it is represented as 'Christ', the eternal 'breaks up into past and present and future'.[101] Once the eternal is abstractly contrasted with time, it takes on its characteristics.

The kingdom of the son inhibits the kingdom of the spirit. In the kingdom of the son

> God exists in a general way for representation or figurative thought in the element of mental pictures or representation by ideas.

It is the 'moment of separation or particularization in general'.[102] The kingdom of the son consists of a series of ways in which finite beings represent the absolute or infinite to themselves. As in the earlier religions the mode of representation is determined by the social and political structure of ethical life, by the relation between law and custom, *Sitte* or ethos.

The discussion of the kingdom of the son and the kingdom of the spirit sounds extremely paradoxical in the lectures on the philosophy of religion. On the one hand, Christ

> is the substantial element in the unity of the divine and human natures of which man attains the consciousness, and, in such a way that man appears as God and God as man.[103]

This substantial unity is man's 'potential nature'. But, on the other hand,

. . . while this potential nature exists for man, it is above and beyond immediate consciousness, ordinary consciousness and knowledge; consequently it must be regarded as existing in a region above that subjective consciousness.[104]

As a result of the misrepresentation of ordinary consciousness, 'this potential nature . . . takes on the form of ordinary consciousness and is determined as such.'[105]

Specifically, the absolute represented as 'Christ' cannot, *ex hypothesi*, be recognized as the unity of the divine and human nature, but

. . . this unity must appear for others in the form of an individual man marked off from or excluding the rest of men, not representing all individual men, but as one from whom they are shut off, though he no longer appears as representing the potentiality or true essence which is above, but as individuality in the region of certainty.[106]

The paradox arises between the standpoint of speculation or the philosophical idea and its appearing 'in the form of certainty for men in general'.[107] There exists no form of exoteric apprehension of the absolute, no form for finite beings to apprehend the infinite. This is equally an abstract statement of the impossibility of substantial freedom. There has never been a common (universal) conception of universality which is present in its determination, in its existence.

The paradox emerges most strongly in the Christian religion because of the greater opposition between the speculative meaning and its representation and real history. In pre-Christian religions the lack of freedom in ethical life was directly presented in the religion. But the Christian religion, the religion with the most substantial idea of freedom in its doctrine of spirit as witness to spirit, is the religion which

is in the very heart of its nature detached from civil and state life and the substantial basis of the latter is taken away, so that the whole structure has no longer any reality, but is an empty appearance . . .[108]

This religious 'freedom' from the real world cannot be maintained. If the real world is denied, then God can only be represented as negative, in opposition to the finite world. The basic Christian experience is not of Christ, the mediator, of freedom, but of spiritual bondage to a dead God.[109] Christ's resurrection and Christian love should restore the unity and freedom of human and divine nature, but they can only do so 'if God is known as trinity'.[110] However, reconciliation in religion always remains implicit and abstract, because it is only achieved as religion, as a spiritual and not as a worldly community.

Christianity thus cannot realize the reconciliation between the human and the divine which would be freedom. It can only repeat the dreadful experience that

> God has died, God is dead, – this is the most frightful of all thoughts, that all that is true is not, that negation itself is found in God; the deepest sorrow, the feeling of something completely irretrievable, the renunciation of everything of a higher kind, are connected with this.[111]

The contradiction between speculative truth and religious misrepresentation is repeatedly presented as a paradox:

> In order that the reconciliation be real, it is necessary that in this development, in this totality, the reconciliation should also be consciously known, be present and be brought forward into actuality. The principles which apply to this worldly element actually exist in this spiritual element.[112]

When religion is presented in this way as an eternal paradox between the speculative standpoint and the subjective standpoint, it cannot appear as *necessary*, as the 'object producing itself'.[113] For misrepresentation of the absolute is laid at the door of feeling, faith, intuition. It is attributed to the 'forms of religious consciousness', to ordinary consciousness as such.[114] Thus, contrary to Hegel's aim, the religious standpoint *does* appear to be a 'subjective business', an inherent characteristic of finite consciousness.

> God would thus be an historical product of weakness, of fear, of joy, or of interested hopes, cupidity, and lust of power. What has its roots in my feeling, is only for me; it is mine, but not its own; it has no independent existence in and for itself.[115]

This criticism of Fichte's founding of faith on feeling applies with equal force to Feuerbach's critique of religion in general.[116] To reduce religion to the feelings of a finite species produces a weak account of the contingency of religious representation. How did Hegel avoid this position?

To conceive of the *necessity* of the religious standpoint, of the object producing itself, the relation between ethical life and religious representation of pre-Christian religions must be compared with the relation between ethical life and religious representation of the Christian religion. Subjectivity (religious representation) must be seen as the historical fate, determination (*Bestimmung*) of substance. This fate is not the fate of the spiritual community, the determination of worship, but the fate or determination of absolute ethical life itself.

To conceive of the necessity of religious representation is to eschew Fichte's 'moral sentimentalism', his lamentations in the face of the eternal, unchangeable evil of the world. To conceive of the necessity of religious representation is to derive historically specific representation from the contradictions of ethical life. This is to treat religion not with a bounded reason, but with a reason which does not indulge in the irrational 'litany of lamentations' which accompanies the never-ending tasks of morality.[117]

The End of Religion

In the speculative proposition that the state and religion are identical, 'everything depends on how they are determined.'[118]

One way in which the state and religion are identical is the Greek *polis*. The Greek *polis* 'has in religion the supreme consciousness of its life as state and as ethical life and is indebted to the Gods for the general arrangements connected with the state, such as agriculture, property, marriage.'[119] How are the state and religion determined in this case? There is no distinction between law and custom in the state, and religion is worldly. Religion sanctions political institutions, but this does not mean that it legitimizes or serves them. For in a society in which law is not separate from custom, political and religious custom and sanction are not separable as 'legitimation' implies. In such a society, custom and law are not means to an end, they are present,

Athena herself is Athenian life – the happiness and well-being of the state is not her end ... These beings which have divine nature are those very powers and activities themselves ... [they] rule in as immanent a way in the reality with which they are connected as the law acts within the planets.[120]

Hegel calls this a 'political religion',[121] for the state, political unity, is revered:

> The principles of the state must be regarded as valid in and for them-
> selves which can only be in so far as they are recognized as deter-
> minate manifestations of a divine nature.[122]

Thus,

> Among the Athenians the word Athens had a double import, sug-
> gesting primarily, a complex of political institutions, but no less, in
> the second place, that Goddess who represented the spirit of the
> people and its unity.[123]

Athens as the real, concrete identity of state and religion is contrasted with the other determinate religions of spiritual individuality, Judaism and the Roman religion. In all of them the divine has the characteristic of being an individual or individuals who recognize others in different ways and are thus spirit. In Judaism and in the Roman religion the divine and human natures are not united.

However, the problem with Athens as the exemplar of the identity of state and religion, of a people which recognizes its ethical life as divine, is that in such a society there is no subjectivity and no religious 'representation' as such. Greece plays an impossible rôle in Hegel's thought. It is the only historical case where the state and religion are one, in the sense that custom and law are united, but, *ex hypothesi*, if the state and religion are one in this sense, there will be no religious representation. The name 'Athena' means immediately both the *polis* and the God. Athena is an *individual*, that is, the universal and particular are unified in her. Hence she is not a subject, for to be a subject means that the universal and particular are not unified. A subject understands itself as infinite (universal) precisely by excluding the finite (determina-tion, or, the particular) and then misrepresents universality to itself in the form of religion. Athena is not a subject because in the Greek *polis* law and custom, legal forms and all other areas of social life, are not distinct from each other. This is a presentation of substantial not formal freedom in a society where subjectivity is not known. People are not determined as subjects, for subjects have to distinguish between, and relate to, separated aspects of themselves and of others.

The political and legal precondition of the development of the

Christian religion is the Roman state and Roman religion. They are of the foremost importance in determining the *aporias* of Christianity.

The Roman form of private property was enshrined in a legal system which separated law, in the form of private property law, from custom, from the other relations of social life. Those other relations, such as the family, were defined in terms of the same property law, by its distinction between 'persons' with the right to bear property, and 'things' who have no such right, such as women and children. The result was not a 'political religion' as in Greece, but a 'religion of the state', a religion which served the particular ends of rulers.[124] The state and religion are identical, but determined differently from Greece. The Roman religion is 'a sovereignty of the world', but it embraces the world 'in an external way'.[125] It does not see the world as divine and the people as substantially free. Instead

> The end which exists in this sovereignty is one which lies outside the individual, and the more it is realized the more external does it become, so that the individual is brought into subjection to this end and serves it.[126]

Law and custom are separate. The state acts, too, as an individual bearer of private property right with its own particular ends and interests which are imposed on the people. The state actively represents the gods to the people in a way which enables it to impose its own ends on them.

In Roman society the contradiction first developed between the formal freedom of private property law, that all are free who have the right to bear property and thus many are not free, with the 'spritual' freedom of all. The formal equality of property rights is represented as the religious freedom of all. The real inequality is reproduced in the merely formal or external equality of all in worship, in the 'freedom' to serve the ends of the Gods of the Roman state.

This is the ground on which the Christian religion developed. Christ's life, his teaching, his death, the Christian community and the Christian Church, produce a new notion of freedom made possible by the abstract, Roman notion of the subject. They produce, too, a new kind of divorce between religion and state.

The life of Christ, however, signifies the aspiration for a new kind of substantial freedom, for the reunification of subjectivity with the totality, for the developed unity of God with reality ... with a subjectivity which has been separated from him,[127]

by Roman legal institutions. But this unity is 'not yet of a concrete order, but simply the first abstract principles'.[128]

The Christian religion inherits the 'infinite value' of personality from the Romans. It is a legal value on the one hand, but, on the other, a principle of 'inwardness and subjectivity', 'soulless personality',[129] which is given a soul by the aspiration of Christianity. Yet this soul is acquired by a conscious and vigorous rejection of the corrupt institutions of Rome. Hence it is even more difficult to realize the aspiration, the unity of God and the world. The unity represented by Christ's life is displaced into a realm which is divorced from both law and custom. As a result both the meaning (representation) of Christ and the real existence of Christianity changed.

This contradiction between the aspiration for substantial freedom and the rejection of ethical life is represented in the story of Christ's life and teaching. Christ taught that all ethical bonds, both the family, natural ethical life, and politics, public ethical life, are unimportant compared with the duty of discipleship. In Greek society the burial of one's kin is a task of supreme political importance, a duty of both natural and public ethical life. To a youth who wishes to delay the duties of discipleship until he has buried his father, Christ says

> Let the dead bury their dead – follow thou me ... He that loveth father and mother more than me is not worthy of me.[130]

Hegel comments

> Here then is an abstraction from all that belongs to reality, even from ethical ties ... everything that had been respected is treated as a matter of indifference – as worthy of no regard.[131]

The gain is to liberate everyone from the external authority of a corrupt society,

> The [Christian] subjectivity which has come to understand its infinite worth has thereby abandoned all distinctions of authority, power, position and even of race; before God all men are equal. It is in the negation of infinite sorrow that love is found, and there, too, is found the possibility and the root of truly universal right, of the realization of freedom.[132]

This cosmopolitan subjectivity can understand its 'infinite worth', but nothing else. The religion which is potentially the realization of substantial freedom becomes the religion of real bondage, a religion of political misrepresentation, because subjectivity, as God and as man, has no determination in it. The cosmopolitan idea of freedom cannot re-affirm the freedom of the *polis*, for it no longer recognizes ethical life as divine, as triune, but rejects it as corrupt and remains in the agony, the passion, of religious and political dualism, of religious separation and political domination.

Christ said 'Give to Caesar's what is Caesar's and to God what is God's.'[133] In the first place, since Caesar, the state, was there, and

> neither Jesus nor his followers could annul it, the fate of Jesus and his following remains a loss of freedom, a restriction of life, passivity under the domination of an alien might which was despised . . .[134]

The result was that Jesus could 'find freedom only in his heart, only in the void'.[135] In the second place, this precept to give to Caesar what is his and to God what is his is 'not enough'.[136] It leaves the questions un-answered what belongs to Caesar and what belongs to God. If this question is not answered, the answer will be 'imperialism', the encroach-ment of Caesar on God, or God on Caesar.[137] Each will be corrupted by this domination and rendered incapable of achieving real unity, and capable only of suppressing.

This encroachment occurred repeatedly. It changed the meaning and structure of both religious and civil institutions. It united the two in different successive ways by suppressing one, and thereby equally cor-rupting and depraving the other. This has been the culture or formation, *die Bildung*, of the Christian religion and the state, ethical life. It has been a series of formative experiences in which religious and political con-sciousness' definition of itself comes into contradiction with its real existence. This experience of the repeatedly enforced unity of the definition on the reality has caused changes in both the definition and the existence.

The contradiction between the Christian ideal of freedom and the Christian rejection of ethical life has made the Christian church into an ethical power. But this cannot be acknowledged by a church which debases the ethical, and Christian doctrine has therefore justified both the evil and the just acts committed in its name. The history of the Christian religion is the history of its relation to secular power and to ethical life, and this history is the history of the perversion of the Christian ideal of freedom. Christianity perpetuated the lack of freedom of Roman institutions, and the even greater bondage of feudal property forms and political institutions.

In each case of encroachment and corruption by church or state the definition of religious subjectivity and its relation to the ethical world has changed. This has been the formation or culture of the Christian religion, its dialectic. In the lectures on the *Philosophy of History* and in *The Phenomenology of Spirit*, Hegel presents the connection between Christian religious civilization and Christian political barbarity at specific historical periods. Whatever the cost of these contradictions, of these various forms of domination, they are comprehended as formative, as educating abstract subjectivity towards an ethical realization of the trinity, of substantial freedom without domination.

The Reformation is a watershed in this education. On one reading of the lectures on the *Philosophy of History*, the Reformation is the final stage of education, for it brings about a change in the concept of subjectivity. Ethical life is once again sanctified, and is no longer repelled or dominated. This opens up the possibility of the 'divine interpenetration of the secular life':[138]

> The Christian principle has now passed through the terrible discipline of culture and first attains truth and reality through the reformation.[139]

The philosophy of history seems to have a happy ending:

> The principle of free spirit is here made the banner of the world, and from this principle are evolved the universal axioms of reason . . . From that epoch thought began to gain a culture properly its own: principles were derived from it which were to be the norm for the constitution of the state. Political life was now to be consciously regulated by reason. Customary morality, traditional usage lost its validity; the various claims insisted upon must prove their legitimacy as based on rational principles. Not till this era is the freedom of spirit realized.[140]

It is clear in the *Philosophy of History* that this freedom could not be realized in France. For the French had a revolution without a reformation. This rationality will only prevail where both a reformation and a revolution have occurred, otherwise the encroachments and domination of Christian history will continue.

In Germany the Enlightenment worked *with* the reformed Church and not *against* an unreformed one as in France.[141] Hegel implies at the end of the text of the lectures on the philosophy of history that the principle of Christianity has been realized in Germany. But it is clear from the lectures on the philosophy of religion and other writings that Hegel did not believe that this had occurred. Germany had had a reformation and an Enlightenment but no revolution.[142] As a result, the meaning of the Enlightenment in Germany, like the meaning of the Revolution in France, became distorted. In France, the encroachment of political on religious life continued and the result was the failure of the revolution. In Germany, the Enlightenment did not contribute to the realization of substantial freedom, of the Christian principle, but became more dualistic than before. The thought of Kant and Fichte is the culmination of this development and has produced a concept of subjectivity which Hegel compares, with consideration, with the Roman concept of subjectivity.

The modern concept of subjectivity is the natural law correlate of Roman private property law, as is especially clear in the case of Kant's *Metaphysic of Morals*. This concept of subjectivity is both a flight from the world and instrumental, as the Roman concept was. It is no longer formative in the way the history of Christian religion has been. It is like the Roman in that it has no vocation to impose itself on the state, for it serves the state,

> Just as in the time of the Roman empire political life [is] universally devoid of principle.[143]

It is no longer formative in the further, unique sense that it is no longer exoteric. It has destroyed, in its 'critique of all revelation', even the religious representation of Christian freedom. It no longer merely depraves people politically, it has abandoned them.[144]

> When the Gospel is no longer preached to the poor, when the salt has lost its savour, and all the foundations have been tacitly removed, then the people, for whose ever-solid reason truth can exist only in representation, no longer know how to assist the impulse and emotions they feel within them. They are nearest to the condition of infinite sorrow; but since love has been perverted to a love and

enjoyment from which all sorrow is absent, they seem to themselves to be deserted by their teachers. The latter have, it is true, brought life to themselves by means of reflection, have found their satisfaction in finitude, in subjectivity and its virtuosity, and consequently in what is empty and vain, but the substantial kernel of the people cannot find its satisfaction there.[145]

The 'Gospel' does not mean the preaching of religious faith, nor the 'faith' of Kant and Fichte. It does not refer to the end of religion in the sense that nothing passes any more for religion. It refers to the way in which religion offers no political guidance to people. The Christian religion has always been inherently unable to offer rational political guidance, but the present way of separating religion and reason, faith and rational political life, is particularly debilitating and depraved.

This final and culminating point thus reached by the formal culture of our day is at the same time the most extreme *crudeness* because it possesses *merely the form of culture*.[146]

This is a 'new spiritual bondage'.[147]

These are rare and revealing passages in which Hegel does not disguise a *Sollen* as the rationality of the real, but simply despairs.

This reconciliation [by philosophy] is itself merely a partial one without universality. Philosophy forms in this relation a sanctuary apart and those who serve in it constitute an isolated order of priests, who must not mix with the world, and whose work is to protect the possession of truth. How the actual present-day world is to find its way out of this state of dualism and what form it is to take, are questions which must be left to itself to settle and to deal with them is not the immediate and practical business of philosophy.[148]

Under present social and political conditions, for the historic Good Friday to become the speculative Good Friday, philosophy must form 'a sanctuary apart', 'an isolated order of priests'. Hegel draws attention to this *status* of philosophy in order not to impose its concept. The priests are *not* to act as Christian priests have done; they are to remain isolated.

This is how the philosophy of history should be conceived, not as a teleology of reconciliation, not as replacing the exhausted attempt to create a Christian civilization, but as perpetual repetition, as the perpetual completing of the historic Good Friday by the speculative Good

Friday. There is no end of religion and no end of history, but a per-petual 'speculative justification' to complete the faith which 'justifies nothing'.[149]

Hegel is not sanguine that the rational completing of the meaning of religion will make possible a rational ethical life in the way a realization of the principle of the Christian religion would have done. But he is sure that misrepresentation and irrational political life will continue in history, and that philosophy will have to be more armed against its irrationality not less. But this philosophic rationality may not bring freedom.

Religion is no longer formative, because it no longer has, even potentially and apolitically in the forms of love and worship, a triune structure, because 'faith' in its contemporary philosophical justifications has no content. The pain and sorrow of the absent God has been trans-formed into an uncritical reconciliation with the immediate present, with the forms of political domination and servitude of specific prop-erty relations. Because religion has lost its vocation, even its barbaric one, it has lost, too, its critical edge, and become completely assimilated.

While the Christian religion as such is no longer formative, the question of 'subjective disposition' remains, of the 'impulses and emo-tions' of the 'ever-solid reason' of the people. For only if this 'ever-solid reason' is formed is any realization of reason, of rational political life, of freedom, possible.

The thesis of the end of religion implies 'end' in the sense of *telos*, in the sense of religion as ethical life, and in the sense of *finis*, the cessation of religion as formative experience, but it does not imply the end of representation. The thesis of the end of religion in modern culture thus provides an analysis of the ideological formation and deformation of modern culture.

Why is it the fate (determination) of the substance (absolute) to become subject? Before Hegel developed a philosophy of history this question was answered by reference to the private property relations of bourgeois society with allusions to and comparisons with other prop-erty forms. These references to different property relations are later elaborated by sustained historical accounts which connect illusion and representation with the division of labour on the one hand, and the experience of work on the other. The fate of substance and the forma-tion of subjectivity are presented in these forms in the *Aesthetics* and the *Phenomenology*.

4

The Division of
Labour and Illusion

The End of Art

This extension of symbolism to every *sphere* of mythology and art [by Friedrich Schlegel] is by no means what we have in view here in considering the symbolic form of art. For our endeavour does not rise to finding out how far artistic configuration could be interpreted symbolically or allegorically in this sense of the word 'symbol'; instead, we have to ask, conversely, how far the symbolic itself is to be reckoned an *art-form*. We want to establish the artistic relation between meaning and its configuration, in so far as that relation is *symbolic* in distinction from other modes of presentation, especially the classical and romantic.[1]

First, the question arises about what character the general world-situation must have if it is to provide a ground on which an epic event can be adequately presented.[2]

The *Aesthetics* presents the speculative experience of the opposition between the state and religion *in a transcendental exposition*. Hence it is Hegel's most 'sociological' work.

The thesis of the end of art, like the thesis of the end of religion, does not mean that works of art are no longer created. It means that art is no longer a formative, educative, political experience. But, in the case of art, the end of art has two meanings, for there are two ends of art. The first 'end' of art refers to the end of a society, Greece, in which life is 'lived aesthetically', in which social institutions are themselves aesthetic. It thus signifies the *beginning* of art in the sense in which we understand art, as relatively autonomous from other social institutions. It signifies the beginning of artistic re-presentation, of art as a *relation* between meaning and configuration, between concept and intuition. Art ceased to be the fundamental politically formative mode of experience at this point: it lost its end in the sense of *telos*.[3] The second 'end' of art refers to modern art, to art in post-revolutionary, bourgeois society. This end of art means 'end' in the sense of *finis*. Art has fallen into such a contradiction between meaning and configuration, between concept and intuition, that it is no longer art in the second sense of a relation, a partial lack of unity, between them.[4]

The *Aesthetics* is a philosophy not a phenomenology of art. It does not present the standpoint of natural consciousness, the experiences of the contradiction between its definition of itself and its real existence, in its transitions to different conceptions of itself and of its existence, from a purely individual to a moral and to an ethical apprehension. In the *Aesthetics* the formation and deformation of art, not of consciousness, is *known* to be over in the two senses specified. Thus the history of this formation and deformation is presented from the standpoint of ethical life, of the collectivity, not from the subjective standpoint. The speculative experience of the opposition between state and religion is presented as 'the doctrine of art-forms [*die Lehre von Kunstformen*]'.[5] Hegel inquires into the possibility of art-forms. He asks which forms of art and which individual arts are possible under specific historical and social preconditions. This enquiry is transcendental because it assumes actual art-forms and individual arts as given and examines their possibility. The enquiry is sociological because it connects social structure (precondition) to art-forms (the conditioned).[6] But the answer to the enquiry has a metaphysical form in the strict Kantian sense that it sets out the specific forms which fall under the justified principles. It is, in Hegel's terms, a doctrine, for it demonstrates the necessity of art-forms and of the system of individual arts. 'Aesthetics' is thus not concerned with the 'interpretation' of art.[7]

The *Aesthetics* is the inverse of the *Phenomenology*. Natural consciousness in the *Phenomenology* gradually discovers the determinations of its limited definitions of itself, culminating in the experiences of art and religion which are still limited experiences, but which are misapprehensions of the absolute, of collective experience, and not misapprehensions of experience as solely individual. In the penultimate sections of the *Phenomenology* on art and religion, the earlier stages which were misunderstood by natural consciousness as individual or 'moral' experiences are re-experienced in their specific historical locations in the opposition between state and religion. But there cannot be a *doctrine* of experience, only its presentation.

As with all transcendental enquiries, Hegel's argument in the *Aesthetics* is circular. He derives the social preconditions for an art-form, for example, the epic, from instances of that form, for example, Homer. Hegel treats artistic genres, in effect, as ritual, as direct evidence of law and custom in Greece, and as indirect and inverse evidence of law and custom in post-Greek societies. Collective determinations are presented in chronological order, in the 'sequence' of art-forms: symbolic, classical and romantic; and in the 'system' of individual arts: architecture (symbolic), sculpture (classical), painting, music and poetry (romantic).[8] Chronology is only defied in the case of poetry, for poetry, 'the universal art', is formative in every precondition.[9]

The *Aesthetics* expounds formative experience from the standpoint of ethical life. From the ethical standpoint the division of labour is seen to determine the individual's experience of work. The *Phenomenology* expounds formative experience from the standpoint of subjective consciousness according to which work is misapprehended as a relation between individuals. Formative experience is the relation to transforming nature, to work, to actuality. Work is a means of recognition of oneself and others. The mode of appropriation of nature in a society, its division of labour and the corresponding work experience of individuals, is ethical. It determines the mutual recognition or lack of it between individuals, and the corresponding media of representation, art and religion.

Beauty and Illusion

Just as the unity of law and custom in Greek society made it incorrect to speak of religious representation in that society, it also makes it incorrect to speak of artistic representation. Artistic representation occurs only when the state and religion become divorced. In Greek society there are 'no Gods in advance of poetry'.[10] Poetry and sculpture do not re-present the Gods of a religion which exists independently of the art-form. Poetry and sculpture *present* the God, they do not *represent* them: 'The Gods are made, invented, but not fictitious.'[11] The Gods are 'made' or 'invented' means that they do not have an independent origin and are re-presented or re-produced in the form of art as occurs in later societies. The Gods, however, are not 'fictitious', not the *mere* invention of the artist, but the direct presentation by artists of the ethical life of the society, of the harmony not the *relation* between spirit and nature, of real, concrete recognition between individuals. Art is *Schein* not *Vorstellung*. In the context of Greek society, *Schein* means the 'shining forth' of meaning in a sensuous medium, not the re-presentation of an external meaning which is not at one with the medium of presentation. In societies where religious representation is the dominant mode of self-consciousness, of self-misapprehension, artistic *Schein* means illusion, the illusion which corresponds to the re-presentation. *Schein* in the latter case means the relation, not the harmony or the shining forth, of nature and spirit, of concept and intuition, of meaning and configuration.[12]

Schein as the unity, not the relation, of spirit and nature presented as an individual is beauty. Beauty is not a harmony between *concept* and nature, for such a harmony or real unity could not appear in a sensuous medium. 'Beauty' refers to a harmony between the natural or sensuous and the individual; a harmony which is not known as such by those who live it: 'It is not free self-determining spirituality; but sheer naturalness formed to spirituality – spiritual individuality.'[13] The beautiful 'is determined as the shining [*Scheinen*] of the Idea to sense'.[14] It is an ideal, 'an inherent unity', recognized *by us* as a harmony.[15] It cannot be a concept, for the concept is abstract and *known* and cancels intuition or nature,[16] and because the unity of concept and intuition cannot occur in a sensuous medium, but can only be *known* as substantial freedom. Beauty is the concrete unity between the individual and his or her physical appearance. It occurs when nature is regarded as divine, not simply in its natural and sensuous form, but in the form of an individual who has specific characteristics, physical and ethical, which are realized in his or her manifestation.[17] The statue of the Greek God is this totality of distinct parts, concrete life, *par excellence*.[18] Beauty occurs in a society with a specific relation to nature and a specific political structure, where 'individual life is substantial life'.[19] Beauty in this society is the 'shining forth' of the specific character of the individual, because it is equally the determination of the whole society in the individual.

Beauty is the real unity of 'meaning' and 'configuration'. 'Configuration' is the 'sensuous appearance' of the work of art; 'meaning' is the 'inner significance' of that appearance. This unity of meaning and configuration is contrasted with art forms where meaning and configuration do not coincide, which are not beautiful. In societies where art re-presents an independent religion, meaning and configuration are not in harmony, and art is not beautiful 'shining' but illusory; it re-presents dominant religious representation for sensuous apprehension.

The contrast between meaning and configuration is not an abstract opposition, nor has Hegel hypostatized a mystical 'inner' meaning. Meaning and configuration correspond to concept and intuition in the sphere of art before concept and intuition have been divorced from each other, before a *relation* to nature, intuition, has arisen, in a society in which nature is suppressed. Relation to nature means a relation to nature as the physical world, work relations, and a relation to nature as the natural will, ethical and political relations. Substance is now split up and re-presented by art as abstract freedom (meaning) in the very medium, sensuous configuration, which is denied.

Ancient Greece is the society where life is 'aesthetically lived'. The human culture of man himself is the 'subjective' work of art; the shaping of the world of divinities is the 'objective' work of art; and the state and the relations of those who compose it are the 'political' work of art.[20]

Greece, where social institutions are 'aesthetic', plays the rôle in Hegel's thought that the 'state of nature' plays in natural law. It is a *fiction*, because the idea of an Heroic Age is taken from Homeric epic and fifth century tragedy, from literary narrative. This fiction is presented as a *natural condition*, as an historically unique harmony of spirit with nature, human, physical and political (second nature). This fictional status is evidenced by Hegel's preference for Goethe's *Iphigenia in Tauris* to Euripedes' play of the same name.[21] Goethe's play captures for Hegel what he means by Greek *Sittlichkeit*, ethical life, better than Euripedes' play does. Euripedes and Socrates herald the end of ethical life, because they assert the right of subjectivity against the substantial freedom of their society.[22]

Greece, like all the other forms in Hegel's thought, whether artforms, property forms or configurations of consciousness, is not a simple, monolithic type. This is particularly clear in the *Phenomenology* where individual, moral and ethical experience are not presented in chronological order. A form of individual experience may occur in more than one historical society, and several historical societies may give rise to the same form of individual experience.

Greece stands for a society in which there is no subjectivity and hence no representation. It stands for a society which contains conflict and injustice, but which is substantially free, and hence the conflict and injustice are transparent and intelligible. In Greek society only a few are known to be free, but this freedom is concrete and realized. Those who are not free are *known* as slaves, and conflict between equally valid social spheres is recognized by all. In later societies all are re-presented as free, but freedom is not realized for any, and the lack of freedom is not *known*.

Hence Greece provides the fictional but logical basis for the subsequent determination of substance (ethical life) as subject, for the exposition of the relation between subjectivity and representation. It stands for a just society, for a limited but realized form of justice. The exposition of the division of labour and work experience reveals the basis of both the justice and the injustice. In this society, meaning and configuration have not yet been separated into concept and intuition. Art is the politically formative experience, *distinct* but not *separate* from work, religion and politics.

The *Aesthetics* appears to be dominated by the ideal of beauty as its prime object. But the presentation of this ideal is the precondition of an exposition of art as we know it, of art as re-presentation of relatively separate spheres of social life. The exposition of the *ideal* of beauty is the precondition of a philosophy of art which does *not idealize* art, which sees art in its symbolic and romantic forms, and as symbolic and romantic individual arts, as illusion, as the re-presentation of the contradiction between state and religion, between real existence and subjective disposition. The exposition of the ideal of beauty is the precondition of a philosophy of art which sees art as we understand it, as an historically specific phenomenon which reproduces social contradiction in the medium of sensuous illusion. Art in this sense is not ideal, not integral, not beautiful.

History commences with the history of states, with the formation of a political unity which distinguishes itself externally from other political unities, and which may be constituted or maintained internally by compulsion, by custom, by formal law, or by subjective disposition.

> The consciousness of freedom first arose among the Greeks . . . but they . . . knew only that *some* are free – not man as such . . . . The Greeks therefore had slaves; and their whole life and the maintenance of their splendid liberty was implicated with the institution of slavery.[23]

The Greek consciousness of freedom is contrasted with oriental despotism where one alone is free, and with patriarchal Judaism where no-one is conceived as free. The kind and the degree of freedom in a society is always derived from the relation of that society to nature. This notion of freedom is, on the one hand, opposed to the natural law position that the 'state of nature' is free. On the contrary, 'society and the state are the very conditions in which freedom is realized.'[24] Freedom is not natural,

> Freedom as the *ideal* of that which is original and natural, does not exist *as original and natural*.[25]

On the other hand, the kind and degree of freedom depends on the *relation* which a society has to nature. For concrete freedom depends not on the *concept* which a society has of freedom, but on whether that concept is realized, whether it is concretely united with the nature or finite which it suppresses by virtue of being a concept as such. Conversely, a society which is concretely free, but has a limited *concept* of freedom will not be substantially free for everyone. Greece is such a society.

From the *System der Sittlichkeit* and the earliest Jena phenomenologies 'nature' or the 'finite' as derived from Kant and Fichte's theoretical philosophy meant physical nature, and, as derived from their practical philosophy, it meant the moral agent as natural will, as desire and inclination. The relation to nature covers both the relation to physical nature and the ethical relation to the other, both parts of oneself and other moral agents. The simplest relation to nature was to transform it in work, an experience in which the relation to the natural world becomes an ethical experience: work as an instrument (mean) to satisfy need becomes a mediation (mean) which determines one's recognition or misrecognition of oneself and others. In this sense the appropriation and transformation of nature *determines* political organization, freedom.

Greek society has a limited concept of freedom, limited in the sense that only some are free, and that those who are free did not have an abstract concept of their freedom. It is only in his discussion of Greek society, and not in the discussion of Oriental or Judaic society, that Hegel first explicates the connection between work as the transformation and appropriation of nature and ethical unity.

The Greeks distinguished human agency from the natural world and then related human agency to the natural world in a way which produced their particular kind of freedom. This is demonstrated by discussion of a putative Heroic Age derived from Homer and from fifth century tragedy.

In the Heroic Age of Greek society, the natural world is not degraded or demeaned. Productive activity is recognized and respected. There is a 'living connection with nature ... be it friendly or hostile'.[26] The Greek mode of appropriating nature results in a specific conception of their own nature and of their relation to each other. The division of labour is simple, and there is no distinction between the social and technical division of labour, between overall class divisions and the division determined by technical imperatives:

> ... the nearest environment of individuals [in the Heroic Age], the satisfaction of their immediate needs, is still their own doing ... the heroes kill and roast their own food; they break in the horse they wish to ride; the utensils they need they more or less make for themselves; plough, weapons for defence, shield, helmet, breastplate, sword, spear, are their own work, or they are familiar with their fabrication. In such a mode of life man has the feeling, in everything he uses and everything he surrounds himself with, that he has produced it from his own resources, and therefore in external things he has to do with what is his own, and not with alienated objects lying outside his own sphere wherein he is master ... everything is domestic, in everything the man has present before his eyes, the power of his arm, the skill of his hand, the cleverness of his own spirit, or a result of his courage and bravery. In this way alone have the means of satisfaction not been degraded to a purely external matter; we see their living origin itself, the living consciousness of the value which man puts on them because in them he has things not dead or killed by custom, but his own closest productions.[27]

Odysseus, an example of such a man, 'carpentered himself his huge marriage bed [Odyssey, XXIII]'.[28] This respect for productive activity, where the productive act and the product remain united, is the basis of the respect which the individual confers on political life. Odysseus and the other princes rallied to support Agamemnon in the Trojan Wars not because they were forced to do so, for 'there is no compelling law to which they are subject'. They are not Agamemnon's

> lieutenants and generals, summoned at his call, but are as independent as he is himself; they have assembled around him of their own free

will. . . . He must take counsel with them, and if they are dissatisfied they stay away from the fight as Achilles did.[29]

The interrelations of this kind of ethical life

the bond of the family, as well as the bond of the people – as an entire nation – in war and peace must all have been discovered, framed and developed; but on the other hand, not yet developed into the form of universal institutions, obligations, and laws valid in themselves without any ratification by the living subjective personality of individuals, and indeed possessed of the power of subsisting even against the will of individuals. On the contrary, the sole origin and support of these relations must clearly be a *sense* of justice and equity, together with custom and the general mind and character so that no intellectualism in the form of a prosaic reality can stand and be consolidated against the heart, individual attitudes of mind and passion. . . . Thus in epic we find an underlying community of objective life and action, but nevertheless a freedom in this action and life which appear to proceed entirely from the subjective will of individuals.[30]

Hegel states this political relation generally in terms of work experience. Just as the Greek hero knows the objects around him as his own work, so the Greek citizens 'know substance as their own work'.[31] Labour (*Arbeit*) and product (*Werk*) are not separated by 'universal mediations', but are simple and united.[32] The individual does not separate himself into a physical and a moral aspect, but sees the whole of himself in the totality of his productions, whether his marriage bed or his valour, and sees both the products of his labour and his individual qualities as immediately ethical, created to further the interests of the *polis* not individual interest. They are a 'second nature', for *Sitte*, custom, and *Sittlichkeit*, ethical life or law, are not distinct. There are no external sanctions and no internal ones. Individual nature is not vastly differentiated, not split up into private and public, natural and moral aspects. Nature, physical and ethical, worked on and transformed, remains second nature.[33]

Yet,

Their whole life and maintenance of their splendid liberty was implicated with the institution of slavery.[34]

It is well-known that in the *Phenomenology* the master's (=the hero) dependence on the labour of the slave limits the freedom of the master.

It is frequently argued that because it is the slave who undergoes the formative experience of productive labour, the future belongs to the slave.[35] This is not the significance of Hegel's discussion of the institution of slavery.

Freedom was expounded as inseparable from the productive activity of the hero (=master), his seeing himself immediately in his physical productions and seeing the ethical whole in his own qualities. But the master's dependence on the slave does not make him into a mere consumer of products with whose 'fabrication' he is not 'familiar'.[36] There *is* a distinction between the social and technical division of labour, but 'everything' remains 'domestic'.[37] The master or hero knows that the slave is a slave, not free. On the other hand, the productive activity, the work experience, of the slave is not formative, because the slave does not attain through it to a knowledge of the validity of his servitude and he will never be free.[38] The hero and master, however, enjoys the achievements of his household as his work, and enjoys the connection between his productive activity and his knowledge of himself.

The future belongs to the master. For in future societies the master will become master *and* slave. He will know himself as master, but not know that he and others are slaves. They will not be called master and slave for that relationship is transparent. They will be called 'persons'. They will know themselves as infinitely free and will not know themselves in opaque bondage to the nature which has been suppressed.

In the Heroic Age of Greek society there is no concept of a law which grants 'universal' property rights. There is no private property, because individuals are not defined by law according to their right to own property, as persons. Productive transformation both of the physical world for the necessities of life, and of the ethical world, valour and courage, occurs according to custom and that custom (*Sitte*) is the unity of the society (*Sittlichkeit*). Unity is not achieved by imposing on custom an external law which grants rights. Thus, although Greek society depends on the labour of those who are not free, it is not based on the labour of those who are known to be infinitely free as persons, but are unknown as specific individuals, and on whose labour therefore others depend but do not enjoy.

The Classical Form of Art: Tragedy and the State

The universal element in ethical life and the abstract freedom of the person in his inner and outer life, remain, in conformity with the principle of Greek life, in undisturbed harmony with one another, and, at the same time, when this principle asserted itself in the actual present there was no question of an independence of the political sphere contrasted with a subjective morality distinct from it; the substance of political life was merged in individuals just as much as they sought this their own freedom only in pursuing the universal aims of the whole.[39]

This is the precondition of the classical form of art in which

> beauty has for its inner meaning the free independent meaning, not a meaning *of* this or that but what means itself and therefore signifies itself.[40]

The classical form of art is a unity of meaning and configuration. Meaning and configuration are distinct but not separate; configuration does not re-present meaning but presents it. When configuration re-presents meaning the relation between the two may be allusion, affinity, allegory, but the presentation of meaning can mean only one kind of unity.[41] Presentation refers to a meaning which both distinguishes itself from the natural world and acknowledges nature. The meaning is *present* in the physical, sensuous world as configuration. The classical form of art is the presentation of Greek custom. Meaning and configuration form a totality not in the sense of a summation but in the sense of a 'living whole' in which every distinct part is essential to the independence of the whole. The statue of the God is the classical individual art *par excellence*. It presents free spirituality as determinate individuality. This is not only a definition of beauty but of happiness,

> because it [classical art] has as its element not that movement and that reconciliation of infinite subjectivity which has been achieved out of opposition and which knows the withdrawal of subjective inwardness into itself, the distraction, the helplessness, the whole series of disunions which produce in their midst the ugly, the hateful, the repulsive in both the sensuous and the spiritual sphere/but instead only the untroubled harmony of determinate free individuality in its adequate existence, this peace in that real existence, this happiness,

this satisfaction and greatness in itself, thus eternal serenity and bliss which even in misfortune and grief do not lose their assured self-repose.[42]

On the other hand,

> The [Greek] community, however, can only maintain itself by suppressing this spirit of individualism, and, because it is an essential moment all the same creates it by its repressive attitude towards it as a hostile moment.[43]

There seems to be a contradiction between these two passages, between the exposition of the necessity of the classical form of art and the reference to suppression, to tragedy. It is not a contradiction. For Greek society is not perfectly just, but its injustice is recognized, and hence transparent and visible. Tragedy not epic poetry or the statue of the god is the form in which a specific kind of conflict is presented.

In the *Aesthetics* this conflict is expounded as the process of formation of the classical form of art.[44] There are two relations to nature in Greek society and therefore two kinds of freedom, two equally valid and necessary spheres of social life which come into conflict. This conflict is immediately presented for both protagonists are known to be ethical.

Tragedy is the art which presents the fundamental collision of Greek society. The tragedies of Aeschylus and Sophocles are a formative, political experience in which the society enacts and resolves its basic conflict and is serene in its grief. Tragedy, the literary genre, is a social institution, and its social preconditions are anachronistically read out of the corpus of Aeschylus' and Sophocles' works.

The battle between the old and the new Gods in Greek mythology, between the Titanic and Olympic Gods, between Chronos and Zeus, is seen as an opposition, preserved even in the victory of Olympus, between a set of Gods which are nature Gods, Gods of natural necessity, and a set of Gods which are active and free, distinct from natural necessity, but united with it.[45]

This battle between the old and the new Gods is not an abstract opposition. The old Gods stand for the human necessity and ability to recognize the forces of nature, such as appetite and death, and to transform nature to human ends, for example, the skill and ability of Prometheus.[46] The new Gods stand for political skill and wisdom, for the formation of political institutions.[47] The transformative powers and abilities of the old Gods are called 'divine', those of the new Gods 'human'. The old Gods are called divine, because their activity is not completely intelligible, whereas the powers of the new Gods are fully intelligible, known as human powers.

These two spheres of communal life, distinct but not separate, come into conflict with each other:

> The old Gods are assigned the right of family situations in so far as these rest on nature and therefore are opposed to the public law and right of the community.[48]

The family is the ethical basis of the community which first makes people into ethical beings. It is called the 'natural' basis of political life, but it also stands for the individual against the communal right when the two conflict. This individual right is not a private interest opposed to the public interest. Hegel calls the family 'the obscure right of the natural element within spiritual relationship',[49] in order to emphasize that the individual's conflict with the state is another aspect of that communal life. To call the family 'natural' prevents 'individual' being misunderstood as infinitely free individuality, as subjectivity or subjective interest.

The new Gods stand for human law, a law which is intelligible, but which still retains a natural basis, while the old Gods are called 'obscure', and 'unconscious'. The latter are not completely intelligible, because they stand for forces not entirely formed by human agency. The old Gods are assigned the right of family, but this does not mean that the family is the inherently 'natural' basis of human community. It expresses the idea that when there is conflict in the midst of a free society the conflicting individuals equally present aspects of communal life, of nature or actuality transformed in two ways, both of which are recognized by each party to the conflict.

The conflicting individuals do not have subjective capricious 'characters', but present the universal substantive interest in its 'divine' and 'human' forms. The individual has a 'pathos' not a character.[50] 'Pathos' means not 'passion' or 'inner conflict', but

> an inherently justified power over the heart, an essential content of rationality and freedom of the will.[51]

Pathos is the domination in an individual of one of the equally but not absolutely valid powers which prevail in communal life.[52] Orestes, for example, kills his mother,

> not at all from an inner movement of the heart such as we would call passion, on the contrary, the pathos which drives him to the deed is well considered and wholly deliberate.[53]

But Orestes' act defies family law and can only be resolved by Athena, the Goddess of the *polis*, granting equal right to the Eumenides, the family Goddesses, who pursue Orestes, and to Apollo, the new, daylight God who seeks to protect Orestes' political right.[54]

Similarly, the tragedy of *Antigone* is not that of the individual in conflict with the state. It is the conflict between family right, the right to bury the dead, and communal right, the law of the society.[55] Antigone pronounces her own judgement,

> Because we suffer, we acknowledge that we have erred.[56]

She thus recognizes that her suffering is not the effect of her personal caprice, nor is it caused by the arbitrary and unjust power of the state. She acknowledges that it arises out of the conflict of two equally just ethical powers. She does not fully comprehend her suffering because her pathos is that of the family, but she acknowledges the right of the powers she defies as she acknowledges her own right to defy.

In Greek society the Gods, both divine and human, were not the 'object of religious consciousness', but were directly active in the world.[57] Tragedy occurs not because one power is natural and uncontrollable but because the powers are active and differentiated. The substance and unity of ethical life is restored either when both powers are appeased as in the *Oresteia*, or when both powers are destroyed (Antigone, Haemon and Eurydice). In this resolution the tragic chorus does not act as a disengaged moralist but as the 'substance' of the living order. A chorus is possible when ethical life exists as direct and living actuality and is not encoded in laws and religious dogmas.[58]

This is a tragic view of human life as eternal conflict, and it is at odds with any interpretation of Hegel's philosophy of history which is based on the resolution and reconciliation of all contradictions. In the *Philosophy of Right*, Hegel says that in a developed, substantially free, society there would be even more collisions because there would be more spheres of social life which would conflict with each other. Collision only occurs with something which is also 'right or freedom in one of its forms'. It does not occur between formal, abstract rights and such con-flict would be merely contingent. Collision occurs between rights which are equally necessary, equally substantial.[59]

This complex collision is *inconceivable* as tragedy, strictly speaking, because aesthetic experience is no longer a formative experience in modern society and substantial freedom cannot be imagined or repre-sented as a new aesthetic life. Substantial freedom can only be thought. Yet it may be considered a tragic point of view in the sense that even in a substantially free, complex society conflict and collision would necessarily arise.

The necessity of fifth century tragedy and of Homeric epic as literary genres is demonstrated by reference to the social organization which they presuppose, and they are themselves social institutions. In this way forms of art whose necessity is demonstrated in the *Aesthetics* are simply presented in the *Philosophy of History* as beautiful institutions, as the subjective, objective and political works of art. In a society in which art is presentation, art-forms are social institutions, and all social insti-tutions are works of art. To argue that the state is the precondition or cause of tragedy is to argue both that the state is the precondition of the tragic form of art, and that tragedy is a social institution which directly presents social and political conflict. Similarly, to say that the Heroic Age is the precondition of Homeric epic is to say both that the Heroic Age is the precondition of the epic form of art, and that epic is a social institution which directly presents the Heroic Age.

The Romantic Form of Art: Poetry and Prose as Social Categories

The 'prosaic' order is the *precondition* of the romantic form of art and the 'poetic' order is the *precondition* of the classical form of art.[60] Literary genres, poetry and prose, are themselves the social and political precon-dition of forms of art. The literary genre as the *precondition* of a form of art is made to describe a kind of social organization. When the genre itself is deduced as an aesthetic category, as the *conditioned*, in the system of individual arts, it has therefore already acquired social and political connotations.

As the precondition, the 'poetic' order describes the productive and political relations of Greek society, while the 'prosaic' order describes a complex division of labour, suppression of productive activity and natural life, a consequent divorce between custom and law and re-presentation in art and religion. The 'prosaic' order is the social pre-condition of art in a society where art becomes the re-presentation of a religion which exists independently of art.

The prosaic order is the precondition of the romantic form of art in general, and, in particular, of the romantic individual art *par excellence*: poetry. In this paradoxical way, *poetry* as artistic configuration is not united with its precondition, the *prosaic* order, but is indirectly deter-mined, by it.

In a society in which the art form has become relatively autonomous from other social institutions which it re-presents, that is, art as we understand it, it loses the integrity of the classical ideal and becomes contradictory. The prevalent social contradiction between real exis-tence and abstract, enforced political unity, the legal state, gives rise to a religion based on a further divorce between real existence, life in the abstract state, and a religious significance or meaning which is infinitely removed from the social and political world. 'Art acquires a totally new position' in such a society.[61] It re-presents the contradiction of religious consciousness between meaning, an infinitely removed deity, and configuration, its appearance in the sensuous medium – a medium which is now debased, and with which such meaning cannot be united. Art re-presents the lack of unity between the abstract ideal of freedom and the abandoned concrete world; it reproduces the real lack of political and social unity. It is illusion: it represents an ethical life which has been determined as subjectivity, which knows itself as in-finitely free and does not know itself as infinitely unfree.

The 'prosaic' order refers to the complex division of labour and formal political institutions which characterize Roman and modern society. Hegel's linking of Roman and modern law is based on the abeyance of Roman law during the feudal era and its re-emergence in the eighteenth century. The 'romantic form of art' refers to the place of art in the cosmopolitan Christian religion and includes the feudal era. Roman social organization and Roman law are seen as the precondition of the contradictions of the Christian religion and of Christian art. Hence the 'romantic' form of art refers to Christian and post-Christian art as such, and not specifically to the late eighteenth century and early nineteenth century Romantic movements. 'Romantic art' stands for art as we know it, art as re-presentation, as relatively autonomous illusion.

The precondition of the romantic form of art is the prosaic order which arose historically when the relation of society to the natural world changed as it did with the rise to domination of the Roman world. Then it was 'all over with the natural side of the spirit'.[62]

> To the Roman world we owe the origin and development of positive law ... the prose of life ... [it] discovered a principle of right which is external, not dependent on disposition and sentiment.[63]

The Roman world was founded on force and continued to rely on force. It was comprised of opposed interests, not unified by free consent. The development of *private* law designed to enforce its political unity 'involved the decay of political life'.[64]

The relation to nature of Roman society was fundamentally different from that of Greek society. In Greek society the household was one's own work and the state was one's own work: custom or law was second nature. Productive activity for the necessities of life and for the political community was a joy. The individuality of the Gods, perfectly at peace in a natural medium, the human body, presented this relation to nature.

The Roman state was based on the conquest of other peoples who always retained their subordinate status. [65] Prior to the introduction of law the state was imposed by force. It was not the people's 'own work', its 'riches [are] not the fruit of industry and honest activity'.[66] It represents divided interests, 'an aristocracy of a rigid order, in a state of opposition to the people'.[67] The relation between patrician and plebian was a form of vassalage: the wealthy patrician offered protection to those poorer than him. The patrician's soil was cultivated by slaves and assigned to clients as tenant cultivators who paid taxes and contributions.[68] These clients were further indebted to the patrician because as free citizens they had to maintain themselves as soldiers.[69]

Political relations were based on the 'dominion' of the patricians, on their superior economic power which depended on the labour of a dependent class. The fruits and means of productive activity were not one's own, but were handed over to the patricians who maintained their clients in debt-bondage.[70] When the law was subsequently developed the *arbitrary* relation between patrician and plebian ceased; it was now *legally* enforceable. The law was developed to codify the rights of private property, the *status quo* of inequality.[71] It was restricted to a specific and narrow aspect of life, the legal 'person' as the bearer of the right to property.

The person was opposed to the thing, *res*, who did not bear such rights, such as women and children and slaves. The distinction between *persona* and *res* is as transparent as the distinction between master and slave. It turns marriage and the family into institutions of private property. But the definition of people as 'persons', the right to law as right to property, means that others who are equally 'persons' are dependent. Their labour is appropriated, and this appropriation cannot be seen. This form of property, of one's *own* (*eigen*), is fundamentally different from Greek *property* (*Eigentum*), where productive act and product are immediately one's own in the necessities of life and in political life.

Private property is not one's own work. It has been appropriated from other *persons*, and this changes the real political status both of the appropriator and of the appropriated. What is one's own becomes particular not the universal interest of all. Subjective disposition is no longer at one with custom, and the will which arises to further and protect these particular interests is isolated, the subjective will. The law is external to this will, based on abstract equality and therefore enforceable against the will, not based on free consent or free dissent. The abstract attribute of 'person' means that other aspects of the life of the individual have to be dominated 'in order to enforce that *abstractum*'.[72] Others cannot be recognized because they are defined as persons, an abstract form of equality and recognition, which makes real inequality invisible. The legal definitions of Roman society *hide* real existence and relations, whereas the legal definitions of Greek society *revealed* real existence.

The development of the particular will and the decay of political life leads to a 'hypertrophy of the inner life'. For the individual has lost his 'own' in work, productive activity and in politics, and becomes increasingly subjective. This subjectivity is a bondage which cannot be seen for the concept of 'person' hides it. The concept of abstract freedom hides the lack of freedom, the imprisonment in inner life of the 'person' who does not work, who is not mediated by the experience of labour, by a relation to the natural world.

Thus a change in relation to nature is in itself a change in the political relation. The first change may be said to *determine* the second in the specific sense that ethical life becomes subjectivity. The separation of *some* members of society from productive activity results in the definition of *all* of its members as separated from productive activity, as 'persons'. Ethical life is determined as the subjective relations of isolated individuals.

This condition of fixed law and a division of labour in which products are consumed without any comprehension of their production or any acquaintance with their producers is 'the prose of life', a prosaic order which is the precondition of the romantic form of art. It is the situation of universal culture where individuals are 'cut adrift from nature'.[73]

> In this situation the long and complicated connection between needs and work, interests and their satisfaction, is completely developed in all its ramifications, and every individual, losing his independence, is tied down in an endless series of dependence on others. His own requirements are either not at all, or only to a very small extent, his own work, and, apart from this, every one of his activities proceeds not in an individual living way but more and more mechanically according to universal norms. Therefore there now enters into the midst of this industrial civilization, with its mutual exploitation and with people elbowing other people aside, the harshest cruelty of poverty on the one hand; on the other hand, if distress is to be removed, this can only happen by the wealth of individuals who are freed from working to satisfy their needs and can now devote themselves to higher interests. In that event, of course, in this superfluity, the constant reflection of endless dependence is removed, and man is all the more withdrawn from all the accidents of business as he is no longer stuck in the sordidness of gain. But for this reason the individual is not at home even in his immediate environment, because it does not appear as his own work. What he surrounds himself with here has not been brought about by himself; it has been taken from the supply of what was already available, produced by others, and indeed in a most mechanical and therefore formed way, and acquired by him only through a long chain of efforts and needs foreign to himself.[74]

A prosaic relation to productive activity is equally a prosaic relation to political activity, just as a poetic relation to productive activity is a poetic relation to political activity, as, for example, in the Heroic Age when 'the independence of the individual [is preserved] unimpaired and this is what gives the whole relationship its poetic form.'[75] A prosaic political relation involves a 'prosaic cleavage' between the individual's own personality and consciousness of laws, principles and maxims for the general weal.[76] Action, the realization of one's ends, depends on innumerable external means which have to be manipulated, and are only accidentally related to the end of the action. Action in these circumstances demands an instrumental relation to others. The 'individual' must

> make himself a means to others . . . and reduce others to more means to satisfy his own interests.[77]

This is the 'prose of the world' as it appears to individuals. It is a world of finitude and mutability, of entanglement in the relative, of the pressure of necessity from which the individual is in no position to withdraw.[78]

The exposition of poetry and prose as literary genres draws on the contrast of social and political cohesion already elaborated as social precondition. Poetry grasps opposites in their living unity, and hence presents the indwelling reason of events which are meaningful.[79] It has an affinity with speculative thinking.[80] In poetry everything is related to the united whole, concretely and freely in an 'organic articulation'. But the individual parts may become independent of the totality, and, to this extent, poetry no longer presents a classic unity, but becomes increasingly romantic.[81]

Prose is a form of abstract reasoning based on a distinction between means and ends.[82] Events are *related* to each other not unified, and hence appear accidental and meaningless. Prose has an affinity with ordinary thinking and with the understanding, *Verstand*.[83] The particular parts have no independence, and are external and finite, unarticulated.

Poetry precedes prose as a social institution, for Greek society is poetic. But a prosaic order is the precondition of the romantic art form, and of the romantic individual art, poetry, as the conditioned. The romantic form of art, 'this final stage of art', arises in a society where the 'concept of freedom' is in inverse relation to the 'living reality of freedom itself'.[84] The medium of sensuous appearance, of *Schein*, is even less adequate for the representation of infinite freedom than religious representation. But to say that sensuous appearance is inherently incapable of presenting the absolute would be, as with religious representation, to make a merely subjective point. Artistic illusion would be simply attributed to the limitations of finite consciousness as such. But finite consciousness is not such a fixed and ultimate point of reference. The determination of a consciousness which understands itself to be finite is itself historically specific and explicable.

It is the Christian religion itself, on the basis of its prosaic precondition, which first opposes the infinite to the finite, and then degrades the finite as a medium adequate to the re-presentation of the infinite. The whole account of the romantic form of art, that is, of art as a social institution of the kind we know, is an account of how this degradation of nature or the finite in work, religion and politics, degrades art itself as the *relation* between meaning and configuration.

The romantic form of art is traced from its initial religious status to its non-religious status, and this transition is internal to its form. The romantic form of art represents initially a subjectivity, Christ, which is not realized in the sensuous world. This divorce between subjectivity and nature changes the meaning of both the subjectivity and its medium, sensuous appearance. Both become increasingly arbitrary and capricious as a religious meaning removed from the world gives rise to an art which confirms that world in the immediacy of its private property relations. The first end of art was the end of art as a politically formative experience. The second end of art is an art which is totally assimilated and utterly depraving politically. The exposition of the romantic form of art in general, art as a relatively autonomous institution which re-presents subjectivity, becomes an exposition of what is understood more narrowly as 'romanticism' in art.

Christian art has the task of representing the reconciliation of the divine with the human. It re-presents the story of Christ's life as an actual happening in history, and the suffering of Christian detachment from the natural world in order to attain reconciliation with it.[85] If this reconciliation, this reunion of infinite and finite, fails to occur, then a new concept of the natural world as a merely finite world cut off from infinity, is, nevertheless, established. Nature in this new sense 'is emptied of the Gods'.[86] Nature is now considered contingent and external, and, correspondingly, spirit, unrepresentable as infinite freedom, appears in its contingent, mundane interests. 'The scope of subjectivity is infinitely extended', but it is the infinity of subjective caprice.[87] This inner subjectivity is intertwined with the contingency of the external world, and this lack of unity 'gives unfettered play to the bold lines of the ugly'.[88] Art is illusion, not because finite consciousness cannot visualize the absolute, but because the relation of society to nature divides consciousness into an abstract opposition between finite and infinite.

Reconciliation between infinite and finite is represented in ways which still presuppose this abstract opposition. These reconciliations are the *topoi* of Christian romantic art. They are displaced reconciliations which still presuppose a subjectivity which is unable to know itself as substance, for example, love and chivalry, which are not ethical virtues.[89]

The *formative* experiences of culture, of forced reconciliation by the domination of the church or the state, correspond to the *depraving* experiences of a form of art which is no longer the determinant of self-consciousness, and which no longer has the vocation to present basic conflict, but is increasingly limited to its medium, to configuration, to the sensuous and finite interests of a prosaic society – as religion eventually is, too.[90]

The Symbolic Form of Art: The Severe Style and the Modern

Art has become 'pleasing'. It persists in the 'pleasing style'. This is the second 'end' of art when the opposition between meaning and con-figuration which is the meaning of art as re-presentation, the romantic form of art, ceases, for it has been settled by the embrace of immediate, untransformed configuration, the *status quo* legitimized.

> In the presentations of romantic art, therefore everything has a place, every sphere of life, all phenomena, the greatest and the least, the supreme and the trivial, the moral, immoral and evil; and, in particular, the more art becomes secular, the more it makes itself at home in the finite things of the world, is satisfied with them, and grants them complete validity, and the artist does well when he portrays them as they are.[91]

Hegel calls this the 'subjective artistic imitation of the existent present'.[92]

The severe, ideal, and pleasing styles are presented both as aesthetic types and as political relations, as aesthetic conditioned and as political precondition. As political precondition the styles do not refer to social organization, but to the relation between the meaning of the form of art and the spectator, the relation between configuration and the possibility of the spectator having a politically formative or deforma-tive experience which the style in question presupposes. This is why I called Hegel's political writings 'politics in the severe style'.

The 'severe' style 'grants domination to the topic alone', to meaning, and is not concerned with its mode of reception: 'nothing at all is granted to the spectator.'[93]

This severe style is that higher abstraction of beauty which clings to what is important and expresses and presents it in its chief outlines, but still despises grace and charm, grants domination to the topic itself, and above all does not devote much industry and elaboration to accessories. Thus the severe style still limits itself to what is present and available. In other words, while on the one hand, in *content* it rests, in respect of ideas and presentation on the given, for example, on the present sacrosanct religious tradition, on the other hand, for the external *form* it allows complete liberty to the topic and not to its own invention.[94]

The 'ideal' style exists between this 'purely substantial presentation of the topic and the complete emergence of what pleases . . .

This is a liveliness of all points, forms, turns of phrase, movements, limbs; in it there is nothing meaningless or inexpressive; everything is active and effective, and it displays the stir and beating pulse of the free life itself, from whatever side the work of art is considered – a liveliness which essentially presents, however, only a whole, and is only an expression of *one* thing, of one individuality and one action.[95]

This style has a grace: 'Grace is an appeal to the listener or spectator which the severe style despises.'[96] Grace does not imply an eagerness to please, but is a perfect harmony between the substantial topic and the experience of the spectator. The configuration or external form does not become an experience in itself:

. . . it does not let us see any private reflection, any aim or intention; on the contrary, in every expression, every turn of phrase, it hints only at the Idea . . . of the whole.[97]

This style is the only 'complete exposition' of the topic, for the configuration is 'wholly determinate, distinct, living and actual'. The spectator participates fully in this concrete life which he has 'completely before him'.[98] The spectator becomes a witness.

The 'pleasing' or 'agreeable' style refers to a form of art where 'pleasing, an effect produced from without, is declared as an aim and becomes a concern on its own account'.[99] This style aims to produce its effects by concentration on configuration *per se*. This is the 'dominant tendency of turning to the public'.[100] Instead of making the spectator aware of the topic (meaning) it draws attention to the contingent characteristics of the artist.

> In this way the public becomes entirely free from the essential content of the topic and is brought by the work only into conversation with the artist . . .[101]

Romantic art in the modern period has become pleasing. The topic of Christian art was subjectivity and inwardness which cancelled the finite and appeared as the fanaticism of martyrdom, repentence and conversion. This topic resulted in displaced reconciliations with the finite which were based on subjective interest and were fundamentally anti-ethical. In both Christian and modern art the finite itself, unreconciled and unreconcilable, becomes increasingly dominant as a mass of contingent, external detail, the representation of which becomes an end-in-itself. Subjectivity also becomes contingent and capricious because it is cut off from any substantial purpose or aim. It is no longer the inwardness which cancels finitude, but the inwardness which is at one with finitude, and which can be represented because it has become as contingent, capricious and external as finitude itself. Subjectivity is no longer beyond the world, it is sheerly present. Its characteristics are idiosyncrasies. Character is 'personal', and personality not substantial interest is the centre of interest.

The contingent subjectivity of the romantic form of art is not substantial, but it is a determination of substance. Subjectivity is what substance has become and it exists in relation to the substance which is denied.[102] In the early and feudal period of Christian art the meaning of the rejection of the substantial was perverted in the context of its real relation to the substantial:

> Piety thus turns into inhumanity and barbaric cruelty and the same inhumanity which leads to the outbreaks of every selfishness and passion of which men are capable, turns round again into the eternal deep emotion and penitence of spirit which was properly the thing at issue.[103]

In the modern period the contingency of finitude (feudal law) has turned into the prosaic organization of life (formal, bourgeois law).

Subjectivity rejects the finite in this 'substantial order and the prose of actuality',[104] the modern legal state based on private property relations. Art asserts 'the infinite rights of the heart' against this world. It re-presents individuals with purely subjective aims, modern knights of love, a new serious chivalry which rejects family, civil society, law, and and state. This art reproduces the society rejected, the 'subjectivity' of individuals excluded by a legal state who are ultimately corrected by the law of a prosaic world.[105]

Art no longer re-presents the deep cleavage between meaning and configuration, but a reconciliation of a prosaic kind which reasserts the means-ends rationality of a depraving political order.

> In most of these things there is no state of affairs, no situation, no conflict which would make the action necessary. The heart just wants out and looks out for adventures deliberately.[106]

Thus the opposition intrinsic to art as re-presentation, the romantic form of art, becomes exclusive embrace of the world.

> Now romantic art was from the beginning the deeper disunion of the inwardness which was finding its satisfaction in itself and which, since objectivity does not completely correspond with the spirit's inward being, remained broken or indifferent to the objective world. In the course of romantic art this opposition developed up to the point at which we had to arrive at an exclusive interest, either in contingent externality or in equally contingent subjec-tivity.[107]

Another indicator of this decay of art's vocation is the rise of 'Romantic irony' in the last decade of the eighteenth century as a theory of art and as works of art. Hegel attributes this especially to the writings of Friedrich Schlegel.[108] He expounds 'Romantic irony' as akin to Fichte's abstract ego,[109] which values only its own products and acknowledges nothing outside of them, and hence may create and destroy as it wishes. Art is understood as the sheer outpouring of this empty ego, as the virtuosity of an artistic life.[110] This life is totally irresponsible to others, and takes an ironical attitude towards those who do not realize their power as infinite ego but rest content with the prosaic world. This solipsistic vanity is the correlate of Fichte's yearn-ing for God. Its infinite freedom is illusory for it cannot act in the world and remains locked up in a '*morbid* beautiful soul'.[111] In so far as irony produces works of art it concentrates exclusively on the personal, displaying

> only the principle of absolute subjectivity, by showing forth what has worth and dignity for mankind as null in its self-destruction.[112]

Hegel does an injustice to the case for 'Romantic irony' and to the question of the possibility of an artistic challenge to prevalent artistic illusion.

The 'symbolic' form of art is presented in the *Aesthetics* as historically prior to the Greek ideal, as characteristic of Oriental and Judaic socie-ties. It is a form of art in a society which has no subjectivity and no re-presentation but where meaning and configuration are not united. The symbolic form of art arises in a society where nature, the sensuous as such, is regarded as divine.[113] Nature is revered as a power. It is both nature as such, sensuousness, and a power, something on which the individual is dependent, a higher power than himself and hence divine. Nature thus acquires a certain universality, but 'The absolute is natural phenomena.'[114] In his existence man 'divines the absolute', but makes it perceptible to himself in the form of natural objects.[115] In these societies there is no concept of freedom, or, only one is free.

The result is a form of art where meaning (the absolute) and con-figuration (nature) are not unified. Since the idea of the absolute, of universal interest, is unformed, the natural object can only signify it, or refer to it, in an abstract and incomplete way. The symbolic form of art does not *present* the absolute nor *re-present* it, but *refers* to it abstractly and indeterminately.[116] Symbols are thus always ambiguous.[117] They imply things other than the meaning for which they furnish the image.[118] For the meaning is not fully distinct from nature and there-fore cannot be fully captured by it. Symbolic art exists in a number of different forms. 'Unconscious' symbolism is linked to specific religions, while 'conscious' symbolism means general, comparative literary genres, such as allegory or didactiasm.[119]

The exposition of the symbolic form of art can be read as a statement for a new severe style, for an attempt to make art politically formative again in a society *with representation*, in which art has become completely assimilated as pleasing style. The forms listed by Hegel as comparative, conscious symbolism, such as fable, parable, riddle, allegory and didacticism, and defined as art in which the separation and juxtaposition of meaning and its concrete configuration is *expressly emphasized* in the work of art itself in a greater or less degree[120]

are the forms advocated and used by the early Romantics, such as Friedrich Schlegel, in their attempt to make art formative again. The notion of poetry as the 'universal art' was the central notion of Schlegel's attempt to develop a progressive philosophy of art, and Hegel took the phrase from the writings of the early Romantics.[121]

The case for irony as a severe style is that it is not possible to return to the classical ideal, to harmony between meaning and configuration, in a society with a long history of subjectivity and re-presentation. But it might be possible to make substance, the topic, come back into view again if the assimilation of configuration to prosaic meaning, the pseudo-integrity of pleasing art, could be broken by the use of a form of art which rests on a divorce, 'an intended severance', between meaning and configuration.[122] This severance is not romantic and not pleasing, but severe. It emphasizes that nature (prevalent configuration) does not coincide with the absolute and that the prevalent idea of the absolute is itself deficient, that '. . . what is taken as content is no longer the absolute itself but only some determinate and restricted meaning.'[123]

This 'symbolic' form of art provides the case for 'romantic irony'. It is 'romantic' because it acknowledges the history of art as re-presentation and the subsequent pseudo-integrity of meaning and configuration. It is 'ironic' because its aims are substantial not subjective. It seeks to draw attention to substance by playing with the conventions of representation in order to undermine them, to reveal the real divorce between meaning and configuration. The result is a form of art which is not pleasing, nor ideal, but which is severe in the attempt to rebel against dominant assimilation. The is the kind of argument which was taken up again in the twentieth century debates over expressionism and post-expressionism. Thomas Mann, for example, called his use of irony 'the severe style'.[124]

The end of art means *telos*, its goal as politically formative experience, and *finis*, the cessation of art as the contradiction between meaning and configuration. As with the end of religion, it does not mean the end of illusion and representation as such, although they may only continue in forms which grant 'complete validity' to the *status quo*.[125] Hegel does not ask and does not consider how art might become politically formative experience again. Religion is a more dominant determinant of ordinary consciousness than art. Subjective disposition could therefore be reformed, that is, could be politically formative again, by the speculative completion of religion not of art. Art, for Hegel, has no political future. The political future is sought in the combination of reformation and revolution.

5

Work and Representation

> But substance is itself essentially negative, partly as the distinction and determination of the content, partly as a simple distinguishing, i.e. a self and knowledge in general.[1]

> For it is only because the concrete divides itself and makes itself non-actual that it is self-moving. The activity of dividing is the power and work of the understanding (*Verstand*) . . . the tremendous power of the negative; it is the energy of thought, of pure ego . . .[2]

Can these passages from the Preface to the *Phenomenology* be read as speculative propositions? Are they not as abstract in form as the axioms with which Fichte begins his *Wissenschaftslehre*, and as abstract in content in stating a split between subject and substance which may be healed either by fiat, by domination of one by the other, or by 'self-reflection', by a mere change in the standpoint of consciousness which will acknowledge the non-ego as alienated ego, its own creation?

> Now although this negative appears at first as a disparity between the 'Ego' and its object, it is just as much the disparity of substance with itself. What seems to occur outside of it, an activity directed against it, is its own doing and substance shows itself to be essentially subject.[3]

Do these passages not pre-judge a result, and offer it as a 'minted coin which is given ready-made and can be simply pocketed'?[4] Do they not remain external to their object, caught in the illusion of the subjective standpoint? How, in general, can the inconsistency be avoided of stating abstractly and schematically that the truth is not abstract? How can there be a methodological statement that there can be no method? How, in particular, can the subject be said to be substance, and substance be said to be subject, without subordinating one to the other, and thereby affirming their separation, or without a self-reflection which turns their original separation or alienation into a subjective illusion, a mere fact of consciousness?

It is not surprising that the *Phenomenology* has so frequently been misread in Fichtean terms according to which the 'experience' of consciousness is either understood as a cancelling or destroying of the non-ego, as a domination which does not see;[5] or as a change in perspective which sees the non-ego as the ego's own alienated externalization, recaptures it by an act of will, and becomes absolute.[6]

The *Phenomenology* does not consist solely of the presentation of the experiences of natural consciousness, but also of the *science* of that experience.[7] It consists both of a presentation of the contradictions of natural consciousness and a doctrine of that consciousness.[8] This is the distinction between what is experienced by consciousness, 'für es', and what is experienced by us, 'für uns'.[9] At the end of the Introduction a new object arises 'for us, behind its [natural consciousness'] back, as it were'.[10] To natural consciousness this knowledge would appear as a 'loss of itself'.[11] A negative experience for natural consciousness is a positive result for us,[12] for natural consciousness has been presented as phenomenal knowledge.[13] Natural consciousness does not *know* itself to be knowledge, but it experiences the contradiction between its definition and its real existence. It thus contains its own criterion of awareness, the precondition of immanent change.[14] But this change is only a change in perspective and results in further contradictions. Natural consciousness changes its definition of itself and of its existence, but this change is itself determined. It does not abolish the determination of consciousness by substance as such, a consciousness which persists as a natural consciousness in *relation* to the substance which determines it.

The *Phenomenology* is not a teleological development towards the reconciliation of all oppositions between consciousness and its objects, to the abolition of 'natural' consciousness as such, but a speculative presentation of the perpetual deformations of natural consciousness. The *Phenomenology* is the education of *our* abstract philosophical consciousness. Our abstract Kantian and Fichtean consciousness and likely misapprehension is dealt with by being itself accounted for. The need for a doctrine, for an introductory abstract statement at the beginning of a phenomenology, is itself justified as one of the determinations of substance. The abstract beginning which would appear to dominate or deny the opposition it presupposes is itself expounded in the series of experiences. In this way an apparent inconsistency is seen to be consistent. The Preface and Introduction are not simply abstract statements denouncing abstract statement. The abstract rejection of abstraction is the only way to induce abstract consciousness to begin to think nonabstractly. This consistency is the Hegelian *system*.

The *Phenomenology* consists of the presentation of the experience of natural consciousness as the education of our abstract, scientific consciousness. Our abstract consciousness *knows* the oppositions which natural consciousness gradually comes to experience. But abstract consciousness only knows those oppositions and their unity in Kantian and Fichtean terms: either as the Kantian circle of the conditions of experience and of the objects of experience, or, as Fichtean intellectual intuition, and these terms still presuppose the opposition. If the *Phenomenology* is successful it will educate philosophical consciousness to *know* these oppositions in a wholly changed way, by making it look on and *see into* (intuit) their formation as the experiences of a natural consciousness.

Hegel distinguishes between ancient times in which natural consciousness was 'properly' 'educated',[15] by distinguishing its universal activity from sensuous existence, and modern times in which 'the individual finds the abstract form already prepared'.[16] Today the universal does not emerge from the concrete, but

> . . . the labour consists not so much of purifying the individual from an immediate sensuous mode and making him into a thought and thinking substance, but more in the opposite in actualizing and inspiring the universal by removing, fixed, determinate thoughts.[17]

But it is far more difficult to bring fixed thoughts into fluidity than sensuous existence. For the ego has to be induced to give up the fixity of its self-positing, not by leaving itself out, but by giving up

> . . . the fixity of the pure concreteness which the ego is in opposition to various content as much as by giving up the fixity of its differentiations which, posited in the element of pure thinking, share the unconditioned state of the ego.[18]

Thus it turns out to be *less* consistent to begin the *Phenomenology* with natural, sensuous consciousness than to begin with an abstract statement of the argument against abstract statement. For modern consciousness is abstract and methodological. Furthermore, the opposition between subject and substance is not affirmed, but the task is to *give up* the fixity of self-positing both of the ego and of its differentiated moments, to give up the idea that determination is merely differentiation, a creation and extension of the ego. But this transformation cannot be achieved abstractly, by the same kind of subjective fiat or decree which constitutes self-positing. This standpoint can only be given up if its determination is recognized.

The Introduction to the *Phenomenology*, like the Introduction to the *Philosophy of Right*, starts with a presentation of the prevalent, abstract, Fichtean ego or will which is itself socially and historically expounded in the course of the main text. The *Phenomenology* is not the experience of consciousness recapturing its alienated existence, but the presentation of the formation of consciousness as a determination of substance and consciousness' misapprehension of that determination. It is the experience not of alienation, but of the inversions of substance into the various forms of misrepresentation. Natural consciousness does not experience itself as generally alienated, except in one specific period. It experiences itself as 'natural', as not alienated, and this 'naturalness' is the misrepresentation of substance and of subject.

Natural consciousness is presented as phenomenal knowledge, as the determination of substance, for our apprehension, because natural consciousness itself does not know of its determination. It does not know that 'being and knowing' are either an antithesis or a harmony,[19] and *we* do not know how our knowledge of the antithesis and our resolution of it in the Kantian and Fichtean forms which perpetuate it, are also determinations of substance.[20]

The *Phenomenology* does not exhort consciousness to enlighten itself, to travel the path of doubting anything given on authority, and only to trust what it can prove itself. There is no difference in principle between trusting to external authority and establishing one's own authority in this way. The latter is merely the vainer conceit, for it amounts to a superficial, momentary scepticism which re-establishes everything as it was before and merely deludes itself that it has changed the court of appeal.[21]

We have to follow not the path of self-enlightening doubt (*Zweifel*), but the path of despair (*Verzweiflung*).[22] This does not demand that established truths should be suspended until they have been tried and tested. It is the conscious insight into the untruth of phenomenal knowledge for which the supreme reality is what is in truth only the unrealized concept.[23]

This 'self-perficient', self-completing scepticism (*sich vollbringende Skeptizismus*)[24] knows that merely to subject 'so-called natural representations' to doubt is still to presuppose that those representations are natural, but this is precisely what should be doubted.[25] It is not a matter of re-establishing the validity of those representations on one's own conviction, but of a despair which questions representation as such, and which seeks 'conscious insight into the untruth of phenomenal knowledge', into the 'so-called' naturalness of the representation. Re-presentation which appears as knowledge, as truth, cannot be true, but must, by definition, be misrepresentation. It must be 'in truth' the 'unrealized concept', for re-presentation is the concept which is not united with intuition and is hence 'unrealized', a mere concept. This path is self-perficient, self-completing, because it is more radical than mere doubt, and because it presents the 'complete' forms of 'untrue consciousness in its untruth'.[26]

This 'untrue consciousness' contains the criterion of its untruth in itself.[27] Consciousness makes a distinction between that which is true or 'in-itself' and that which is dependent on us or 'for another'. Truth is thus defined as in-itself, as outside any relation to consciousness by consciousness and is hence also for consciousness. When consciousness proceeds to examine the relation of concept to object the 'in-itself' may be taken as the concept and the 'for another' as the object, or what is 'in-itself' may be taken as the object and the 'for us' or knowledge as the concept, but in either case both poles of the comparison occur within consciousness.[28]

Consciousness is always this opposition between itself and its object, for to know an object means that it is both 'in-itself' and 'for us'. This opposition falls within consciousness, because what is considered in-itself is always, whether as the knowledge or as the being of the object, *for* consciousness. Thus when a discrepancy arises between consciousness and its object, the in-itself is now seen as only in-itself *for* consciousness, and consciousness turns to a new in-itself. We, however, know that what was preciously considered in-itself is now defined by consciousness as for it, and that the 'new' object has been defined in opposition to the old one which is now re-cognized by consciousness to be in relation to it. But we re-cognize the relation of the new object to the old one, and hence re-cognize that the new object is equally in relation to consciousness and not outside it as a new 'in-itself'.[29]

This insight into the dependence of the first object *qua* in-itself is our experience of it. This experience is a 'reversal' of consciousness; it is our 'addition', because *we* can see the *necessary* connection between the first and second object, but consciousness itself does not see the connection between the two.[30]

This introductory statement of the distinction between 'in-itself' and 'for itself' is very abstract. It is a general statement of the experiences to be observed, stated in terms which are directed to Kantian and Fichtean self-consciousness which knows that there is an opposition between consciousness and its objects and that the opposition is created by consciousness. The statement is designed to show our Kantian and Fichtean self-consciousness that the path of despair is not negative, because while natural consciousness may not grasp the necessary connection between its first and subsequent objects, we can grasp it, and hence the experience is formative for us. We will gradually see that the experience of natural consciousness is ours too. We think in the same oppositions and although we *know* the oppositions, there is also a sense in which abstract consciousness does not know, and has not experienced, the oppositions which are so 'well-known'.[31] This experience can only be achieved if abstract consciousness follows a natural consciousness which it does not know as itself. In this way abstract consciousness, the dominance of the concept, may come to *see into* (intuit) *the necessity* of the connection between the successive forms of consciousness, between the first and second objects, and thus may ultimately see itself in its creation of abstract oppositions between consciousness or knowledge and its objects.

The Causality of Fate

The 'necessity' of the sequence of the forms of consciousness is not a chronological or historical necessity, an iron law of history. The structure of the *Phenomenology* both displays and defies a chronological reading. The experience of consciousness is repeated as individual experience, as moral experience and as religious experience. If read chronologically this experience culminates in the moment of philosophy which is to re-unite the modern, abstract culture of *Verstand*, and such a philosophy, arising out of the ruins of modern ethical life, would be as abstract and negatively absolute as Kantian and Fichtean 'freedom'.

The necessity of the experience of consciousness is not historical necessity. It is the necessity of the law of ethical life, or 'the causality of fate' as it is called in 'The Spirit of Christianity and its Fate'.[33] In this text, written 1798–9, the idea of the 'causality of fate' is used in *two senses* which correspond to what is meant by the necessity of the sequence of forms of consciousness and the way we can experience that necessity in the *Phenomenology*.

'Fate' does not mean what we usually understand by it, 'blind fate', belief in irrational and uncontrollable ruling forces. It does not mean 'necessity, fate and the like',

> just that about which we cannot say *what* it does, what its specific laws and positive content are, because it is the absolute, pure concept intuited as *being*, a simple and empty, irresistible and imperturbable relation whose work is the nothingness of individuality.[34]

This concept of fate is that of 'abstract necessity' which has 'the character of the merely negative, uncomprehended power of universality on which individuality is smashed to pieces'.[35]

'Fate' as the necessity of fate refers, on the contrary, to rationality and law. The first sense of 'causality of fate' is not *blind* fate but fate *seen* as the rationality of the whole society. The second sense of 'causality of fate' is fate in the sense of destiny, of what happened to that first visible rationality, its determination as subjective consciousness which can no longer see the law of its determination, the rationality of the whole, because the whole has been *determined* or become a concept which denies its concrete existence.

The first fate is experienced as a hostile power which asserts itself against an individual as punishment when a law has been transgressed. This is not a matter of a deed trespassing against a universal, formal law, but

> It is the deed itself which has created a law whose domination now comes on the scene.[36]

This 'law' is the re-unification of the injured life with the trespasser's life. The trespasser knows that he has armed the hostile power himself, that life has been turned into an enemy by himself.[37] This law is only 'lack of life', the defective whole 'appearing as a power', and the trespasser recognizes the deficiency 'as a part of himself, as what was to have been in him and is not'.[38] This is the causality of fate in a society in which the universal interest, ethical life, is recognized as the life of the individual, even in moments of conflict. The individual recognizes the whole in his suffering, in his separation from it. Suffering is not inflicted by an alien might, but is a longing for what has been lost – the harmony of the whole.

The second fate arises when the law precedes the deed. Then the punishment is not recognized as life, as the ethical whole, but is set absolutely against the individual who withdraws into the void, lifting himself 'above fate entirely'.[39] This is to flee from life and its law, to make life the enemy. This response is also a causality of fate, for fate as a formal law has determined a response which denies what has been lost and does not seek to be reconciled with it.

In 'The Spirit of Christianity and its Fate', the first fate is presented as the ideal of Christian love and the second fate as what happened to (i.e. the destiny or determination of) Christian teaching when this ideal of love does not constitute the ethical relation but can only survive by denying ethical life:

> Their love was to remain love and not become life.[40]

As a result

> The fate of Jesus and his following . . . remains a loss of freedom, a restriction of life, passivity under the domination of an alien might which was despised . . .[41]

This fate is separation 'from the world'.[42] It leads to the development of a corrupt consciousness, for Jesus set his fate against a corrupt world and

> the inevitable result was to give a consciousness of corruption both to this corruption itself, and to the spirit still relatively free from it, and then to set this corruption's face at variance with itself.[43]

Jesus foresaw the full horror of this fate, that it meant destruction not reconciliation:

> I came not to bring peace on earth, but a sword: I came to set the son against his father, the daughter against her mother, the bride against her husband's kin.[44]

This fate means both the life denied as corrupt, which consequently corrupted the love set against it, and the history of the community of love which was to misrepresent itself as ideal love although corrupted by its separation from life. This is to be caught in the 'toils of fate',[45] for the community believes that it has escaped fate altogether.

> Its fate however was centred in the fact that the love which shunned all ties was extended over a group; and this fate was all the more developed the more the group expanded, and, owing to this expansion, continually coincided more and more with the world's fate both by unconsciously adopting many of that fate's aspects and also by continually becoming sullied itself in the course of its struggle against that fate.[46]

This fate means, first, destiny, what happened historically to fate as ethical life; secondly, determination, how the first fate, ethical life, changed into the second fate which denied life and hence changed itself as life; thirdly, representation, how the denied concrete existence is misrepresented as ideal, non-worldly love.

The first causality or necessity of fate is the law or necessity which is freedom, the second causality or necessity of fate is the necessity or law which is opposed to freedom.

In the introductory paragraphs of Part B, Chapter Five of the *Phenomenology*, which is entitled 'The Actualization of rational self-consciousness through its own activity', the idea of ethical life is presented as a substantially free and happy nation[47] in which

> The *labour* of the individual for his own needs is just as much a satisfaction of the needs of others as of his own, and the satisfaction of his own needs he obtains only through the labour of others. As the individual in his *individual* work already *unconsciously* performs a *universal* work, so again he also performs the universal work as his conscious object, the whole becomes, as *a* whole, his own work, for which he sacrifices himself and precisely in so doing receives back from it his own self.[48]

This is the first causality of fate. The ethical whole is seen as the foundation, the cause of the individual both in his activity (work) and in his suffering (crime).

However, this happy state is only known as such by us.[49] To achieve it in a way which is known it must be 'lost' as this immediacy, or, 'for both may equally well be said,'[50] it may be 'not yet attained'.[51] The latter expression is the causality of fate in the second sense. It refers to the determination of substance as subject in a way which does not correspond to that substance or existence, which is not yet 'this happy state'. By saying that such a state is both 'lost' and 'not yet attained', *self*-consciousness can be seen both as the result of the loss of that state *and* as the possibility of re-attaining it. Consciousness is now self-consciousness: it does not receive itself back from the whole but only part of itself.

The necessity of the sequence of shapes of consciousness means that substance is the cause of self-consciousness, and that we may *see* the cause of consciousness, the misrepresentations of substance, the untrue forms of consciousness.

Phenomenological necessity means that we can see what consciousness considers 'in-itself', whether the ideal of love, or a characterless God or an abstract principle of political unity, as not 'in-itself', but as 'for it', defined by consciousness *as* 'in-itself'. We can see that this illusion resulted from the *loss* of what was truly 'in-itself' and which became 'for it', solely within consciousness and no longer concrete life itself. The 'for it' is the misrepresentation of an 'in-itself' which cannot appear within self-consciousness because *self*-consciousness can only posit itself and its own determinations.

Thus the reason why ethical life or the whole cannot be stated or pre-judged is the same as the reason why what is 'in-itself' cannot appear within self-consciousness. To state the absolute or define what is 'in-itself' makes it fall within consciousness, makes it 'for us' and not 'in-itself'. What is wrong with the abstract statements in the passages which introduce this chapter is that they make substance, the 'in-itself', for us. All that can be said is that the absolute or substance is 'lost' or 'not yet attained'. This trope is an acknowledgement not a statement that the absolute is present but not pre-judged.

Only in a society where self-consciousness is absolute, where pure and empirical consciousness coincide or where necessity is freedom, will there be an 'in-itself' which is not merely 'for it'. It is the attempt to avoid relapsing into a philosophy of consciousness which determines the allusion to ethical life as equally 'lost' and 'not yet attained'. At the same time abstract philosophical consciousness is addressed by presenting the misrepresented whole in terms of that consciousness' own abstract oppositions between what is 'in-itself' and what is 'for it'.

If the phenomenological experience is successful, then we will see that our abstract culture of *Verstand* is also necessary, a determination of substance, a causality of fate. We will see that the law of our determination can be comprehended and that the determination is the product of a law which is outside the oppositions of our self-consciousness.

The *Phenomenology* is not the revocation of alienated externalization, nor a teleology of reconciliation, nor a dominating absolute knowledge. The *Phenomenology* is not a success, it is a gamble. For the perpetual occurrence of inversion and misrepresentation can only be undermined, or 'brought into fluidity',[52] by *allusion* to the law of their determination, to the causality of fate.

The Grave of Life

The 'lost' substance reappears in the forms of misrepresentation, in the forms of consciousness which misapprehends its relation to that substance. The *Phenomenology* does not trace the misrepresentation of substance, for that is the task of the philosophy of art and the philosophy of religion, but the misapprehension of the relation. Thus the *Phenomenology* is the book of *Verstand*, because natural consciousness in its relations is presented separately from divine history, from the exposition of experience from the standpoint of the whole.[54]

The structure of the *Phenomenology* corresponds to the structure of *The System of Ethical Life*. First, absolute ethical life is presented 'according to its relation', as individual experience (Chapter IV). Secondly, absolute ethical life is presented as 'relative ethical life', which is called 'The negative or freedom or crime' in *The System of Ethical Life*. It is the potency or stage at which individuals recognize each other as constraints, or as means to their particular ends (Chapter V). Finally, absolute ethical life is presented from the prevalent standpoint of the whole in its ethical, cultural and moral forms (Chapter VI).

In the *System of Ethical Life* these potencies pertain to experience within bourgeois, formal, private property law. Central to the *Phenomenology* is the experience of a consciousness whose precondition is formal property law, but whose fate is existence in a lawless order: feudalism.

Absolute ethical life of the feudal order is first presented 'according to its relation' as the 'unhappy consciousness'. This consciousness results from the 'loss of substance',[55] and is characteristic of the pre- and post-Christian as well as of the Christian epochs. It is a dualistic consciousness for which God is dead. This death of the God may refer to the death of the Greek Gods, or to the characterless and hence unknowable modern God, or to a God who is imagined (represented) and imaginable (representable), but who dwells beyond concrete existence and is therefore absent.

When God is represented as Christ, the representation makes God present and immediate and thus mediates him. But what is represented is an image or narrative, a content which is separate from the consciousness which experiences it.[56] This consciousness is unhappy in this separation but it does not recognize its own activity in it.

The modern consciousness which no longer re-presents the absolute, but knows itself as what was represented, knows the other as its own determination, is also unhappy.[57] This self-certain consciousness no longer represents an alien God to itself and has therefore achieved 'infinite power'. But

> This hard saying that God is dead is the expression of innermost simple self-knowledge, the return of consciousness into the depths of the night in which ego = ego, a night which no longer distinguishes or knows anything outside of it. This feeling is, in fact, the loss of substance and of its appearance over against consciousness; but it is at the same time the pure *subjectivity* of substance, or the pure certainty of itself which it lacked when it was object, or the immediate or pure essence.[58]

The Kantian or Fichtean subjectivity which has lost the Christian God even as an opposition to its own subjectivity is as unhappy as the consciousness which was first receptive to the news of the Christian God, but did not know its relation to that news.

The unhappy consciousness arose out of the experience of the death of the Greek Gods. This death does not have the significance of the death of Christ, of a particular individual become universal, nor does it have the significance of the death of Christianity, of the end of religious representation. It means the death of life as divine and gives rise to the denial of existence and of transformative activity and hence of actuality.[59] Life is experienced as the grave.

This experience is prepared by the Roman philosophies of stoicism and scepticism. Stoicism did not reject the world of transformative activity, of productive relations. It neutralized them by disdaining them as riches or as poverty.

> As lord, it does not have its truth in the bondsman, nor as bondsman is its truth in the lord's will and in his service; on the contrary, whether on the throne or in chairs, in the utter dependence of its individual existence, its aim is to be free, and to maintain that lifeless indifference which steadfastly withdraws from the bustle of existence, alike from being active as passive, into the simple essentiality of thought.[60]

This 'freedom' is a universal bondage which treats all social relations indifferently.

Scepticism is more active. It does not remain in the world and disdain its differences, but actively rejects it.

> It is clear that just as stoicism corresponds to the *concept* of the *independent* consciousness which appeared as the lord and bondsman relationship, so scepticism corresponds to its *realization* as a negative stance towards otherness, to desire and work.[61]

Scepticism actively rejects activity and is hence contradictory. It both doubts the reality behind representations and trusts representation as such. Similarly it treats itself as universal (the doubter or authority) and as contingent (as another representation to be subject to doubt).[62]

This consciousness becomes unhappy when it recognizes that this contradiction between the universal and contingent exists within itself: 'the *unhappy consciousness* is the consciousness of self as a dual-natured, merely contradictory being.'[63] Unlike scepticism this consciousness *knows* itself to be 'internally contradictory', and 'inwardly disrupted'.[64] This consciousness increases its unhappiness by thinking that it has discovered a fixed point outside itself, something unchangeable. However, it has merely posited part of the contradiction as external, called it the unchangeable and achieved a relation to it. But this is merely to recreate the contradiction in an even more painful way. For the price of the relation to the unchangeable is an 'agonizing over', a rejection of real existence and activity.[65]

This consciousness knows itself to be an individual, an active and transforming being, which stoicism and scepticism denied. But knowing itself as a living individual, it debases itself to the merely changeable and contingent. As an individual it is 'conscious only of its nothing-ness'.[66] Thus it does not relate to the unchangeable as an independent, active individual, but becomes mere feeling, devotion, infinite yearn-ing.[67] This consciousness is thus destined to fail in its desire for the unchangeable, for feeling or yearning can only feel itself, and cannot form its activity or recognize the other as active and actual.

When this consciousness turns to other particular individuals or to the rest of its own life, it can only relate to a sensuous immediacy which is transitory and insignificant because it does not treat itself as significant in its activity. Hence such a consciousness is not actual, not alive:

> Consciousness can only come to the present as the grave of its life.[68]

All the enterprises of this consciousness are doomed to fail. For the significance accorded to the unchangeable debases the transforming and appropriating activities of life.[69] Consciousness does not even experi-ence the happiness of the Fichtean unhappy consciousness which enjoys self-certainty: 'Its inner life really remains a still incomplete self-certainty.'[70] It is, however, the archetype of our Fichtean consciousness, *broken in two* as consciousness and as activity.[71] It acknowledges work and enjoyment as its own activity, as for itself, and separates this from the being which is in-itself.[72] It then proceeds to thank the in-itself, the unchangeable, for its gift of desire, work and enjoyment.[73] Hence it experiences its activity, its actuality, only in the past tense, when it gives thanks. The unhappy consciousness 'merely finds itself desiring and working'.[74] It denies its activity as its own act when it is acting in the present: 'its actual doing thus becomes a doing of nothing, its enjoyment a feeling of its wretchedness.'[75]

Yet, the more these activities are debased, the greater the importance which is in effect granted them as isolated acts.[76] Before thanks are rendered, they are unsanctified. Life is worse than a grave; it is hell, a perpetual agony:

> Consciousness of life, of its existence and activity, is only an agoniz-ing over this existence and activity, for therein it is conscious that its essence is only its opposite, is conscious only of its own nothingness.[77]

This agony must be eternally repeated; for life is transformative activity, not an unchangeable, so that if life is despised and not enjoyed, the result will be perpetual unhappiness. Furthermore, once productive activity has been cut off from significance, it acquires enormous power to pervert that significance. Productive activity and natural functions become loathsome and the unhappiness, the self-hatred, is self-sustaining.

A further result of this self-hatred in an unhappy consciousness which does not know what it is doing, is its susceptibility to the authority of a mediator who takes over the rôle of castigator. In this way the individual is deprived even more of the fruits of his labour. His property and his will are surrendered to the feudal Church.[78]

Fichte's *Vocation of Man* is a highly self-conscious version of this unhappiness, of the denial of life, of life as the grave. We, Fichteans, recognize this yearning and self-hating unhappiness, although it is not us, not self-certain. This consciousness is unhappy because it does not know itself, and we are still unhappy in spite of 'knowing' ourselves, because we have become our own castigators.

The birth of unhappy consciousness is not expounded as divine history, as the ideal of Christian freedom, but 'according to its relation', as experienced by the individual. The precondition of the unhappy consciousness is the relative ethical life of Roman property law, which is only discussed briefly in the *Phenomenology*. This precondition changes into feudal property relations and feudal law. The consequent re-formation of consciousness is experienced as the relative ethical life of particular feudal relations (Chapter V B), and as the absolute ethical life of universal feudal life (Chapter VI B 1 a).

The Barbarism of Pure Culture

Unhappy consciousness, the archetype of dualistic consciousness, is originally the determination of a substance which is prosaically ordered by Roman private property law. Unhappy consciousness disowns its desire and productive activity. It subordinates itself and others in an opaque bondage by divorcing real existence from the definition of legal persons and retreating to the solitariness of inwardness and the search for an absent God.

This form of consciousness which denies concrete life, this form of misrepresentation of real existence, changes when the law and property relations which determine it change. Between Roman and modern formal property law there was a different form of private property and law: feudalism. Feudal relations display no mutual consensus and custom as in Greece, no abstract, universal law as in Rome. Feudal relations are, by comparison, lawless. The right to possession and the right to appropriate the labour of others is based on force. Ethical life is fragmented, arbitrary and violent.

Determined by this precondition consciousness misrepresents its existence in a different form. It denies the whole scope of its activity not just a part of it, because that activity occurs in the realm of arbitrary and violent social relations. Consciousness attempts to impose its denial of a disorganized social order on that order. The result of this attempt cannot be the successful suppression of everything outside a formal, acknowledged law. The intention to suppress the whole order and to reorganize it on principles which consciousness brings in from outside cannot succeed, and is perverted in its real effects. Consciousness' intention to reform the social order becomes a re-forming of itself. The predominance of specific social relations changes the meaning of the re-forming intent, changes it into a reinforcement of that order in all its lawlessness and barbarism.

The result is a 'false' reconciliation or harmony of subject and substance, of self-consciousness and ethical life. Substance is determined as a misrepresenting subject which imposes itself on that substance in its misrepresentation. This is a 'false' reconciliation, or 'inversion' or 'pure culture'. It is an experience of the unity of consciousness and the world, but of a misrepresenting consciousness and a lawless world. Thus the unity is utterly false or 'pure'.[79]

Dualistic consciousness was originally determined by a universal, formal law. The dualism is recreated when consciousness is determined by a lawless order. But the lawless order gives consciousness the vocation (Bestimmung – determination) to re-form its lawless precondition. In carrying out this vocation, consciousness is itself re-formed by that precondition, and this re-formation is its culture. This new form of consciousness which denies the whole order not just part of it, and is perpetually re-formed or inverted, is called 'alienated spirit'. Thus the idea that Hegel equated 'alienation' with 'externalization' in general is fundamentally mistaken. 'Alienated spirit' is a specific determination of spirit which does not characterize the modern period.

The exposition of a social order based on private possession, but without universal property law, in the lectures on The Philosophy of History is the precondition of the experiences of the re-forming and re-formed consciousness of culture in the Phenomenology.

The dissolution of the Roman empire and of Roman private property and law is accompanied by the development of the Christian Church as a cosmopolitan possessor of property and as the authority which, under the guise of mediator, reinforces the lack of freedom. Property passed into the hands of the church and the invaders. In both cases the property was held subject only to the law and juridical institutions of each estate.[80]

It was in Western not Eastern Europe that the Church found itself amidst uncultured tribes, a people with no universal law, and it was here that the re-forming vocation of the Church developed. In the East Christianity found itself in the midst of an independent civilization with universal law and guaranteed property forms and hence did not develop a re-forming intent.[81]

As a property holding and legal institution the Church did not coincide with any nation or people in the West. After the dissolution of the Roman Empire it became increasingly cosmopolitan. Thus it could re-present the absolute as distinct from any specific ethical life and re-present the realization of the absolute as its own specific vocation.

However, the concrete existence of the Church was determined by the new form of social and political organization. This organization consisted of particular privileges and rights which were not encoded in abstract, universal law but were based on the 'laws' of isolated estates, religious and secular.[82] The property of the Church and its spiritual and legal power depended on this politically decentred base. The Church condoned the lawlessness of the feudal order, for the power of each estate or court to establish its own law was the precondition of the Church's own law.

The lack of any national definition of ethical life lent support to the abstract universality of Christian freedom, to a concept of the freedom of all which cannot be realized in any particular nation or *polis*, and therefore can exist alongside real lack of freedom. The real bondage of the feudal system is even less visible than the bondage hidden by the definition of people as legal persons. The relation of vassal to vassal is based on the purely subjective relationship of one individual to another. There is no law to guarantee this relationship, no Greek consensus and no Roman legality. The state is a 'patchwork' of private interest.[83]

Ostensibly the lack of universal law meant that individuals were isolated and defenceless and thus sought the 'protection' of others who were more powerful. However, the relation between vassals was not one of protection, but of appropriation, because the conditions of protection were arbitrarily defined and 'tried' in the courts of the protector.

The feudal system was thus 'a condition of universal dependence'. The state and law become a matter of 'private possession and personal sovereignty'.[84] Fiefs were not 'conferred' on vassals. The weaker were expropriated by the stronger and then received their possessions back encumbered with feudal obligations.[85]

> Instead of freemen, they became vassals – feudal dependents . . . *Feudum* is connected with *fides*; the fidelity implied in this case is a bond established on unjust principles . . . for the fidelity of vassals is not an obligation to the commonwealth, but a private one – *ipso facto* therefore subject to the sway of chance, caprice and violence.[86]

The Church promoted the general reaction against this lawlessness which took the form of the turn to a religion which refuses to sanctify the real world. All the secular evils are thereby recreated within the Church. The servile dependencies of feudal relations are reinforced by a religion which also rejects the idea of rational law, of a just ethical life. Thus flight from utter lawlessness resulted in submission to a Church which reproduced secular vassalage in its separation between clergy and laity.

The rejection of rational law and ethical life by the Church was enshrined in the three vows of poverty, chastity and obedience.[87] The vow of poverty meant the denial of work and productive activity. As a result of this vow the Church accrued great riches because people who wished to live in penance bestowed their wealth on it. The vow of chastity demeaned the natural ethical life of the family and gave rise to an obsession with physicality and sexuality divorced from the meaning of natural ethical life. The vow of obedience amounted to the justification of acceptance of blind, external authority. It prevented the realization of the concept of freedom and reinforced the prevailing arbitrary dependencies.

The clergy as owner of property became a secular power with special spiritual dignity to enforce that power.[88] Thus the clergy became implicated in all the arbitrariness of prevalent, personal power relations, such as simony and nepotism. The vow of obedience reinforces, above all, the general lawlessness, the universal injustice:

A condition the very reverse of freedom is intruded into the principle of freedom itself.[89]

By imposing abstract, non-worldly freedom on a lawless society, the concept of freedom itself becomes a positive reinforcement of the prevalent lack of freedom. In its opposition to the prevalent lack of freedom, consciousness is re-formed by that lack of freedom. It represents freedom in a way which cannot in principle be realized. This consciousness is not assimilated to a dominant, universal law, but itself *forms* the prevalent lawlessness. It is re-formed as the dominant principle of political life: anarchy.

> The reaction of the spiritual against the secular life of the time . . . is so constituted that it only subjects to itself that against which it reacts and does not reform it.[90]

As a result,

> Far from abolishing lawless caprice and violence and supplanting them by a virtuous rule of its own, it has even enlisted them in the service of ecclesiastical authority.[91]

The determination of consciousness by lawlessness, not by abstract law, gives rise to the vocation of culture and the result of pure inversion. These cultures, re-formations, become more violent and extreme, for the greater the opposition between reality and consciousness, the greater the violence of their enforced unity.

In the *System of Ethical Life*, 'relative ethical life' was presented as 'the negative or freedom or crime'.[92] In a society with formal property law, individuals recognize each other according to their own particular ends and interests in a way which they experience as 'negative', or 'freedom' or 'crime'. In a society with *no* formal law, feudal society, 'relative ethical life' is also experienced as 'negative', or 'freedom' or 'crime'. In the *Phenomenology*, the experience of the 'negative' is this experience of 'pleasure and necessity'; the experience of freedom is the experience of 'the law of the heart and the frenzy of self-deceit'; and the experience of 'crime' is the opposition between 'virtue' and the vicious 'way of the world'.

In 'relative ethical life' the individual holds itself to be 'qua *being for self*, essential being . . . the *negativity* of the other'.[93]

In its consciousness, therefore, it appears as the positive in contrast to something which certainly *is*, but which has for it the significance of something without intrinsic being. . . . Its primary goal, however, is its immediate, abstract *being-for-self*; or, to see itself as this *particular individual* in another, or seeing another self-consciousness as itself.[94]

In a society with formal property law, individuals experience each other according to their own particular ends which are guaranteed by that law. In a society without formal law, individuals experience each other according to their own particular interests either by completely rejecting the other as an alien law (pleasure *versus* necessity, virtue *versus* the way of the world), or, by attempting to make their own particular interests into the dominant law (the 'law' of the heart). In no case does this 'law' attain any universality, not even formal, abstract universality, but remains either the antagonist or the servant of particular individual interests. As a result the consciousness which opposes or imposes the 'law' is always perverted, always defeated by the particular interests which it combats as an equally particular interest. Instead of making its interests prevail in a corrupt world the interests of that corrupt world prevail, and enlist the particular interests of consciousness, for consciousness and the world share the same particular interests. But consciousness experiences this enlistment as a perversion of its re-forming intent.

The world is experienced as the 'negative' when self-consciousness makes 'pleasure' its particular goal.[95] The other is only recognized as something to be consumed and enjoyed, not as productive activity, nor as universal law, nor as ethical life. Hence the transitoriness of consumption, the contingent and intrinsic impossibility of continually satisfying the desire for pleasure, is experienced as an utterly alien and incomprehensible law or necessity. This necessity or law is experienced as a blind fate, 'irresistible and impeturbable', whose work is the destruction of individuality, for it thwarts its only goal, that of pleasure.[96]

Consciousness experiences its intention or goal to enjoy pleasure as completely perverted. It does not enjoy life, but experiences the denial of its demands to be as dreadful as death, because it has no other aim or goal than the enjoyment which is denied. Consciousness thought it would plunge into life, a life of pleasure, but it has

really only plunged into consciousness of its own lifelessness and has as its lot only empty and alien necessity, a *dead* actuality.[97]

However, consciousness does not understand that by defining actuality as pleasure, as passive enjoyment, it has itself brought about its own necessity, which it considers to be an absolutely inexplicable fate.[98]

Consciousness therefore attempts to assert its own 'freedom' in the face of this alien law. This is not the 'freedom' guaranteed by a formal law, but an attempt to make the particular interest of pleasure into a law in order to combat the uncomprehended and alien law of necessity. This 'freedom' is not based on a formally universal law, but on the 'law' of each individual. It is a 'law of the heart', a law which is granted to all other hearts, and which thus appears to have a certain universality. But this law is not universal in either form or content.[99]

It cannot be universal in form, for if another particular individual realizes the law of *his* heart, then, *ipso facto*, I cannot realize the law of my heart. Even if an individual realizes the law of his heart, the achievement is immediately lost. For once the law is universal or recognized, it is no longer solely the law of his own heart, and may be enforced against the dictates of his heart.[100]

The 'law' of the heart does not in fact establish universal right, but means the assertion of the particular content of each individual's heart. But these particular contents necessarily conflict, and thus individuals find themselves not only combating the alien necessity of the world, but also combating each other as alien necessities. Whereas initially the assertion of the *law* of the heart was undertaken on behalf of all hearts, of humanity, in face of an hostile, uncomprehended world, now heart is ranged against heart. All others as well as the world as such become the antagonist.[101]

Thus this consciousness also experiences the perversion of its goal and intent. It sought 'freedom', the right of the heart, on behalf of humanity, but it finds that humanity has become the enemy. It also fails to understand that it has itself created its enemy as a result of its own definition of actuality and its own definition of the law. It considered the world to be an alien necessity or law against which it had to assert an immediate right of the heart. Instead it should have sought to comprehend that alien law, its history and its formation. It should have sought to recognize and reform it as ethical life. This consciousness remains especially deranged and perverted, raving in self-righteous indignation. But it is a vain conceit which hates all others, because it can only recognize them as equally vain hearts in opposition to both the alien world and to its own heart. It clings to the idea that the unrealized and unrealizable law of its own heart is the only justice, and can see no possibility of justice in the reform of ethical life as a whole.[102]

Ethical life is experienced as the war of all against all, the law of each heart against the law of each vain heart. Consciousness comes to see that the 'law' of its own heart does not further the common interests of individuals, but pits them against each other as particular individuals.[103] Hence it experiences itself as 'criminal' or vicious, and sets out to transform its vice into virtue. Virtue is another attempt to impose a 'law' on those aspects of the individual which are now seen to be lawless. The previous pursuit of pleasure and the law of that pleasure pursued as the freedom of the heart are now seen as intrinsically lawless, as the 'way of the world', and as incapable of founding any universal law.[104] But instead of looking for the law of virtue in ethical life, 'virtue' is defined as the denial of the previous pursuit of pleasure and of the law of the heart. 'Virtue' becomes the denial not the realization of individuality in the social order. Hence it merely creates a new form of particularity opposed to the law or 'way of the world'. The inner sanctum of personality is to be reformed by the stifling of its former desire and pleasure, by further restriction of its activity not by the extension of activity into ethical life.[105]

The law of this virtue is also perverted and does not understand that it has brought this experience of perversion upon itself. 'Virtue' consists in destroying desire and activity which are condemned as 'the way of the world'. But this vocation demands an active opposition to the world, for it cannot remain passive and prevail. But to act is to act in the world on the basis of desire and goals. Hence the very individuality which virtue claims it wants to harness is exercised. In this way nonworldly virtue preserves its enemy – its own desire, pleasure and action, its individuality, in the world, 'the way of the world', when, at the same time, it claims it is sacrificing that individuality.[106]

'Relative ethical life' in a society with no formal, property law consists of the recognition of oneself and others as desire and pleasure, as passive consumers, not as possessors of property, nor as politically active or ethical. This 'relative' ethical life is the correlate of an 'absolute' ethical life where the polity is also misrecognized according to the 'law' of wealth and its consumption, and not according to any universal, productive, active, ethical interest. When absolute ethical life and the individual's relation to it is defined in accordance with the particular interests of wealth and enjoyment and not according to universal law the result is the perversion of consciousness. For in a society with formal property law, that *part* of life not included in the law is suppressed, but in a society with no formal law, where recognition is based on wealth and passivity, the *whole of* life or actuality is both confirmed as wealth, and denied as productive activity or actuality. Under these conditions any ostensibly 'universal' intention in relation to the polity may 'change' into its opposite since its basis in particular interest may be revealed. This particular interest or wealth has not been created by the self-consciousness which enjoys it.[107]

Thus individuals recognize themselves in the state power. They recognize it as the universal which they have not produced themselves, but which they seek to enjoy.[108] As a form of universal recognition the state is recognized as good, but as the appropriation of wealth it is recognized as bad.[109] This equivocation attaches to wealth itself, too, for if it is universally distributed and enjoyed, it is a good, but as the basis of unequal, self-centred and transitory consumption, it is bad.[110] The impossibility of a stable law of recognition when the universality of ethical life depends on particular interests makes the dichotomy between nobility and ignobility unstable. For it is 'noble' to act in the service of the ethical interest, but this nobility is not heroic, not based on the production and creation of that interest. It is equally 'ignoble' because it is dependent on the wealth of the state power and acts in the latter's interest solely to maintain its own distinct material interests.[111]

In a society without formal law the exercise of state power depends on the counsel of 'nobles', not on the execution of the law. But the 'nobles' have conflicting interests in relation to ethical life. They have an interest in promoting the whole only to the extent that it serves their particular interest of maintaining their wealth. 'Counsel' is, by definition, suspicious, and conflicts with the general interest. The ignoble noble behaves as if he is in conformity with the universal interest, but 'actually sets aside and rends in pieces the universal substance'.[112] 'Honour' retains its own dishonourable will.

This general inversion brought about by service to the universal on the basis of particular interest characterizes the relation of vassal to vassal. The relation of monarch to retainer displays the inversion not in the form of insincere counsel but in the form of flattery. The increased dependence of monarch and retainer leaves the retainer only the form of language to pervert, for he has no independent wealth on which to base the nobility or ignobility, the faith or infidelity, of his particular relation to the ostensible universal, the monarch.[113]

This inversion of language itself is 'pure culture'.[114]

The inversions of 'pure culture' culminate in the experiences of the German Reformation and the French Revolution, or '*satisfied* Enlightenment' and '*unsatisfied* Enlightenment', respectively.[115] The Enlightenment in Germany brings about a Reformation without a revolution, while the Enlightenment in France brings about a Revolution, without a Reformation. The abstract spiritualism of the German Enlightenment and the abstract materialism of the French Enlightenment both continue to deny and not to re-form ethical life. They are themselves re-formed by the ethical life which they fail to acknowledge, and recreate and reaffirm the blind faith which they sought to transform. These re-formations are the 'last and grandest' cultures.[116]

The French Revolution occurred among a people which had experienced no Reformation. In France the re-forming of consciousness, the inversions of its intentions by a lawless social order based on the 'law' of wealth, was not terminated by the development of modern, abstract, formal, bourgeois property law. The development of such law potentially opens up the possibility of an acknowledgement and sanctification of at least part of ethical life. But in France the anarchy of the 'law' of wealth and the hypocrisy of its servile and dependent retainers persisted under the absolute monarchy of the eighteenth century. As a result the attempts at reform continued to be inverted and re-formed and not to achieve a Reformation. The opposition of the Enlightenment in France to the power of the monarch and of the Church was an absolute opposition to those lawless institutions. But an absolute opposition to lawless institutions denies the actuality of ethical life and becomes itself equally absolute and abstract as what it opposes: it becomes another form of faith or superstition.

Similarly, the German Reformation did not succeed in reforming ethical life. The German Enlightenment, which receives its supreme statement in the opposition between reason and faith in Kant and Fichte, was determined by the re-development of abstract, formal property law. This effected a change in consciousness. It changed from a complete denial of lawless reality to an acknowledgement of the new formal law and a denial of the residual as illegal. It thus acknowledges part of ethical life and is no longer inverted or re-formed by a reality which it totally denies. Instead it supports the dominant law of that reality and is assimilated to it. Consciousness turns from fighting law-lessness to becoming a law-giver. This consciousness is no longer re-formed or inverted, but has become certain of itself. It has become certain of itself because it has acquired a law again, albeit a formal one. The large void of uncertainty which still remains, the rest of ethical life which is suppressed, is called 'God' or 'Faith' by this enlightened and reformed consciousness.

The Enlightenment takes the guise of abstract materialism in a society with no law, and of abstract idealism in a society with formal law. In both cases Enlightenment turns out to be a new abstract faith, but the consequences of affirming this faith lead to Revolution in France, and to 'morality' in Germany. The materialist Enlightenment starts from im-mediate sensuous, finite reality, abstracts from all its specific character-istics and affirms this 'absolute matter' as the sole reality. The idealist Enlightenment also affirms a characterless Being or Spirit as its abso-lute.[117] Since neither of these concepts of matter and spirit have any differentiations or characteristics there is no way in principle of distin-guishing between them. The French Enlightenment considered that its affirmation of the sole reality of the finite was in opposition to a faith which believed in an unknowable infinite. But the German Enlighten-ment precisely affirmed an unknowable absolute as the precondition of a 'rational faith'.[118] In effect the French affirmation of the finite as such as the ultimate reality also strips it of all characteristics and makes it into a product of pure thinking,

> ... *pure* being, is not something *concretely actual* but a *pure abstrac-tion*.[119]

But to be a product of pure thinking is precisely the criticism which the French Enlightenment makes of pre-Enlightenment faith. The French Enlightenment is thus indistinguishable from the pure thinking of faith in an 'unknown and unknowable' Absolute.[120] As a form of pure think-ing it is indistinguishable from both pre-Enlightenment faith and from the faith whish is justified by the German Enlightenment.

> But there is this difference, the *latter* is *satisfied* Enlightenment, but *faith* is *unsatisfied* Enlightenment.[121]

There is a difference between defining the absolute as characterless nature or material and defining it as characterless God or spirit. For the

Enlightenment which affirms the absolute to be matter arises in opposition to a lawless faith which it has the vocation to destroy. The abstract materialism of this Enlightenment becomes an instrumentalist and violent idealism:

> the thing counts for it [for cultured self-consciousness] as something which *exists on its own account*; it declares sense-certainty to be absolute truth, but this *being-for-self* is itself declared to be a moment that merely vanishes and passes over into its opposite, into a being that is at the disposal of an other.[122]

If reality is defined as material not as ethical, then the idea of revolutionizing it becomes the question of imposing a different form on that material, of altering its use or utility. The idea that reality is merely material is the illusion of a consciousness which misunderstands itself as solely spiritual, and which *acts* as if it considered reality to be solely spiritual too.[123]

The French Revolution was not an attempt to abolish formal private property. It was the act of a consciousness determined by pre-bourgeois, lawless, private property. The revolution was the denial of a lawless feudal order, not the reality of a different property relation. The revolution was the act of a pure consciousness which did not acknowledge any reality outside itself, any ethical life, and was perverted by the lawlessness which it sought to abolish.[124]

A revolution or Reformation could only succeed if it starts from an acknowledgement of ethical life, from a comprehension of the determination of subjectivity by substance as it has been historically formed, from a re-cognition of the differences and unity of ethical relations. Otherwise reform becomes the act of a 'pure' general will which is condemned to reaffirm the lawlessness or the law against which it turns. The formation of revolutionary consciousness resulted from the struggle of faith with pure insight and of Enlightenment with superstition. It developed as a result of a battle between forms of consciousness which have in common their denial of ethical life, their ignorance of what really determines them.

The End of Ethical Life

The transition from the experience of culture to the experience of morality appears to consciousness itself as a release from the destruction which absolute freedom occasioned. Consciousness believed that it had removed the antithesis between the individual and the universal will, that it was absolutely free, but this resulted in the experience of ferocious destruction.[125] This experience of destruction made the real opposition between the individual and the universal will transparent to consciousness.[126] Consciousness now knows that it is separate from reality and therefore no longer destroys that reality. It makes this very knowledge of its separation from the real world into a new form of 'freedom', a freedom which exists in an 'unreal', unconditioned realm.[127]

This form of self-consciousness represents a transition from the 'particular accident of private possession' to the formal law of private property – the 'accident' fixed (*gesetzt*) and guaranteed as law (*Gesetz*).[128]

Consciousness acquires a law which it considers to be unconditioned in opposition to the conditioned law of the real, phenomenal world. It imposes this unconditioned law on itself and hence acquires 'moral' autonomy. This law or freedom is opposed to the law of the phenomenal world, but consciousness is no longer opposed to the whole of lawless reality. It no longer misre-presents that lawless reality as an imagined deity to be re-imposed on that reality (culture), but misunderstands the conditioned law now prevalent, the accident of private possession formalized as property, to be an absolutely unconditioned law of freedom, which is found as an inexplicable fact of reason. This absolute is not an imagined deity in opposition to the world, but the absolute law of the subject in opposition to the law of nature. The deity is no longer imagined but is the characterless guarantor of the law of the subject. This misunderstanding of ethical life *knows itself* to be the source of its law, but does *not know* the law which it wrongly believes to be absolute and unconditioned. This subjectivity is the culture of *Verstand*, of the understanding, of a known, abstract opposition between itself and the world. It understands itself to be a 'moral' subject which applies an unconditioned law to itself.

Moral consciousness does not have the vocation (*Bestimmung*, determination) to enforce the absolute on the world, to culture it. Its vocation is to impose the law on itself, and thereby to strive continually for autonomy in the face of the inescapable threat of heteronomy. However, the legislation of the will which universalizes the will's subjective maxims does not guarantee the unconditioned nature of the legislation. The subjective maxims are topics of the prevalent social reality which cannot be neutralized by the formula of the categorical imperative. The prevalent law of private property is reinforced by an abstract moral law which legislates indiscriminately on the basis of maxims determined by that prevalent law. The basis of the law in subjective maxims is an 'invalid' establishing of the law, and universalizing or 'testing' those maxims is an 'invalid' way of achieving 'immunity' from their specific, conditioned nature.[129]

As 'relative ethical life' and as 'absolute ethical life' this consciousness deceives itself and becomes a deceiving consciousness. Unlike alienated consciousness it does not deny the whole world, but acknowledges part of it, the partial or formal law of private property relations. It thus *looks as if* it recognizes the universal or ethical. But since it is really only acknowledging the world to the extent that it is determined by the formal law of private property relations, it is only really acknowledging its own particular interests. For formal, universal law (*Gesetz*) is the fixing (*gesetzt*) of the particular, but the fixed, legal categories prevent this from being seen. The law is thus deceptive, and consciousness, too, deceives itself and others.

This consciousness does not become inverted in the course of carrying out its vocation to re-form itself, it becomes subverted and subverting. It subverts the meaning of the moral law to which it ostensibly submits because that law is abstract and not absolute as it claims. The law defines *actuality* as an infinite task and thus draws attention away from the real significance of the *acts* of the moral subject. Consciousness becomes deceiving: it con-forms to a moral law which it does not comprehend, and denies the actuality of its con-formity to the real, abstract law.

'Relative ethical life' is experienced when the acknowledgement of the other *looks as if* it is universal, but is determined by the clash of particular interests. In alienated culture there was no formal law to give rise to the deception that a particular action was universal.

Under the conditions of formal property law 'relative ethical life' is determined by the relation of individuals to their productive activity and property, and not solely to wealth and its consumption. The relation to work looks universal. It looks as if the work of one is the work of all. But although this self-consciousness acknowledges its activity, its actuality, it acknowledges it only as its own activity and excludes others from it.[130] This is a 'spiritual animal kingdom' because transformative activity fuses the universal and the individual, or, the concept subsumes intuition, and produces something which others recognize. It is hence 'spiritual', the apparent harmony of universal and individual, or concept and intuition. But this harmony turns out to be a deceptive appearance, an 'animal world' which excludes and does not recognize the other or the product. Instead of a universal work, what is produced is a mere 'matter in hand' (die Sache selbst) which serves the particular ends of individuals and not the whole society.[131]

This is a 'spiritual animal kingdom', not a master-slave bondage, because of the strength of the deception that the work is universal. Deception is different from the immediacy of bondage because it appears that the work is transparent and universal. To be deceived is to know wrongly, whereas bondage is transparent.

Since individuals can only recognize themselves in their own and not in each other's work, the work has no permanence. The same certainty of self-consciousness which created the actuality of the work for the individual consciousness destroys the certainty of that work. For a work which is certain for one consciousness alone cannot attain any permanence or certainty outside that consciousness, nor hence for that consciousness itself.[132] The Sache selbst is both an honest purpose, willed and acted into reality, and a deceit – for its creator and for others who are excluded if they become interested in it. Since they deceive, too, in their relation to their work, a limited but common experience of the conditioned and particular nature of these apparently universal works is attained.[133] This experience itself is a recognition of ethical life albeit based on relative or particular interests and ends.[134]

It is on this conditioned basis, or relative ethical life, that reason believes it is legislating and testing an absolute law. The absolute formal law arises out of the content of the relative ethical life which is based on formal property law. Each example of universalizing is shown to depend on institutions specifically determined by that law.[135]

As 'absolute ethical life' in a society with formal law the 'moral' not the productive relation of consciousness to actuality is presented. This relation is called the moral Weltanschauung, because morality or duty is known and created by self-consciousness which is certain of itself.

> It is absolutely free in that it knows its freedom, and just this knowledge is its substance and purpose and sole content.[136]

What it does not know 'would have no meaning and can have no power over it'.[137] But what it does not know does have great power over it, the power to change the meaning of what this self-consciousness thinks it 'knows'.

Since 'moral' freedom is defined in opposition to the laws of nature the actualization of that freedom cannot occur in nature which is non-moral.[138] Thus the 'harmony of morality and nature [actuality]' must be 'postulated', that is, merely thought of as actual.[139] This thought of an actuality which does not act, but which guarantees moral actuality 'opens up' 'a whole circle of postulates':[140] a whole series of 'necessary thoughts' about the unity of moral action and actuality (nature) which is actual beyond the realm of individual moral acts. For moral acts are singular events which occur in the non-moral realm of nature and which cannot be complete in the infinite task of morality.

'God' is the supreme 'postulate', the 'postulate' of consciousness which is the law of duty as such as opposed to any specific duty. The unity of nature and morality is present in the actuality of 'God'.[141] But since 'God' is only a 'postulate', He is not actual either. The moral *Weltanschauung* thus rests on a contradiction. We both know and create the moral object, duty, and deny its actuality. We then attribute this actuality to God, an actuality which is beyond actuality, and which is only a postulate, a thought, and not actual.[142]

We know our actions and deny their actuality. This is a form of dissembling.[143] We know each action as the exercise of duty, and we refuse to know its actuality in the phenomenal world. We refuse to know it as 'enjoyment' or 'happiness', for the will which is motivated by these heteronomous ends is not good.[144]

But if we refuse to know nature as the realm of the actualization of our actions, we become incapable of making moral judgements about ourselves or others. If 'morality' is essentially 'imperfect' and un-realizable, then there is no basis for distinguishing between moral and immoral individuals.[145] We can only 'know' a 'pure moral being' who stands above 'the struggle with nature'. But then He cannot be moral, for He would be separated from the reality which is the source of our moral nature.[146] Hence He could not be actual either. Once again the postulate of 'God' is 'an unconscious, unreal, abstraction', a 'dissem-blance of the facts'.[147]

A postulate of 'God' to guarantee the moral law is a contradiction, for he is supposed to be beyond actuality and to be actuality.[148] Hence 'morality' too is both 'essential and devoid of essence'.[149]

Moral self-consciousness becomes aware of the 'antinomy of the moral *Weltanschauung*', but it does not turn to what it 'does not know' to see if it has unrecognized 'power over it'. Instead it 'flees' from this antinomy 'with abhorrence back into itself'. This scornful retreat does not challenge or transform the hypocrisy of the moral *Weltanschauung*. By retreating from action consciousness colludes in the prevailing hypocrisy.[150]

It acquires a *conscience*, 'a content for its previously empty duty'.[151] It is itself able to connect its act and its actualization before the court of conscience, and no longer attributes duty to a non-actual postulate.[152] But moral *consciousness* at least acknowledged an actuality beyond itself which both thwarted and guaranteed the actuality of its acts. [153] Moral *conscience* does not acknowledge any such actuality.

> It is now the law which exists for the sake of the self, not the self which exists for the sake of the law.[154]

Conscience recognizes its own act and the acts of others which moral consciousness was not able to do. For conscience knows that its duty has a content which can be realized and is immediately recognized or self-certain.[155] The pure form of duty has become a multiplicity of duties between which conscience chooses solely on the basis of its pure conviction of its duty. Thus conscience, too, acts on the basis of pure duty, and is indifferent to content. It, too, cannot make moral judgements, for everyone acts on the basis of 'individual conviction', and pure conviction can justify any act.[156]

Moral conscience, like moral consciousness, cannot appeal to the general good as the basis for its actions, for 'duty' as the autonomous law means opposition to 'what already exists as absolute substance as law and right'.[157] The law of morality is opposed to the law of established right, to *Sittlichkeit*. It is opposed not only to conformity to it, but to *knowing* it. Conscience has taken over the 'law' itself:

> It absolves itself from any specific duty which is supposed to have the validity of law. In the strength of its own self-assurance, it possesses the majesty of absolute autarky, to bind and to loose.[158]

As a result moral conscience has become completely uncertain about the significance of the other's equally self-certain action.[159] It comes to depend entirely on what the other says, on the 'language of conscience'.[160] Thus conscience treats its own *voice* as a 'divine voice', but actuality cannot be a mere voice.[161] Conscience utters its morality and does not act. It is a pure ego with no differentiation, and the 'ego equals ego' has become its sole actuality. This cessation of action is a self-willed impotence, the impassivity of a beautiful soul which will not besmirch its beauty by acting.[162]

This beautiful soul acknowledges others by use of a language 'in which all reciprocally acknowledge each other as acting [*sic*] conscientiously'.[163] But in fact no-one is acting at all, and thus this linguistic recognition corresponds to a real 'antithesis of individuality to other individuals'.[164] This discrepancy between mouthing the universal and the real, hostile, particular interests of individuals is utterly hypocritical. This hypocrisy is another 'law of the heart', 'a frenzy of self-deceit', for conscience asserts its particularity as 'law'. It is opposed to others under the guise of furthering their particular interests as if they could be a universal law.[165]

When conscience comes to see the hypocrisy on which the 'law of the heart' is based it proclaims the evil of that conscience in a harsh judgement of the other, for its own voice is still divine. But the 'divine' voice is equally hypocritical and evil, and it must confess this, break its own hard heart, and give and ask for forgiveness. Thus the word of reconciliation is exchanged:

> The word of reconciliation is the *objectively* existent spirit, which sees the pure knowledge of itself *qua universal* essence, in its opposite, in the pure knowledge of itself *qua* absolutely self-contained and exclusive *individuality* – a reciprocal recognition, which is *absolute* spirit.[166]

The experience of moral consciousness culminates in this *abstract* statement of the meaning of the *word* of confession and forgiveness. We, even as abstract Fichtean consciousness, have learnt that more than this is necessary for any ethical reconciliation. We have learnt that words are not actions, that evil, confession and forgiveness are subjective, Christian virtues not ethical ones, and that abstract statements mask ethical actuality. We have learnt that to espouse this position of confession and forgiveness would be to remain in the illusion of absolute subjectivity.

The only other ethical reconciliation was presented at the conclusion of experience of the 'relative ethical life' of a society with formal law. Formal law was contrasted with 'the essential universality of law' by reference to *Antigone*.[167] But we have learnt, too, that Antigone's experience of reconciliation is not a possibility for us, for we *know* ourselves as abstract subjects.

We are left with the realization of the barbarism of our abstract culture, of how we have reproduced that barbarism by denying the ethical, by fixing (positing, *setzen*) the illusion that we are absolute or pure consciousness in our moral law or in the law of our hearts.

We are indeed admonished, contrite, but not ethical: for the possibility of becoming ethical does not depend on our moral decision nor on our words. It does not depend on our Fichtean will.

The Law and the Logic

The reconciliation of forgiveness which concludes the shapes of 'consciousness itself as such' is abstract, a reconciliation of consciousness with self-consciousness which is solely for itself, a form devoid of content. On the other hand, religion represents this reconciliation in itself, as content, as image. It represents the whole or absolute by misrepresenting it as separate from the self-consciousness which knows itself.[168]

The absolute has still not been prejudged, not stated abstractly and thus not turned into either another formal, empty concept, nor into an image.

Our own act here has been simply to gather together the separate moments.[169]

The moments have been gathered in order to *see* the absolute by presenting the series of its determinations, of its misapprehensions. *Der Begriff* is usually translated as 'the Notion' when it alludes to this absolute or substance which cannot be stated.

However, once the shapes of consciousness have been experienced, one thing can be stated. It can be stated that the absolute or substance is negative, which means that it is determined as the knowing and acting self-consciousness which does not know itself to be substance, but which knows itself by denying or negating substance, and is certain of itself in opposition to its objects. This is not an abstract statement about the absolute, but an observation to which we have now attained, by looking at the experiences of a consciousness which knows itself as an antithesis, as negative, and thus 'participates' in this antithesis as its own act.[170]

This perspective is comprehensive, *Begreifendes*, conceptual in the sense of complete, not in the sense of the abstract concept.[171] It conceives or grasps the absolute as it is determined in all the shapes of consciousness. It is not a static or prejudged knowledge but comprehends the shapes of consciousness as they appear in their contradictions.

The absolute or substance appears as consciousness and its oppositions or differentiations. To know that consciousness divides itself into abstract concept and oppositions is not the same as consciousness' knowledge of that opposition. It is a knowing which knows consciousness and its oppositions and is therefore comprehensive. This comprehension is not the concept which is opposed to nature or intuition, but the concept or Idea which includes the opposition between the formal concept and its determinations.

This knowing or *science* only exists now, as our Fichtean consciousness transformed into science, but the absolute or substance which is now determined as this knowing has existed as previous forms of knowing or misrecognition, as misrepresentation.[172]

The *Phenomenology* culminates in science. Yet even though the oppositions of consciousness have been surmounted, we still cannot have an abstract statement of the absolute or substance. As science we still have to continue to rediscover 'the passage of the concept into consciousness', into misrepresentation, and this, too, is a process which eludes statement.[173] The attainment of science is no end,

> for the self-knowing spirit, just because it graps its concept, is the immediate identity with itself, which, in its difference, is the certainty of immediacy, or sense–consciousness, – the beginning from which we started.[174]

Self-knowing spirit is a relation and this knowing whether presented in the historical shapes of consciousness or as science is perpetual and never-ending. Absolute knowledge is a path which must be continually traversed, re-collecting the forms of consciousness and the forms of science. This idea of a whole which cannot be grasped in one moment or in one statement for it must be experienced is the idea of the system.

In the *Phenomenology* the system starts from 'subjective' spirit which is purely subjective, which has no concept or knowledge of itself, but which considers itself to exist in opposition. It has an actuality which we see and which it comes to see by achieving a perspective on its own simple subjectivity. Consciousness first becomes objective to itself by coming to comprehend itself as also 'simply' subjective.[175] It may equally well be said that consciousness becomes subjective by comprehending its 'simple' objectivity. This is the path of the *Logic*. In both cases we see spirit from the beginning as both subjective and objective, and the development from its simple subjectivity or simple objectivity is both objective and subjective.

To comprehend subjectivity as determined is to go beyond subjectivity. It is to acknowledge determination: that we are determined and that the determination is ours. This acknowledgement cannot occur in ethical life for the same reason that the only idea we have of it is ethical: the ethical is the realm of law (*Gesetz*), that is, of positing (*setzen*). Simple subjective consciousness exists in relation to the other and is thus unfree, or only free in principle. It attains freedom as objective spirit:

> Spirit that is objective is a person and as such has an actuality of its freedom in property . . .[176]

Subjective spirit which knows itself to be free in the actual world is objective. But the actual world as property or as ethical life is still only posited (*gesetzt*), only law (*Gesetz*), only put there, and thus still subjective not fully objective.[177] To know fully the determination of consciousness, what is *posited* must be known as having an *immediate being* too, not as put there by us, determined by us, but as what determines itself as us and is there in the determination.

The *Logic* has to vindicate the idea of a positing, of a law, which is not put there by us but which determines us. It thus has to expound the actuality of positing or law and go beyond the logic and the terminology of positing and law to show that positing and the law can be comprehended outside the simple subjective viewpoint. In other words, the *Logic* has to yield a 'Subjective Logic', a logic of spirit which has become fully subjective. It has to comprehend its simple or immediate subjectivity *without* once again positing it.

The *Phenomenology* consists of the experience of positing, of coming to see that the laws (*Gesetze*) are put there (*gesetzt*) and thus of becoming increasingly conscious of the positing of law, for example, the laws of nature, the moral law, the law of the heart. These apparently 'universal' laws turn out to be the fixing (*setzen*) of particularity.

Natural consciousness' experience of positing law is abstract consciousness' experience of the determination of law, of substance determined as 'law' and misapprehended as posited or universal, for example, the Greek distinction between human and divine law; Roman legal status; feudal lawlessness; modern, formal law.

Ultimately natural consciousness' experience of positing coincides with abstract consciousness' experience of the determination of natural consciousness. This coincidence is encountered not as morality, not as religion, but as philosophy. It is philosophy which now has the vocation (determination) to present a notion of law to our abstract consciousness which will re-form the ethical without being re-formed by it, which will comprehend itself, its positing, as the law of substance, of absolute ethical life.

This law is the law which *is*, which has immediate being, Antigone's law:

> The law is valid in and for itself: it is the absolute pure will which has the form of immediate being. . . . Laws are the thoughts of its own absolute self-consciousness, thoughts which are immediately its own.[178]

It does not matter whether this immediacy is that of sense-certainty or self-certainty,[179] whether it is the beginning or the end, not because we cannot distinguish between the beginning and the end, but because we live between the two, in the experience of lack of freedom, of representation and abstract understanding.

But the fate of this philosophy has been to be re-formed by the ethical life which it re-presents. The absolute philosophy has not been read speculatively, because the reality of unfreedom has determined its reading. It has been read as the negative absolute which it sought to undermine, as an imposed *Sollen*. This *Sollen* has either reinforced prevailing law and thus has brought about the 'end of philosophy' just like the end of art and the end of religion. This is known as Right-wing Hegelianism. Or this *Sollen* has been imposed on the capricious law of bourgeois society. Known as Left-wing Hegelianism, this has created the new culture of Marxism which has been perpetually re-formed in its vocation.

6

Rewriting the Logic

Beyond the Bounds of Morality

The *Logic* essays again the simplest and most difficult task: the speculative rereading of Kant and Fichte. This rereading seeks to educate our abstract philosophical thinking by expounding the process of its determination. It returns to the basic dichotomies, rules and axioms of Kant and of Fichte's thought which were examined in the earlier critique of their theories of natural law.[1] Once again it is shown how these dichotomies, rules, and axioms abstract from real relations, and how our positing of these abstractions is itself determined.

In *Faith and Knowledge* Hegel demonstrates how Kant's formal rule 'Thoughts without contents are empty, intuitions without concepts are blind' re-presents a real lack of identity between concept and intuition, the domination of relative identity.[2] This lack of identity is also presupposed by Fichte's primacy of practical reason. The 'perennial ought' depends on the same domination.[3] In the essay on natural law and in the *System of Ethical Life* the specific social institutions and relations to which these abstractions correspond are derived. In the *philosophies* of art and religion, the social institutions and laws which determine representation and illusion are expounded. In the *Philosophy of Right* and the *Phenomenology*, the exposition of abstract thinking and the derivation of the social institutions which determine it are completely integrated in the tracing of the education of self-consciousness at specific historical moments. This educative integration means that the determining law is only visible in the interstices and transformations of self-consciousness.

The unity of the *Logic* is forged by the attempt to expound yet again how the opposition between concept and intuition is the basis both of the opposition between theoretical and practical reason, and of the primacy of Fichtean practical reason, of abstract Fichtean domination. The *Logic* seeks to show how we might comprehend what has been dominated and suppressed without dominating it once again.

In the first section of the *Logic*, 'The Doctrine of Being', the connection of the opposition between concept and intuition and of the opposition between theoretical and practical reason is expounded. The dichotomies are discussed by us, in their abstract opposition as they have appeared to the philosophical consciousness of the external Kantian observer.

The central section of the *Logic*, 'The Doctrine of Essence', concerns Fichte's attempt to unify the Kantian dichotomies by the act and deed (*Tat-handlung*) of positing. As a result, in Fichte, these dichotomies are no longer viewed externally, but from the perspective of their self-generation. Hegel shows that Fichte's 'absolute positing' is an illusion, that absolute positing does not determine anything. To comprehend actual determination, the determination of the illusion that positing determines must be seen.

The final section of the *Logic* is 'Subjective Logic', or 'The Doctrine of the Concept'. It both acknowledges the determination and illusion of positing, and is beyond the standpoint of positing, beyond the standpoint of an abstract (modern, bourgeois, property) law which determines abstract illusion. The subjective logic seeks to present a different law which is not posited but which has determinate existence. The unity of theoretical and practical reason is built in this way out of the unity of the logic of being and the logic of essence. This unity re-cognizes the moment of intuition outside the concept in Kant's theoretical philosophy and restores real determination to the empty Fichtean self-determination. From this perspective 'practical reason' is no longer a formal law, but the 'idea of the good'. The 'idea of the good' is the realization of substantial freedom, not the mere concept of a formal law.[4]

This unity acknowledges the partial perspectives of the doctrine of being and the doctrine of essence. It thus seeks to avoid making itself into another abstract imposition as Kant and Fichte's 'unities' are. The unity of being (theory, nature) and essence (practice, concept) yields the overall unity by continuing to recognize the lack of unity and without justifying or stating the unity.

Yet, the paradox remains that the end of the *Logic* is as abstract as the beginning. It ends in fact with an abstract *statement* of the procedure of 'absolute method'.[5] Absolute method is the method which is only expoundable at the end of a science, and which acknowledges both its circularity and the breaks in the circle. Furthermore, the penultimate chapter *states* the unity of theoretical and practical reason, of concept and intuition, in a way which remains fully within these abstract oppositions.

The beginning of the *Logic loses* its abstract character when recognized from the standpoint of the subjective logic, for it becomes the idea of the good, of a law which 'simply is'.[6] But the abstract character of the beginning is *restored* in the discussion of 'absolute method'. For if the good, the law which *is* and includes all relations, has not been attained, then it must be conceded that the 'beginning' and the 'end' are still abstract. Even the idea of an *absolute* method is abstract once it is stated or even needed. Thus the beginning and the end of the system are abstract. The end is both a result, and it is just the same as the beginning: an abstraction.

Hegel did not believe that freedom could be achieved in the pages of the *Logic*, nor did he have the ambition or vocation to *impose* it. He did not believe that there was any natural beginning or any utopian end. He recognized the continuing domination of formal law and that *his* recognition was not enough to change it. But in between the beginning and the end, the speculative exposition demonstrates the domination of abstraction and urges *us* to transform ethical life by re-cognizing the law of its determination. Hegel urges us not to try to transform solely our way of thinking, our abstract concepts.

The 'Logic of Being' is the first section of the Logic. 'Being' means absence of determination or characteristic. The concept of being is achieved by abstracting from all characteristics, and is therefore empty and formal. The section discusses the abstract oppositions which are the corollary of this initial abstraction. It does not discuss the *relation* between the terms of the oppositions, but the way in which they exclude and are opposed to each other. The dichotomies between concept and intuition, thought and being, are shown to lead to a moral standpoint which claims to unite the dichotomies but which reinforces them, and implies further dichotomies such as finite/infinite. The dichotomies of Kant's theoretical philosophy are reinforced by Fichte's transformation of the justification of objective validity into the primacy of practical reason.

'Die Schranke und das Sollen', the limit and the ought, is the title of a seminal section of 'The Doctrine of Being'.[7] It consists of a speculative reading of Kant's distinction between a boundary (*Grenze*) and a limit (*Schranke*).[8] Kant made the distinction in order both to establish the idea of a boundary and to acknowledge something unknowable beyond the boundary, 'things-in-themselves'. Hegel shows how the connection between the boundary and the limit is the precondition of the 'moral' standpoint, of a standpoint which also both acknowledges and denies an actuality which is beyond our apprehension.

Hegel resumes the exposition of the 'moral *Weltanschauung*' from the *Phenomenology* where it *appears* as the standpoint of the present age,[9] and returns to the non-phenomenological standpoint of the *Differenz-schrift*, or of the essay on natural law, to point out again to our abstract, philosophical consciousness, as egregiously as he did then, the pre-suppositions and implications of 'morality'.

However, the *Logic* is a phenomenology of abstract philosophical consciousness. It is thus phenomenologically consistent to expound the *Schranke* and the *Sollen* abstractly since we are at the stage of established and customary abstractions. Nevertheless the exposition depends on two ideas which cannot be expounded in the logic of being because they have yet to be discovered by abstract philosophical consciousness as the precondition of its abstractness. They are 'actuality' and 'positing'. This anticipation is quite legitimate. For the abstract standpoint has precisely this uneasy relation to actuality and to its positing which it both acknowledges and disowns. Thus 'actuality' and 'positing' may *appear* at this point, although they cannot yet be explicated.

In the *Prolegomena* Kant distinguishes between a boundary (*Grenze*) and a limit (*Schranke*). A boundary presupposes a space to be found outside a determined and determinable space which encloses whatever is inside the boundary. A limit is quantitative and does not imply any specific or determinable space beyond the limit, but implies a mere negative, a quantity or series which is not complete. A limit does not imply something beyond the limit which is qualitatively attainable, which is unavailable to knowledge, but knowable as such. It implies simply an absence of any expectation of completing an infinite series in any inner progression.[10] According to Kant, mathematics, for example, recognizes limits, while it is the task of metaphysics to lead to the boundaries of knowledge and to determine them without being able to determine what is beyond them.[11]

Hegel produces a speculative commentary on the distinction between boundary and limit, and shows how the distinction implies the standpoint of the infinite, unrealizable ought (*Sollen*). The distinction between boundary and limit re-presents a displacement of actuality.[12]

A boundary means the way in which a specific determination (characteristic) distinguishes something from something else with a different specific determination, and thus forms its boundary. The boundary is the determination considered 'in general', 'relatively to an other'. 'The boundary is the non-being of the other, not of something itself.'[13] But the other has the same relation to the first determination or boundary. The other's own boundary or determination makes it into something, as well as making the other into an other. Hence the boundary is not just a negative relation to something else in general which bounds it, but '. . . *through the boundary something is what it is, and in the boundary it has its quality.*'[14]

The boundary is a quality. Hegel agrees with Kant that a boundary has its 'determinate being *outside* . . . of its boundary' in a negative, relative sense, and, 'as it is also put, on the *inside* . . . of its boundary' in a positive sense.[15] Kant explicated the idea of a boundary by use of spatial metaphors, and Hegel points out how the boundary tends to be imagined or (mis)re-presented by reference to spatial objects.

The metaphor tends to be extended, as in Kant, to imagine something *in general* outside the boundary, determinate being in general. In a sense this has already happened with the idea of something in general as the other of the boundary. But, now, 'boundary' points not to something in general which it is equally itself in relation to that something, but points beyond itself 'to its non-being, declaring this to be its being'.[16] Now the abstract opposition between two things as something and its boundary becomes a relation in which one thing is the 'element' of the other.[17] In spatial terms, it is the difference between the point as the boundary of the line, its characteristic, and the point as the constituent element of the line. In these spatial terms the boundary is discrete, contingent, and external. The point is abstracted; it is not considered in a determinate being, the line, but as the element of 'abstract space', 'a pure continuous asunderness'.[18] Even as an element, a point is not considered to have anything immanent in it, but is opposed to its abstract negation which is a characterless continuity. This is Kant's explication of the boundary which is determinable as a boundary, but what is outside it is unknowable, abstract negation as such.[19]

The notion of limit (*Schranke*) is implied by this notion of boundary (*Grenze*). Kant distinguishes limit from boundary by reference to mathematics, to a series which is never complete but is infinite and unending. Hegel shows how this notion of limit follows from the notion of a boundary, when the boundary is thought in terms of a spatial metaphor. He shows how Kant's metaphysical boundary, expounded by Kant in physical terms, leads to a limit, expounded by Kant in mathematical terms of an infinite series, which is the infinitely unattainable actuality delineated by the moral ought, *das Sollen*.

The boundary is the way something distinguishes itself negatively from something else. At the same time, this external other also belongs to the first thing as its otherness, as the determination which forms the boundary. The combination of externality and owness becomes 'a relation turned towards its own self'.[20] The thing (self) knows that the boundary which distinguishes itself from the other is its way of knowing itself. In this way it acquires a self-identity: by making the opposition (negation) of something else the way of relating itself to itself. It 'relates to itself' by knowing itself to be 'its own non-being'.[21]

> Something's own limit thus posited by it as a negative which is at the same time essential, is not merely a boundary as such but a limit.[22]

This limit is Kant's limit: something outside a determination which is infinitely incomplete, a 'mere negation', the 'recognition of something which can never be reached'.[23] The limit is the boundary known as the negative of itself, but also as essential to itself, and hence a determination of itself. An essential determination which something knows to be a negative relation to itself, a limit which is infinite, is the relation of 'ought'.

For the thing (self) relates to its limit not as something which is (boundary), but as something which it is *not*, but which is essential to what it is. When we say 'X ought to be', we know that it both is and is not. It *is to be* and it *is not*, because otherwise we would not say that it ought to be.[24] Something is both in-itself an ought *to be* and a non-being, an *ought* to be. It both has an essential determination, *to be*, and posits it as its own negative: *ought* to be. This is a limit which can be momentarily transcended. Something can raise itself above its limit and pass from the ought to be to the existence of whatever ought to be. But 'it is only as the *ought* that it has its limit', its self-identity.[25]

This is what Kant's limit implies, a perpetual raising above the limit which by that very act recreates the limit, the infinite series of negative self-relation posited as negative. This limit, the series, is implied by the idea of boundary from which Kant wanted to distinguish it: the spatial re-presentation of a general negative somethingwhich is the boundary becomes a limit when the something which knew its characteristic as itself separates the negative determination from the positive and posits it as a negative, but still as essential, as a determination of itself.

A speculative reading of Kant's re-presentational exposition of the distinction between boundary and limit reveals the contradictory relation to actuality in that distinction as the foundation of 'morality'.

The 'ought', the inexplicable fact of reason in Kant, is said to imply 'can'.[26] It implies that one is superior to the limit of the ought *to be* which *is not*. But it is equally valid to say 'you cannot precisely because you ought',[27] because if you could you would, and then it would not be a case of 'you ought'. The 'can' means merely *formal* possibility. 'You ought to do x' implies that 'x' is not a contradiction and therefore logically impossible. But the sense in which 'ought' implies something is not implies a *real* not being of it, and thus a cannot, or, rather, an impossibility. It is this impossibility, this cannot, which is always implied in 'ought' which makes it into a 'progress to infinity', that is, Kant's limit.[28]

The ought is a pre-judging which asserts that the limit cannot be transcended. We have to live in the limit of what ought to be. This is a proposition of the understanding (*Verstand*) which also says that reason cannot transcend its boundaries. The understanding makes a boundary into a limit because it makes thought superior to actuality, and then says that thought can only be an ought-to-be, inferior to actuality. In this way an untrue and contradictory relation to actuality is maintained.[29]

Hegel then gives a representational example of a limit which can be overcome. Hunger is a limit or negation which determines the sentient creature to overcome it and to realize or actualize itself. A limit can be overcome if actuality is acknowledged as both determination and as act. The limit is transcended by transforming the specific determination in relation to the totality of its real possibilities. However, this is to use notions not yet presented. So Hegel concludes that at this stage an abstract reference to a wholly abstract universal is a sufficient riposte to the abstract assertion that limit cannot be transcended.[30]

It has been shown at this stage how the standpoint of morality depends on spatial and mathematical metaphors for actuality. The ought is transcended in a finite way, for it always recurs, and this is the definition of being finite.[31] 'Being-in-itself', what is, actuality, is opposed 'to limitedness', what *ought* to be.[32] This being-in-itself is regulative and essential, and what is subject to the ought is limited and null. The being-in-itself is called 'duty', and is held superior not only to thought but to particularity, to 'self-seeking desire' and 'capricious interest'.[33]

Thus the perennial ought confirms the perennial finite,

> But in the world of actuality itself, reason and law are not in such a bad way that they only *ought* to be.[34]

The speculative reading of boundary, limit and ought reveals the contradiction in the concept of actuality. To theoretical reason actuality is 'acknowledged' and unknowable, and to practical reason it is 'acknowledged' and unattainable.

Illusion and Actuality

The doctrine of essence is a speculative reading of Fichte's transformation of Kant's *Schranke* and *Sollen*, the limit and the ought.

> Thus the positing of the ego by itself is the pure activity of it. The ego *posits itself* and it *is* by virtue of this sheer positing of itself; and vice versa, the ego *is* and it posits its being by virtue of its sheer being – it is at the same time the agent and the product of the act; the active, and what the activity brings about; action [*Handlung*] and deed [*Tat*] are one and the same, and hence 'I am' is an expression of a fact [*Tathandlung*], and the only one possible . . .[35]

For Fichte, the ego must posit a boundary (*Grenze*) because it is finite, but it is not limited (*eingeschränkt*) by this boundary because the boundary is posited absolutely. The positing is dependent on the ego alone. Thus the boundary, which makes the ego finite, lies *wherever* in the infinite the ego posits it to be: it depends entirely on the spontaneity of the ego.[36]

This notion of a boundary is incoherent: 'The ego simply posits an object, a boundary point; but where the boundary lies is undetermined.'[37] The concept of a boundary is inconceivable if it does not refer to something which is distinct from something else, that is, to a determination. According to Fichte a spontaneous act becomes determinate or posited 'insofar as there is a resistance to an activity of the ego; no such activity of the ego, no object – it is related as determinans to determinate.'[38] But this 'resistance' is also inconceivable. It is an empty resistance, as empty as the Kantian thing-in-itself.[39]

On the one hand, the absolute and unconditioned produces an object and the product must be distinct from the act. On the other hand, the act and the deed, the *Tathandlung*, are 'absolutely connected . . . absolutely alike.' But since, according to the first proposition, they cannot be absolutely alike, 'we can only say that their likeness is absolutely demanded: they *ought* to be absolutely alike.'[40] Fichte's absolute ego 'demands the conformity of the object with the ego precisely in the name of its absolute being'.[41] The *limit* of theoretical reason is broken by the practical ought.[42]

Fichte himself claims that this is the significance of Kant's categorical imperative:

> How could he ever have arrived at a categorical imperative as an absolute postulate of conformity with the pure ego without presupposing the absolute being of the ego, whereby everything is posited, and so far as it *is* not, at least *ought* to be?[43]

This is a statement of Kantian morality where actuality is attributed to the imperative of duty: 'The ground of authority of the absolute postulate . . . is absoluteness of the ego . . . from which everything else is deduced.'[44] Fichte thus attributes actuality to the ego. The *Sollen* is thus not an 'inexplicable fact of consciousness'[45] as it is in Kant, but the basis of the *Science of Knowledge*, of the relation between the absolute positing of the ego and the boundaries or objects which are posited. The *Sollen* reconnects act and deed, ego and object. It reconnects what has been bounded or limited with its precondition.

Thus 'positing reflection' is both absolute and finite. The ego is absolute because it posits the boundaries itself, and it is finite because it is subject to those boundaries. This 'positing reflection' is the target of 'The Doctrine of Essence'. According to Hegel, absolute positing or positing reflection as the spontaneous act of the ego is an illusion. The illusion is that positing is the source of determination. Either Fichte's positing is determinate, in which case it would not be absolute; or, if it is absolute, then it must be indeterminate and 'then, too, it has nothing with which it could bridge the gap between itself and an other. . . . It is just as impossible for anything to break forth from it as to break into it . . .'[46]

'Positing' cannot acknowledge determinate being or actuality.

Hegel's speculative commentary derives the determination of this positing:

> ... the determinate being which essence gives itself is not yet determinate being as in and for itself, but as *given* by essence to itself, or as *posited*, and is consequently still distinct from the determinate being of the concept.[47]

Positing reflection thus differs from external reflection of the logic of being, the reflection of dichotomies where something is determined in relation to something else as a boundary. Positing reflection cannot achieve a determination which is not merely posited and which thus has no independence or actuality. In Fichte determination is revoked, summoned back, by the absolute ego which has posited it.

In the logic of essence, something is not determined by something else by virtue of its boundary, but the determination is posited, put there, by something itself. This something is not an unconditioned absolute ego but something determinate. The relation of something itself positing something else is the relation of essence to what it posits. What essence posits 'its determining, remains within this unity [of being in itself (absolute) and being for itself (posited)] and is neither a becoming nor a transition'.[48]

The exposition of essence and its positing shows that what is posited is an illusion not a determinate being. Positing reflection disowns and displaces actuality as much as the external reflection of the logic of being, of the limit and the ought. It produces 'a non-essence or illusory being, an immediate which is in and for itself a nullity'.[49] Hegel calls positing 'illusory being' when the stress is on its immediacy, on the deed (*Tat*) posited. When this immediacy is seen as illusory, as unessential, as posited (*Handlung*), it is called reflection: 'Illusory being is the same thing as reflection; but it is reflection as immediate.'[50]

For Fichte, the determination or boundary is created by the spontaneous act of the absolute ego. But it is impossible to conceive this determination, for the relation of determinans to determinate is unspecified.[51] For Hegel, this is to make being into illusory being. For being now consists of negative determination. It is a boundary of the absolute and hence a reflected immediacy: 'one which *is* only by means of its negation and which when contrasted with its mediation, is nothing but the empty determination of the immediacy of negated determinate being.'[52] Being is robbed of any positive determination.

Even this negative immediacy is not the boundary of essence which would confer on it a determination in relation to essence. Since being has no characteristic beyond being posited, even the immediacy of negative being is lost, for there is only the negativity of essence itself. The negative immediacy of being is indistinguishable from essence, or, it is reflected and mediated not immediate.[53] Thus there is not an illusory being of essence (a determination), nor an illusory essence in being (a determination), but the illusory being of essence itself.[54]

Essence is the unity of absolute negativity (Fichte's absolute ego which bounds itself) and immediacy (Fichte's boundary). But neither essence nor immediacy have any determination: 'the negative self-relation, a negating that is a repelling of itself is negative or determinate', but this determinateness is absolutely negative. Thus it cannot be said to be a determination but is 'the absolute sublating [removing] of the determinateness itself'.[55]

This process of taking illusory being as immediate being and seeing that the immediacy or determination is an illusion is to see that being is reflected.[56] The other of this being is not a being with a boundary or determination but the negation of any determination, the negation of negation. Fichte's account of positing cannot employ the notion of boundary for the relation of determinans to determinate acknowledges no other, only the spontaneous act of the ego, which is unconditioned and independent. Hegel shows that this account of positing makes being into illusory being. The claim that absolute positing results in determinate objects is incoherent.

Under the title 'Positing Reflection', Hegel shows that the claim that positing is absolute, unconditioned and dependent on itself alone is also incoherent. For Fichte, positing is an immediate, underivable, unconditioned, spontaneous act which accounts for the possibility of objects. On this account, however, no determinate object can be posited but only an immediate being whose immediacy as a determination is illusory, since the absolute act *gives itself* 'boundaries', and hence has none. Fichte was giving an account of how and why we represent objects to ourselves as external and independent. This question presupposes the existence of the very objects whose determinate being is dissolved in the subsequent account of their positing.

Hence the immediacy of '*posited* being' is not the starting point of a reflection which comes to see that immediate being as illusory being.[57] The reflection or positing has *already* posited the immediate as negative

– as dependent on essence, on being posited. Reflection has *presupposed* (*vorausgesetzt*) what it claims it is *positing* (*setzen*). It is not a spontaneous act of positing, but has presupposed the negative, illusory nature of immediacy. Thus positing is not unconditional and underived. It depends on the reflection which already knows immediacy as 'that negative which is the illusory being of the beginning'.[58]

This applies to all 'immediate beginnings': the immediacy is an illusion which is not posited, not put there as immediate, but presupposed as negative. Immediacy is presupposed 'as a returning moment . . . as a coincidence of the negative with itself'.[59] Thus positing is a presupposing. It is not unconditioned but depends on an immediate which it *finds* and sublates:

What is thus found only *comes to be* through being *left behind*.[60]

Far from being unconditioned and absolute, posited*ness* is presupposed.

The Unity of Theoretical and Practical Reason

The actuality or real determination which positing presupposes has now appeared. This is now presented as the unity of external and positing reflection which is determining reflection. The exposition is still within the discourse of essence and thus cannot fully acknowledge actuality.

External reflection, the Kantian determination of something by its boundary in relation to something else, is reconsidered within the discourse of essence. Positing reflection which claims to start from nothing and to determine something, 'is determined as negative, as immediately opposed to something else, therefore to an other'.[61] External reflection knows that it presupposes a being unlike positing reflection which claims it presupposes nothing. Positing reflection knows that it has a presupposition which it finds before it as its starting point, but which it negates as it returns into itself and asserts that it has created itself what is found.[62]

External reflection knows that it has posited determination, such as the distinction between finite and infinite, but leaves the determination as external. It does not claim to have determined the infinite, and contents itself with taking the finite 'as the first, as the real; as the foundation, the abiding foundation'; and not as the starting point of a negating reflection.[63]

External reflection within the logic of essence, the opposition between something and something else, between finite and infinite, is not just *for us*, not just external as in the logic of being. It is restated as a reflection which posits the immediate and then withdraws from its positing. This positing presupposes the immediate and does not claim to have determined it. It acknowledges the immediate as a presupposition, as *found*, and withdraws from its own determining. Hence 'the externality of reflection over against the immediate is sublated',[64] and

External reflection is not external, but is no less the immanent reflection of immediacy itself.[65]

Thus external reflection, re-considered within the discourse of positing reflection, can be seen as a reflection which determines. The determination is not the immediate determination of being, nor the illusory determination of positing, but determination which has an independence, albeit still that of the logic of essence.[66]

The determination of external reflection is not 'put in the place of an other'. It does not find an immediacy and replace it by itself, 'the positing has no presupposition'.[67] It is determinate, because the something posited is opposed to something else. Within the logic of essence, the positing is 'superior' to the determination, whereas, in the logic of being, the determination was 'superior' to the positing.[68]

Positing reflection is now united with external reflection. Reflection has become determinate. It acknowledges its presupposition because external reflection 'repels' its positing for the sake of the determination.[69] Hence posited*ness* (not positing but what is posited) is a determination of reflection. It is determinate but as a reflection, 'a relation to other'.[70] This is not the relation to other of the logic of being, but relation to other as 'reflection-into-self'. It is not our doing, nor the doing of the absolute, unconditioned ego, but the conditioning or determination of the negation of something itself.[71] This determination is thus essential, not transitory, not posited by us, not illusory. The determining has 'come forth from itself'. It is posited: 'Reflection is immanent determining.'[72] But it is determinate not indeterminate, because the illusion of indeterminate positing has been acknowledged as the determination which external positing concedes and indeterminate positing presupposes.[73]

Both external reflection, positedness, and positing, 'negation as such, a non-being over against an other', constitute determining reflection.

The latter is the 'subsistence' of the former. It is a relation (*Beziehung*) to its otherness within itself, not to the other as 'something else'. It is thus determinate.[74] Although positing only achieves a real determination by including external determination, positing is an internal relation. It relates to its determination, that is, to its negation, not as a spatial, external boundary, but

> It is *positedness*, negation, which however bends back into itself, the relation to other, and negation which is equal to itself, the unity of itself and its other, and only through this is an *essentiality*. It is, therefore, positedness, negation, but as reflection into self it is at the same time the sublatedness of this positedness, infinite self-relation.[75]

Determining reflection has thus been expounded by reuniting Fichte's primacy of practical reason with Kant's theoretical reason, positing with external reflection, concept with intuition. The result is that actuality, determination, is re-cognized.

The 'subjective logic' unites the logic of being and the logic of essence within the logic or discourse of the idea in order to re-cognize actuality without positing it again. The subjective logic is the doctrine of the concept. The 'concept' is carefully distinguished from Kant and from Fichte's 'concept' and is called the 'idea':

> It must now certainly be admitted that the concept *as such* is not yet complete, but must raise itself to the idea which alone is the unity of concept and reality.[76]

The logic of the concept is the doctrine of the idea. It is the unity of the speculative readings of the logic of being and the logic of essence.

The logic of being turned out to be an abstract immediacy, an intuition without a concept, and hence blind – external reflection. The logic of essence turned out to be a 'concept without intuition', and hence 'empty' – positing reflection.[77] The idea of a reflection which determines was expounded by uniting external and positing reflection, or theoretical and practical reason, or intuition and concept.

This unity is re-attained within the discourse of the concept, beyond the discourses of being, positing and reflection. The penultimate chapter of the subjective logic is entitled 'The Idea of Cognition', and is divided into two parts, 'The Idea of the True' and 'The Idea of the Good'. It is the idea of spirit that the dichotomy between 'true' and 'good' expresses.[78] As a dichotomy the distinction between the idea of the true and the idea of the good belongs to external reflection. But the *eminent* use of 'true' and 'good' does not belong to a critical philosophy, a canon, but to a doctrine, an organon.

The chapter entitled 'The Idea of Cognition' is in effect the ultimate not the penultimate chapter of the *Logic*. For the last chapter, entitled 'The Absolute Idea' is a survey of method. It is striking how much the former chapter, too, remains within the terms of Kantian and Fichtean dichotomies of theoretical and practical reason, concept and intuition. Prevailing dichotomies must be acknowledged not suppressed, but a unity of a different kind which includes their relations has to be expounded. Hegel's concluding statement of that unity is necessarily abstract, because, as a *statement*, it depends on the Kantian and Fichtean oppositions.

Hegel could not find an alternative discourse to the *speculative discourse* of rereading the dichotomies of theoretical and practical reason, concept and intuition. He thus used the discourse of positing. For Fichte, positing originates in the absolute, unconditioned ego. For Hegel, actuality is posited or reflected in the ego. Fichte dissolves the world in the ego; Hegel dissolves and maintains the ego in the world. Hegel cannot find another discourse because positing (*setzen*) is not the unconditioned act of the ego, but the law (*Gesetz*) of the formation of the ego and of its cognition and miscognition. Thus to explicate this law Hegel needs the discourse of positing. However, to explicate a law which is there, determinate, not put there, which is the unity of concept and intuition, of practical and theoretical reason, he needs another discourse which he cannot find, and thus he cannot expound that law. Antigone's law had no concept, and positing, modern law, has no intuition.

The unity of the theoretical and the practical idea is expounded so as to re-unite the actuality which each idea by itself presents and suppresses in a different way. The theoretical idea is an empty idea, which takes 'a determinate content and filling' from the world. The practical idea is certain of itself as actual, but denies the actuality of the world.[79]

Hegel distinguishes between the notion of 'good' of the moral standpoint, the 'ought to be' opposed to being, and his own notion of '*realized* good',

. . . good in its concrete existence is not simply subject to destruction by external contingency, but by the collision and conflict of the good itself.[80]

The unresolved contradiction between the *Sollen*, the unrealized good, and the limit, when actuality is conceived as an 'externally manifold actuality that is an undisclosed realm of darkness' which cannot be seen or intuited, has been expounded in the *Phenomenology* to which Hegel refers.[81]

Unlike the discussion in the *Phenomenology*, Hegel goes on to *state* how the opposition between the good of morality and its displacement of actuality may be overcome. A way of 'regarding this defect is that the *practical* idea still lacks the moment of the theoretical idea'.[82] It is the theoretical idea which knows itself to be an indeterminate universal and that what 'truly *is* is the actuality there before it *independently of subjective positing*'.[83] For the practical idea either *posits* itself, certain of its own actuality and of the world's non-actuality, or posits the world as an insuperable limit (*Schranke*) to its end of the good. Hence 'the idea of the good can therefore find its integration through the idea of the true.'[84] It can find an actuality which it has not posited but which is recognized as the law of the good and is determinate. When this occurs 'the end [of practical action] communicates itself to actuality without meeting any resistance and is in simple identity with it'.[85] But this is not Antigone's beginning. Phenomenal reality has been 'altered by the activity of the objective concept: it has been *posited* as being in and for itself'.[86]

In this process of alteration the general presupposition is sublated, both what is immediately and at first found there (Greek law) and 'the determination of the good as a merely subjective end . . . and the necessity of realizing it by subjective activity (bourgeois law)';

> In the result the mediation sublates itself; the result is an *immediacy* that is not the restoration of the presupposition but rather its accomplished sublation.[87]

It is no accident that this was not *stated* at the end of the *Phenomenology* which traced the historical shapes of consciousness for it has never existed in history. This statement is abstract, a statement of absolute ethical life, conceivable but impossible, and hence a *Sollen*. It is not a *Sollen* within the *Logic*, for the *Logic* affirms the good as actual, and the actual as good. '. . . the actuality found as given is at the same time determined as the realized absolute end . . . This is the absolute idea.'[88]

The end is abstract like the beginning. Thus Hegel has not imposed a concept on intuition, but has recognized the abstraction, the reality of unfreedom. This recognition itself *commends* a different way of transforming that unfreedom.

The first paragraph of 'The Absolute Idea', the last chapter of the *Logic*, and the rest of the chapter, admits and *justifies* this abstraction in the exposition of absolute method.

> The absolute idea has shown itself to be the identity of the theoretical and the practical idea. Each of these by itself is still one-sided, possessing the idea itself as a sought-for-beyond and an unattainable goal; each, therefore, is a *synthesis of endeavour*, and has, but equally has *not*, the idea in it; each passes from one to the other without bringing the two together, and so remains fixed in their contradiction.[89]

The Victory of Reflection

When Hegel died (1831) he was engaged in revising the *Logic*. He had completed the revision of the logic of being and the logic of essence, but had not yet revised the 'Subjective Logic', the logic of the concept. He was in effect still engrossed in meeting the challenge which he had set himself as early as the *Differenzschrift* (1801):

> As to the need of the times, Fichte's philosophy has caused so much of a stir and has made an epoch to the extent that even those who declare themselves against it and strain themselves to get speculative systems of their own on the road, still cling to its principle, though in a more turbid and impure way, and are incapable of resisting it. The most obvious symptoms of an epoch-making system are the misunderstandings and the awkward conduct of its adversaries. However, when one can say of a system that fortune has smiled on it, it is because some widespread philosophical need, itself unable to give birth to philosophy – for otherwise it would have achieved fulfilment through the creation of a system – turns to it with an instinct-like propensity. The acceptance of the system seems to be passive but this is because what it articulates is already present in the time's inner core and everyone will soon be proclaiming it in his sphere or science of life.[91]

To resist this thought successfully it is necessary to present actuality in such a way that

> ... will recompense nature for the mishandling that it suffered in Kant and Fichte's systems, and set reason itself in harmony with nature, not by having reason renounce itself or become an insipid imitator of nature, but by reason recasting itself into nature out of its own inner strength.[92]

Hegel's battle with Fichte was fought on two fronts. It was fought against Fichte's positing reflection (*setzen*), because positing was indeterminate and could not recognize real determinations. As a result the tyrannous *Sollen* dominated and suppressed the determinations which positing refused to recognize. It was fought against Fichte's theory of (natural) law (*Gesetz*), for Fichte gave *legality*, not morality, the prime task of welding together the ego and non-ego, the general will and the community of rational beings, concept and intuition.

In Fichte,

> Every relation is one of domination and being dominated according to the laws of a consistent understanding [*Verstand*]. The whole edifice of the community of living beings is built by reflection.[93]

It is built by positing reflection which posits nothing, but which sanctifies prevailing bourgeois law with the sanction of the *Sollen*:

> ... when limitation [*Beschränkung*] by the common will is raised to the status of law [*Gesetz*] fixed as a concept, true freedom, the possibility of suspending a determinate relation is nullified. The living relation can no longer be indeterminate and is therefore no longer rational but absolutely determined and fixed fast [*festgesetzt*] by the understanding. Life has given itself up to servitude. Reflection dominates it and has gained the victory over reason.
>
> This state of indigence is stated to be natural law . . .[94]

For Hegel substantial or real freedom is not a bounding [*Beschränken*]:

> In a living relation, insofar as it is free, the indeterminate is nothing but the possible, it is neither something actual made dominant, nor a concept which commands.[95]

Absolute ethical life, the unjustifiable and unstatable alternative, is neither the legitimation of 'something actual', but not visible, nor a new imposed *Sollen*, 'a concept which commands'.

Hegel devoted the *Phenomenology* to the struggle with the various concepts of law, *Gesetz*, in Kant and Fichte: natural law, the laws of nature, the law of the heart, human and divine law, Roman legality, reason as law-giver and as law-tester. He devoted the *Logic* to the struggle with positing (*setzen*). But he was 'awkward' in his 'conduct'.[96]

> This essay [the *Differenzschrift*] begins with general reflections about the need, presupposition, basic principles etc. of philosophy. It is a fault in them that they are general reflections, but they are occasioned by the fact that presuppositions, principles, and such like forms still adorn the entrance to philosophy with their cobwebs. So, up to a point it is necessary to deal with them until the day comes when from beginning to end it is philosophy itself whose voice will be heard....[97]

If ethical life is abstract, then it can only be recognized by recognizing its abstractions, the cobwebs, and their determination. In this way actuality is recognized and another indeterminate, non-actuality is not posited.

However, since the day of philosophy, of freedom, has not yet come, the 'system' fell victim to the three fates which Hegel himself identified. The first fate is the continuing victory of reflection over reason and, in this sense, Hegel proved himself to be the most awkward of Fichte's adversaries. The second fate is that the Hegelian alternative would itself become 'something actual made dominant'; the third fate is that it would become 'a concept which commands'.[98] In the second and third case it is the 'awkwardness' and 'misunderstandings' of Hegel's adversaries which are important.[99] For if Hegel's thought is treated as a *Sollen*, a concept, this concept may be turned against illegality, thus presupposing the existing law and assimilated to its purpose. Or, this *Sollen*, this concept, may be invoked in opposition to the real lawlessness of the prevailing social order. In the former case, this fate heralds the end of philosophy; in the latter case, it heralds the dawn of a new vocation, which may, in its turn, be re-formed and perverted. All three of these fates are determined by the continuing domination of the relations of bourgeois private property and law.

7

With What Must the Science End?

The End of Philosophy

Hegel's philosophy has no social import if the absolute cannot be thought.[1] If we cannot *think* the absolute this means that it is therefore not our *thought* in the sense of not realized. The absolute is the comprehensive thinking which transcends the dichotomies between concept and intuition, theoretical and practical reason. It cannot be thought (realized) because these dichotomies and their determination are not transcended.

Once we realize this we can think the absolute by acknowledging the element of *Sollen* in such a thinking, by acknowledging the subjective element, the limits on our thinking the absolute. This is to think the absolute and to fail to think it quite differently from Kant and Fichte's thinking and failing to think it.

Thinking the absolute means recognizing actuality as *determinans* of our acting by recognizing it in our acts. Thus recognizing our transformative or productive activity has a special claim as a mode of acknowledging actuality which transcends the dichotomies between theoretical and practical reason, between positing and posited. Transformative activity acknowledges actuality in the act and does not oppose act to non-act.

Thinking the absolute is the basis for the critique of different kinds of property relations and for the critique of different kinds of law, for the social import of this philosophy. A society's *relation* to nature, to transformative activity determines its political and property relations, its concept of law, and its subjective or natural consciousness. For the *relation* to actuality, which, by definition, excludes part of it, is negative, and determines the relation to self and relation to other. Actuality is not something posited (put there) and not nature, not-posited or outside the act (not put there). Actuality can be known because it is experienced both as a dichotomy and as beyond the dichotomy. The lack of identity between actuality and specific act gives rise to experience, to a re-cognition which sees what the act did not immediately see. To see the determination of the act is to see beyond the dichotomy between act and non-act.

In the *Logic* 'actuality' and 'relation' appear at the end of the logic of essence as the exposition of the absolute.[2] The universal and particular on which the critique of law and property depend are expounded at the beginning of the subjective logic as 'The Concept'.[3] Actuality, relation and concept (law), the components of the absolute, are integrated in the subsequent exposition of 'Teleology' and 'Life'.[4]

The 'absolute' in the *Logic* is a category of essence, and the 'idea' is the corresponding category in the subjective logic. The idea is the unity of concept and reality, that is, the realization of the concept.[5] Thus the place of appearance of the 'absolute' in the *Logic* is an admission of its limitation, of the element of abstractness, or *Sollen*, or subjectivity, in its exposition. However, the same limitation applies to the exposition of the 'idea' and, in the final chapter, Hegel deliberately draws attention to the abstract status of the 'idea'.[6]

> What is actual *can act*; something manifests its actuality through what it produces. Its relating [*Verhalten*] to another is the manifestation *of itself* . . .[7]

This relating is not a transition, a relation of the logic of being, nor a relation of the logic of essence where the relation to self depends on another self-subsistent.[8] It is real or substantial actuality, not the merely formal actuality of what is actual is possible, that is, not logically contradictory.[9] Real actuality manifests itself 'through what it produces'. This is a critique of Fichte's unconditioned actuality of the ego which 'posits' the non-ego and leaves unexplicated and inexplicable how this positing or production occurs.

Hegel's proposition may sound like a mere reversal of Fichte's position. Not the ego but actuality produces, and this leaves the problem of positing exactly as it is in Fichte: inexplicable. The agent or unconditioned has simply changed its name. But real actuality means real possibility, 'the real possibility of something is therefore the existing multiplicity of circumstances which are related to it.'[10] Real actuality is not an unconditioned, inexplicable agent, but a recognition of '*the totality of conditions*, a dispersed actuality' which more or less reappears in our subjective acts or productions.[11] A 'dispersed actuality' is in opposition to Fichte's 'dispersed self':[12]

... a dispersed actuality which is not reflected into itself but is determined as being the in-itself, but the in-itself of another, ought to return back into itself.[13]

Actuality is more or less acknowledged in our actions. It is acknowledged as our in-itself, as the in-itself of another. It ought to return back into itself. But it is not so determined by that other that it can return back into itself, that is, we only partially recognize it.

The exposition of real necessity makes it clear that Hegel has not reproduced the Fichtean problem. What is necessary 'cannot be otherwise', but real necessity is also 'relative': it has a 'presupposition from which it begins, it has its starting point in the contingent'.[14] This is to acknowledge actuality as determinate, 'as immediate being in the fact that it is a multiplicity of existing circumstances', and as real possibility, as the negative of this immediate being, as realized.[15]

Necessity is real as the combination of necessity as form, it could not be otherwise, and as content, 'a *limited actuality* which on account of this limitation, is also only a contingent in some other respect'.[16] Specific or limited actuality is recognized as real necessity and not simply posited.

[Actuality's] negative positing of these moments is thereby itself the *presupposing* or positing *of itself as sublated*, or of *immediacy*.[17]

Actuality simply is and it acts or produces. It is the lack of identity between the simple existence of actuality and the 'limited' or specific 'content' of any real necessity which is the basis of all speculative exposition.

Actuality is the foundation of the critique of law and of property relations, of the social import of Hegel's thought. In the logic of the concept the exposition of 'teleology' and of 'life' fuse a 'concrete' law or concept with 'real actuality'.[18] The exposition of the universal concept is the exposition of substantial law, of a universal which is not abstract but concrete, which is equally particular and individual. For, historically, the law is either bourgeois law, the universal (concept) which dominates the particular (intuition), or the law of Athens, which is individual, Athena, the goddess of the *polis*, but not universal. The law which is both universal and individual has never existed. Thus it can only be thought in the *Logic*. The subjective logic, the logic of the concept, is the logic of the law.

The universal concept is expounded as a 'becoming' or 'outcome' which is unconditioned and original'.[19] In the universal concept, essence has 'restored itself as a being that is *not posited*, that is *original'*.[20]

> By virtue of this original unity it follows, in the first place, that the first negative, or the determination is not a limit [*Schranke*] for the universal which, on the contrary, *maintains itself therein*, and is positively identical with itself.[21]

This universal 'is free power [*Macht*]; it is itself and takes its other within its embrace, but without *doing violence* to it'.[22] It is 'as absolute negativity . . . both shaper and creator, and because the determination is not a limit but is just as much utterly sublated or posited being, so illusion [*Schein*] is now appearance as the identical'.[23] This universal 'is thus the totality of the concept; it is concrete, and far from being empty, it has through its concept a content, and a content in which it not only maintains itself but one which is its own and immanent in it'.[24]

This concrete universal is not a simple identity. The 'determinateness' is the 'total reflection', the 'double negation' or double illusion. It is the negation of the logic of being, 'shining outwards' or 'reflection-into another', relation to another; and the negation of the logic of essence, 'shining inwards' or 'reflection-into-self', relation to self.[25] Hence the universal is distinguished from and at one with the other, its particularity or intuition.

> Thus even the determinate concept remains within itself infinitely free concept.[26]

> This concept is not empty, nor the intuition blind.[27] The exposition

fully acknowledges the lack of identity of universal and particular, concept and intuition, that the universal

> is a process in which it posits the differences themselves as universal and self-related. They thereby become *fixed*, isolated differences.[28]

The unity of universal and particular is an individual or a totality, a self-related determinateness. The totality or determinateness which is related to others and to itself is actuality.[29] Actuality is thus both determinate and abstract. Determinations become fixed and actuality is no longer united. Its individuality becomes '*posited abstraction*'.[30] Abstraction is both the precondition of the concrete universal and prevents its realization.

'Teleology' and 'Life' continue the exposition of actuality as a law (universal) which is united with the particular. 'Life' appears as the first chapter of the final part of the logic of the concept. In this chapter Hegel repeats some of the points which appeared in the *System of Ethical Life*. The 'life-process' is expounded as need, as feeling, as violence and as appropriation.[31] It is the final attempt to expound the concrete before the exposition from the 'subjective' point of view of the last two chapters.

The exposition of life depends on the exposition of means and end of teleology:

> At this first stage the idea is life: the concept that, distinguished from its objectivity, simple within itself, pervades its objectivity and, as its own end, possesses its means in the objectivity and posits the latter as means, yet is immanent in this means and is there in the realized end that is identical with itself.[32]

A living being contains potentially or in itself what it will become in and for itself, as the seed is potentially the plant, and the plant is potentially many plants.

It may seem odd to have a 'natural' category such as life appear at the end of the subjective logic. This is a way of tempering the reliance on positing, a way of stressing that 'positing' at this stage is an acknow-ledging of actuality as presupposition not an absolute positing of it:

> ... finite, that is, subjective spirit, *makes* for itself the *presupposition* of an objective world, just as life *has* such a presupposition; but its activity consists in sublating this presupposition and converting it into positedness. In this way its reality is for it the objective world, or conversely, the objective world is the ideality in which it cognizes itself.[33]

The overall intention of Hegel's thought is to make a different ethical life possible by providing insight into the displacement of actuality in those dominant philosophies which are assimilated to and reinforce bourgeois law and bourgeois property relations. This is why Hegel's thought has no social import if the absolute cannot be thought.

However, as long as these relations and law prevails the absolute can only be thought by an abstract consciousness and hence any specification of it, as the 'in-itself' is in effect 'for us' and not 'in-itself'. This accounts for the difference between the unconvincing nature of Hegel's attempts to state the absolute by comparison with the powerful speculative rereadings of law.

Hegel had no 'solution' to the contradictions of bourgeois productive and property relations. He searched for a different concept of law but it could only be explicated abstractly. Marx did not resolve these aporias in Hegel's position. He inherited them and returned to a pre-Hegelian position by reading Hegel non-speculatively and by reviving the dichotomies which Hegel had sought to expose as rooted in bourgeois social relations.

A speculative reading of social and philosophical contradictions anticipates and accounts for subsequent non-speculative misreadings of the speculative discourse. Speculative discourse recognizes the difference between concept and reality. But Marx's non-speculative presentation does not anticipate and cannot account for the subsequent fate of the ideas represented.

Have art, religion, ethical life, philosophy come to an end? In each case there are two 'ends': *telos*, the end of art, religion, philosophy as presentation, as the definitive political experience; *finis*, the end of art, (religion, philosophy) as re-presentation of the relation between subject and substance, meaning and configuration, that is, the end of art, (religion, philosophy) as a culture and their assimilation to prevailing formal law.

Was Hegel wrong about art and religion: religion has come to an end, but art, the image, has persisted? Art has been marked by the attempt to avoid Hegel's second end. From the Romantics on, where Hegel's account of art concludes, it may be argued that art has striven, consciously or unconsciously, to be politically effective but has been subverted in this ambition by the actuality of bourgeois society which has re-formed its vocation. Art with such ambitions is a culture and hence not over in Hegel's second sense of 'end', although it may not achieve its 'end' in the first sense of *telos*. But there is no time for any new cultures in Hegel's thought except for the time of philosophy and that was not to be a culture but a *telos*: a presentation of political experience.

Hegel underestimated the power of art in bourgeois society to renew itself at least as a culture, to re-form itself as different modes of representing the contradiction between meaning and configuration. He thus failed to provide any account of the experience afforded by the images (*Vorstellungen*) of such a culture, or any account of the different forms of non-classical beauty which are powerful in such a society.

Hegel was not wrong to distinguish the end of art from the end of religion. For 'religion' in modern, bourgeois society means the formation of subjective disposition in general, whereas art means its formation in a limited and specific realm. Hegel thereby wished to draw attention to the problem of combining reformation, the transformation of subjective disposition, with revolution. The prevalent formal law determines subjectivity or subjective disposition and the illusions of subjective freedom and of subjective bondage. For any revolution to succeed it must acknowledge and re-form this aspect of ethical life even though it is de-formed and hidden by bourgeois law.

When Marx called for the 'end of philosophy'[34] he meant both that philosophy as theory must be realized in practice (*telos*) and that the time of philosophy as passive, contemplative, autonomous theory was over (*finis*), Both of these points are formulated by Marx as critiques of Feuerbach and are already conceded by Hegel. Hegel showed that the concept of reason in Kant and Fichte was not autonomous and self-evident but a re-presentation of subjectivity determined by bourgeois property relations and law. Hegel's thought was directed against the dichotomy of theory and practice for it is precisely this distinction which prevents the realization of philosophy and condemns it to being the unrealizable *concept* of unity or freedom which is imposed or which dominates. Marx draws on the distinction between theory and practice in a pre-Hegelian or in a Feuerbachian manner and thus presupposes the structure of the thinking which he is rejecting. It is the social determination of philosophy not its specious autonomy which makes philosophy abstract and powerful, able to suppress intuition or the particular.

In Hegel's terms the 'end' of philosophy would mean that it is not yet politically formative, that it is not yet time for its realization (*telos*). Hence this philosophy, too, becomes a *Sollen*. It may then be imposed in a way which reinforces existing law, and which suppresses whatever that law suppresses (*finis*). Or it may be imposed against existing law and aspire to an end (*telos*) but only achieve a vocation or culture. Philosophy in this case re-presents the lack of identity or contradiction between subject and substance and seeks to re-form the lack of identity on the basis of its own re-presentation of it.

In both cases Hegel's thought has been read non-speculatively. In the first case, this is to derive the right Hegelian reading, the real is rational, which reinforces law and religion. In the second case, this is to derive the left Hegelian reading, the rational is real, which seeks to abolish the state and religion. Speculative discourse was thus turned back into the discourse of abstract opposition.

Hegel was not utopian in thinking that the time of philosophy had come, for he knew that the time of philosophy had not come. He acknowledged the domination of abstract thinking especially in its Fichtean mode, the 'cobwebs' at the portals of philosophy. He knew, too, that a consequence of the ineffectiveness of his own thought would be the continued domination of Fichteanism. Lukács was thus very close to Hegel when he argued in his discussion of 'The Antinomies of Bourgeois Thought' in *History and Class Consciousness* that Fichte is the supreme representative of bourgeois thought.[35] But the details of Lukács' argument are quite different from Hegel's position.

The Repetition of Sociology

It is thus Hegel himself who provides an account of the 'historical barriers' which stand in the way of rereading him, an account of the continually renewed victory of Fichtean reflection.[36]

The two main kinds of neo-Kantianism in sociology met at the Fichtean station on the road between Kant and Hegel.[37] The foundations of this sociological Fichteanism were laid in the Marburg and Heidelberg Schools of neo-Kantianism.

The Marburg School replaced the primacy of Kant's processes of discursive consciousness by an *original unity* out of which both subjective consciousness and its objects arise, or, to put it in Fichtean terms, which is the precondition of the positing of the ego and the positing of the non-ego. For the Marburg School the relation between consciousness and its objects is no longer an epistemological question. It pertains to the different realms of scientific constitution whose validity is presupposed. Thus the critical philosophy becomes a *Geltungslogik*.

The Heidelberg School replaced Kantian justification of objective validity by the primacy of 'values' which transcend the spatio-temporal forms of intuition of discursive consciousness, or, to put it in Fichtean terms, by the primacy of underivable, original *faith*. The critical, epistemological question is destroyed by giving practical reason primacy over theoretical reason. However, this primacy of practical reason in the Heidelberg School, as in Fichte, reproduces the dichotomy of theoretical and practical reason and does not transform it.

The sociological metacritiques of Marburg and of Heidelberg neo-Kantianism inherited and drew out this latent Fichteanism in the opposition between the structural metacritique of validity (Durkheim) and the action-oriented metacritique of values (Weber).

The sociological antinomy of the primacy of validity over value and the primacy of value over validity, of Durkheim and Weber, of structure and action, has been reproduced time and time again. The various attempts to incorporate both poles of the antinomy within a systematic framework have also reproduced it.[38]

The sociological antinomy of action and structure reproduces the Fichtean antinomy of the positing ego and the posited non-ego. The non-ego is the deed or the structure, the *Tathandlung*, which is initially there and considered to be independent of consciousness. The ego is the action, the *Handlung*, which has insight into its own agency as the highest 'fact of consciousness', and thus comes to know the non-ego as its own positing. The idea that something is independent of consciousness, not posited, not put there, can be seen in Fichte to imply the idea of an agency which posits it, which puts it there. The opposition between structure and agency, or between not-posited and positing is abstract. It is a dichotomy the poles of which collapse into each other: the not-posited becomes indistinguishable from the positing. But the dichotomy is perpetually reconstituted, for an abstract opposition is a bad infinite which is therefore repeated but never sublated or transcended.

Within Marxist theory, too, the development of subjective or voluntarist Marxism and of structuralist Marxism has reproduced the same antinomy and this has brought both kinds of Marxism into the confines of sociological legitimacy. The more recent revival of a philosophy of social science which addresses itself to the question 'How is social science possible' and understands itself as a 'transcendental realism' which is securing the basis for a Marxist or a non-Marxist science is a repetition of a traditional *Geltungslogik* which assumes the *validity* of scientific realms.[39]

This Fichtean antinomy, which is repeatedly established by sociology, persists because its historical and social preconditions persist, the actuality which it refuses to acknowledge. The principle of unity in sociology, its concept of law, reproduces and hence reinforces the dominant formally universal laws which correspond to particular property relations. The relation of society to transformative activity, to nature, determines the law and defines the realm of personality and subjectivity in that society.

The principle of unity or social cohesion in structuralism, collective conscience (Durkheim) or functions, pattern maintenance (Parsons), is posited as underivable and absolute, as independent of and prior to subjective meanings and actions. The 'individual' is posited as the opposite pole of this collective determining force. The relation bet-ween the *determinans* and the individual remains inexplicable for the sake of maintaining the *sui generis* status of the collectivity. The 'individual' can only be subordinated to, or dominated by, the collec-tivity or structures. The postulate of social cohesion is maintained in the face of its perceived absence which is conceptualized as anomie or as dysfunctions. As a postulate, 'social cohesion' reproduces the real domination of individuals but cannot explain it because the postulate is formal and empty. It is a mere postulate, and lack of cohesion can only be postulated too. This sociology reproduces the contradiction of a formally universal law which fixes arbitrary and unequal relations between persons conceived as agents by positing abstract collective postulates. The postulate of social cohesion excludes any reference to actuality as the relation of society to its transformative activity, and to the definition of law which results from that activity.

Prima facie, action theory refuses a principle of unity as such, and transforms any apparent institutional unity into the discourse of action oriented to subjectively-meaningful ends, or, into the sum of legitima-tions. Social reality is posited by actors and no actuality outside that positing is acknowledged. This subjective emphasis is blind to the real determinants of action or positing: transformative activity, property relations and law. It reproduces the subjective illusion of free, uncon-strained action which is the correlate of a formal law which 'liberates' a residual realm of subjectivity by dominating the rest of social activity. Social reality is read as a collection of intended meanings, but there can be no examination of how meaning may re-present an actuality which is inverted in that meaning. 'Subjective meaning' can only re-present actuality, it cannot present it. Thus the inversion of actuality in the media of re-presentation should be the point of departure. Action theory makes meaning into its absolute, its principle of unity, and thereby reproduces the illusion of subjectivity, the unconditioned ego which 'determines' its own boundaries and denies its presupposition: its relation to actuality.

Structural sociology is 'empty', action theory is 'blind'. The former imposes abstract postulates on social reality and confirms by simplifying the contradictions of dominant law. The latter confirms social reality as a mass of random meanings in its immediate mode of representation. The lack in both cases of any references to transformative activity, property relations, law and the corresponding media of representation results in the absolutizing of the unconditioned actor on the one hand and of the totally conditioned agent on the other.

If actuality is not thought, then thinking has no social import. The suppression of actuality results in sociologies which confirm dominant law and representation and which have no means of knowing or recognizing the real relations which determine that law and the media of re-presentation.

The Culture and Fate of Marxism

Marx produces a Fichtean reading of Hegel's system as the unconditioned absolute idea which pours forth nature, which does not recognize but creates determination, but presents in his turn a dichotomous Fichtean actuality which is divided into activity and nature, which is either created by the act or is external to the act.[40]

There are passages in Marx's writings and in Hegel's writings where it seems that history has a natural beginning, the natural ethical life of the family, and an utopian end, the realization of freedom, when universal and particular interests are reconciled in a community united with nature. There are also passages in Hegel's writings where the abstractness of the beginning and the end is emphasized, and passages in Marx where the idea of any immediately accessible nature is undermined, and where the idea of any 'end' is unstated, unjustified, not pre-judged:

> But man is not only a natural being; he is a *human*, natural being; that is, he is a being for himself and hence a *species being*, as which he must confirm and express himself as much in his being as in his knowing. Consequently, *human* objects are not natural objects as they

immediately present themselves, nor is *human* sense as it immediately and objectively *is human* sensibility, human objectivity. Neither objective nor subjective nature is immediately presented in a form adequate to the *human* being.[41]

This problem with the beginning and the end, the problem of nature and the natural, is the problem of thinking the absolute or actuality, or of thinking the relation between activity and actuality.

The first thesis on Feuerbach displays clearly a problem in Marx's presentation of actuality:

> The chief defect of all previous materialism (including Feuerbach's) is that the object, actuality, sensuousness is conceived only in the form of the *object* or *intuition*, but not as *sensuous human activity*, praxis, not subjectively. Hence in opposition to materialism, the *active* side was developed by idealism – but only abstractly since idealism naturally does not know actual, sensuous activity as such.[42]

The thesis has an antinomical form: materialism/idealism; actuality as object/actuality as active, as subjectivity, as praxis; theory/praxis. Marx's own position is presented by taking activity from idealism, and sensuousness from materialism to compound 'actual sensuous activity' as actuality. In this thesis Marx reinforces the abstract oppositions between idealism and materialism, theory and praxis, which he claims to be transcending. In the fourth thesis on Feuerbach Marx says that theory 'finds the secrets' and praxis 'nullifies' and 'revolutionizes'.[43] This is a Kantian or Fichtean opposition of theory and practice. It is not the Hegelian position according to which theory re-cognizes the intuition or object which practice suppresses. In the first thesis Marx dissolves actuality in activity, and 'materialism' consists solely in the 'sensuousness' of activity. This reference to sensuousness is abstract, for the notion of activity as that of a '*human*, natural being' already includes it. Any reference to sensuousness or to the sentient being can only be the first stage in the exposition of productive and social relations which develop from that stage as, for example, in the *System of Ethical Life* or the *Phenomenology*.

When Marx is not self-conscious about his relation to Hegel's philosophy or to Feuerbach's materialism he does not think actuality by means of Kantian and Fichtean dichotomies:

> For this third object I am thus an *other actuality* than it, that is, *its*

object. To assume a being which is not the object of another is thus to suppose that *no* objective being exists.[44]

This captures what Hegel means by actuality or spirit. But when Marx desires to dissociate himself from Hegel's actuality, 'the absolute spirit which nullifies the object', and from Feuerbach's 'passive' materialism, he relies on and affirms abstract dichotomies between being and consciousness, theory and practice, etc.

Marx's reading of Hegel overlooks the discourse or logic of the speculative proposition. He refuses to see the lack of identity in Hegel's thought, and therefore tries to establish his own discourse of lack of identity by using the ordinary proposition. But instead of developing a logic or discourse of lack of identity he produced an ambiguous dichotomy of activity/nature which relies on a natural beginning and an utopian end.

'... the critique of religion is the prerequisite of every critique.'[45] Marx read the speculative proposition of the identity of the state and religion as an ordinary proposition. The legitimacy of religion must be exposed and related to its base in the class structure on which the state rests, to the ensemble of social relations, and not to some eternal human essence (Feuerbach). However, Marx's position is as abstract and ahistorical as Feuerbach's. The referring of religion to productive relations remains merely a reference. Marx never examined the relation between historically-specific productive relations and particular religions. For the relation would always be the same once the general proposition is accepted that religion masks and legitimizes prevailing social relations. Similarly, Marx saw the appeal of art as eternal and ahistorical and considered that the mystery of the universal appeal of Greek art needed to be explained.[46]

Marx's failure to understand Hegel's actuality meant that he did not develop any notion of subjectivity. Subjects are merely 'bearers' of economic functions, such as, 'capitalist' and 'worker', and the remainder of human personality is *directly* reduced to this defining function. For Hegel, the social and legal definition of people *indirectly* liberated and enslaved the remainder of human 'personality'. Hence art and religion could be read as re-presentation of an inverse relation to law, property relations and productive activity. The thesis that religion or art serves and legitimizes prevailing social relations posits an abstract identity between the relations and the superstructure by comparison with the speculative exposition of religion and art as media of re-presentation of those relations. For re-presentation is always misrepresentation, lack of identity.

This accounts for the weakness in Marx's concept of ideology. Marx's thinking about the relation between productive relations and other social institutions is couched in abstract and historically general oppositions between base and superstructure, being and consciousness. This prevented him from developing a comprehensive view of actuality and its re-presentation. This is why the theory of commodity fetishism has become central to the neo-Marxist theory of domination, aesthetics, and ideology. The theory of commodity fetishism is the most speculative moment in Marx's exposition of capital. It comes nearest to demonstrating in the historically-specific case of commodity producing society how substance is ((mis)-represented as) subject, how necessary illusion arises out of productive activity.

For Hegel, 'natural consciousness' is subjective consciousness which does not know its subjectivity and does not know that its subjectivity is determined by the prevalent relation to nature and activity. Natural consciousness is presented in its relations and misapprehensions as individual sense-consciousness, as related to one other (master-slave), as political consciousness, as religious consciousness, as aesthetic consciousness and as abstract philosophical consciousness, at different points in history, as the 'complete forms of untrue consciousness in its untruth'.[47] What is presented at each point is an aspect of the formation of *our* consciousness. The presentation has a phenomenological, that is, an educative, a *political* intent.

Marx did not appreciate the politics of Hegel's presentation, the politics of a phenomenology which aims to re-form consciousness in a way which would not itself be re-formed. Phenomenology acknowledges the actuality which determines the formation of consciousness. The recognition of actuality takes the form of a presentation of the various attempts at reform and revolution which displace the real determinants of consciousness and action and therefore do not effectively change those determinants but reinforce them. This includes a presentation of illusions of acting in the communal interest which turn out to be forms of individualism, a frenzy of self-deceit; a presentation of the different possibilities of change in societies without formal law and in societies with formal law, and of the different ways change might be perverted in each case; a presentation of the illusion that consciousness is reality (abstract materialism) and that a change in the former, *ipso facto*, means a change in the latter.

Marx's notion of political education was less systematic than this. 'It is not enough that thought strive to actualize itself; actuality must itself strive toward thought.'[48] The opposition between thought and reality is abstract and unexplicated here, with the result that the unity of thought and reality is an ought, a *Sollen*. Lukács' *History and Class Consciousness* is an attempt to give *Capital* a phenomenological form: to read Marx's analysis of capital as the potential consciousness of a universal class. But Lukács' emphasis on change in consciousness as *per se* revolutionary, separate from the analysis of change in capitalism, gives his appeal to the proletariat or the party the status of an appeal to a Fichtean will. The question of the relation between *Capital* and politics is thus not an abstract question about the relation between theory and practice, but a phenomenological question about the relationship between acknowledgement of actuality and the possibility of change. This is why the theory of commodity fetishism, the presentation of a contradiction between substance and subject, remains more impressive than any abstract statements about the relation between theory and practice or between capitalist crisis and the formation of revolutionary consciousness. It acknowledges actuality and its misrepresentation as consciousness.

Missing from Marx's *oeuvre* is any concept of culture, of formation and re-formation (*Bildung*). There is no idea of a vocation which may be assimilated or re-formed by the determinations or law which it fails to acknowledge or the strength of which it underestimates. Because Marx did not relate actuality to representation and subjectivity, his account of structural change in capitalism is abstractly related to possible change in consciousness. This resulted in gross oversimplification regarding the likelihood and the inhibition of change. This is not the argument that Marx's predictions about the conditions of the formation of revolutionary consciousness were wrong. It is an argument to the effect that the very concept of consciousness and, *a fortiori*, of revolutionary consciousness, are insufficiently established in Marx.

This absence of any account of the formation of 'natural consciousness' or 'subjective disposition' in its modern, individualistic, moral, religious, aesthetic, political and philosophical misapprehensions has meant that Marxism is especially susceptible to re-formation. For revolutionary consciousness is subjective consciousness, just as natural consciousness is, that is, it is a determination or re-presentation of substance, ethical life, actuality, in the form of an abstract consciousness. An abstract consciousness is one which *knows* that it is not united with ethical life. It is determined by abstract law to know itself as formally free, identical and empty. It is only such an abstract consciousness which can be potentially revolutionary, which can conceive the ambition to acquire a universal content or determination which is not that of the bourgeois property law which bestowed universality and subjectivity on it in the first place.

The very notion of Marx*ism*, that is, that Marx's ideas are not realized, implies that Marxism is a culture, the very thing of which it has no idea. Furthermore Marxism has been 'applied' or imposed as a revolutionary theory both in societies with no formal, bourgeois law and in societies with formal bourgeois law. Marx's use of 'alienation' as characteristic of capitalist society has obscured the force of Hegel's historically-specific use of alienation to present the antinomies of revolutionary intention in *pre-bourgeois* societies.

Strictly speaking, Hegel only analysed cultures in pre-bourgeois societies. In bourgeois, capitalist society the cultures of art and religion culminating in the culture of the French Revolution were over. Philosophy is attributed the vocation which other forms of re-presentation held previously, and, as we have seen, in places Hegel intimated that philosophy might be equally perverted, 'awkward in its conduct', and in others he seemed to be announcing its success.

Both Hegel's and Marx's discourse has been misread and has been either assimilated to the prevalent law or lawlessness or imposed on it. Hegel anticipated this, but Marx, who made the relation of theory and practice so central, misunderstood the relation between his discourse and the possibility of a transformed politics.

This is to point to a flaw not in Marx's analysis of *Capital*, but in any presentation of that analysis as a comprehensive account of *capitalism*, and in any pre-judged, imposed 'realization' of that theory, any using it *as a theory, as Marxism*. This is the utility which Hegel analysed in the French Revolution: an instrumental use of a 'materialist' theory rests in fact on the idealist assumption that social reality is an object and that its definition depends on revolutionary consciousness. This is to fail to acknowledge that reality is ethical, and it is to risk recreating a terror, or reinforcing lawlessness, or strengthening bourgeois law in its universality and arbitrariness.

This critique of Marxism itself yields the project of a critical Marxism.

The Hegelian exposition of the re-formation of a vocation in a society in which reflection dominates is an exposition of the perpetually renewed victory of forms of bourgeois cultural domination or hegemony. It provides the possibility of re-examining the changing relation between Marx's presentation of the contradictions of Capital and a comprehensive exposition of capitalism – of capitalism itself as a culture in both its formative and destructive potencies.

To expound capitalism as a culture is thus not to abandon the classical Marxist interests in political economy and in revolutionary practice. On the contrary, a presentation of the contradictory relations between Capital and culture is the only way to link the analysis of the economy to comprehension of the conditions for revolutionary practice.

NOTES

For texts and translations used, see *Select Bibliography*, p. 249
Where I have retranslated or altered the translation of a passage I have indicated
this by the addition of (G.R.).

1. The Antinomies of Sociological Reason

1 For a different discussion of neo-Kantianism and sociology, see Andrew
Arato, 'The Neo-Idealist Defence of Subjectivity', *Telos*, 21 (Fall 1974),,
108–61.

2 For overall accounts, see Traugott Konstantin Oesterreich, *Die deutsche Philosophie des XIX Jahrhunderts und der Gegenwart, Friedrich Ueberwegs Grundriss
der Geschichte der Philosophie*, Pt IV, Berlin, E. S. Mittler & Sohn, 1923;
Willy Moog, *Die deutsche Philosophie des 20. Jahrhunderts in ihren Hauptrich-
tungen und ihren Grundproblemen*, Stuttgart, Ferdinand Encke, 1922.

3 Jacob Friedrich Fries (1773–1843), a colleague of Hegel's at the University of
Berlin, defended a psychological interpretation of Kant.

4 *Critique of Pure Reason*, 1781, 1787. I use the standard A and B references so
that any edition may be consulted. B116–17.

5 *Ibid.*, B120.

6 *Ibid.*, B122.

7 *Ibid.*

8 *Ibid.*, B118.

9 *Ibid.*, B195.

10 *Ibid.*, B196.

11 *Prolegomena to Any Future Metaphysics that will be able to Present Itself as a
Science*, 1783, sec. 20.

12 *Ibid.*, sec. 20n. (G.R.).

13 *Critique of Pure Reason*, B351.

14 *Ibid.*

15 *Ibid.*, A105.

16 *Ibid.*, A108.

17 *Ibid.*, B140 and 133.

18 *Ibid.*, B152-3-7.

19 *Ibid.*, B164, my italics.

20 *Ibid.*, B197.

21 Nicolai Hartmann, *Die Philosophie des deutschen Idealismus* (1923-9), Berlin,
Walter de Gruyter, 1960, Abschnitt 1, 'Kantianer und Antikantianer', pp.
8–39; Richard Kroner, *Von Kant bis Hegel* (1921–4), Tübingen, J. C. B. Mohr,
1961, pp. 303–61.

22 For example Alois Riehl, *Der philosophische Kritizismus und seine Bedeutungen
für die positive Wissenschaft*, 2 vols, Leipzig, Wilhelm Engelman, 1876; Paul

Natorp, *Die logischen Grundlagen der exakten Wissenschaften*, Leipzig, B. G. Teuchner, 1910; Raymund Schmidt (ed.), *Die Philosophie der Gegenwart in Selbstdarstellungen*, 4 vols, Leipzig, Felix Meiner, 1922–3.

23 Compare Talcott Parsons' famous remarks on Spencer, in *The Structure of Social Action* (1937), vol. I, New York, Free Press, 1968, p. 3, quoting Crane Brinton, *English Political Thought in the Nineteenth Century*, London, Ernest Benn, 1933, pp. 226–7.

24 See Paul Grimley Kuntz' Introduction to George Santayana, *Lotze's System of Philosophy* (1889), Bloomington, Indiana University Press, 1971, pp. 3–105.

25 Rudolf Hermann Lotze, *System der Philosophie*, I, *Logik Drei Bücher vom Denken, vom Untersuchen, und vom Erkennen*, 1874; II, *Metaphysik*, 1879. I have used the 1928 edition of the *Logik*, edited and with an Introduction by Georg Misch, Leipzig, Felix Meiner. English translation edited by Bernard Bosanquet, *Lotze's System of Philosophy*, Pt I, *Logic in Three Books of Thought, of Investigation and of Knowledge*, 2 vols; Pt II, *Metaphysic in Three Books, Ontology, Cosmology and Psychology*, Oxford, Clarendon Press, 1888, 2nd edn.

26 *Logik*, vol. II, sec. 321, p. 521, tr. p. 220.

27 *Ibid.*, sec. 316, p. 512, tr. p. 208.

28 *Ibid.*, sec. 317, p. 513, tr. p. 210.

29 *Ibid.*, sec. 316, pp. 512–13, tr. p. 209.

30 This aspect of Lotze's argument was developed in his earlier work, *Mikrokosmos. Ideen zur Naturgeschichte und Geschichte der Menschheit*, 3 vols, 1856–64, Leipzig, E. Hirzel, 5th edn, 1896; tr. *Microcosmos. An Essay Concerning Man and His Relation to the World*, 2 vols, Elizabeth Hamilton and E. E. Constance Jones, Edinburgh, T. & T. Clark, 4th edn, 1894.

31 *Microcosmos*, vol. II p. 265, tr. vol. I p. 244 and vol. I p. 447, tr. vol. I p. 396.

32 *Ibid.*

33 *Ibid.*, vol. II p. 267, tr. vol. I pp. 245–6.

34 *Ibid.*, vol. II p. 269, tr. vol. II pp. 247–8.

35 *Critique of Pure Reason*, B372.

36 See Georg Misch, Introduction to Lotze, *Logik*, pp. LXI–LXIII.

37 *Microcosmos*, vol. III p. 561, tr. vol. II p. 670.

38 *Ibid.*, vol. III p. 461, tr. vol. II p. 575 (G.R.).

39 Hermann Cohen, *System der Philosophie*, Pt I, *Logik der reinen Erkenntnis*, Berlin, Bruno Cassirer, 1902, 'Einleitung und Disposition', pp. 1–64. Compare Paul Natorp, *Philosophie in Selbstdarstellungen*, vol. I, 161–81 and Natorp, 'Das Problem einer Logik der exakten Wissenschaften', *Die Logischen Grundlagen der exakten Wissenschaft*, pp. 1–34.

40 *Critique of Pure Reason*, B174.

41 Cohen, *Logik der reinen Erkenntnis*, p. 6.

42 *Ibid.*, pp. 11, 24.

43 *Ibid.*, p. 28.

44 *Ibid.*, p. 25.

45 *Ibid.*, p. 12.

46 *Ibid.*, p. 15.

48 *Ibid.*, pp. 45, 56–64.

49 *Ibid.*, pp. 38–9.

50 *Ibid.*, p. 40.

51 *Critique of Pure Reason*, A126.

52 Heinrich Rickert, *Der Gegenstand der Erkenntnis Einführung in die Transzen-dentalphilosophie*, first published 1892, substantially rewritten, 1915 and 1928. I have used the 1928 edition, Tübingen, J. C. B. Mohr, pp. 15–22.

53 *Ibid.*, pp. 209, 211–12.

54 *Ibid.*, pp. 6, 19, 65n.

55 *Ibid.*, pp. 207, 202.

56 *Ibid.*, p. 202.

57 *Ibid.*, p. 207.

58 *Ibid.*, p. 235.

59 Rickert objected to this interpretation, p. 62; for an example, see W. Moog, *Die deutsche Philosophie des 20. Jahrhunderts*, pp. 241–8.

60 Rickert, *Der Gegenstand der Erkenntnis*, p. 215.

61 *Ibid.*, p. 213.

62 *Ibid.*

63 *Ibid.*, p. 218.

64 *Ibid.*, p. 206.

65 See Marianne Weber, *Max Weber: A Biography*, 1926, tr. Harry Zohn, New York, John Wiley, 1975; Paul Honigsheim, *On Max Weber*, tr. Joan Tytina, New York, The Free Press, 1968.

66 Steven Lukes, *Emile Durkheim His Life and Work A Historical and Critical Study*, London, Allen Lane, 1973, pp. 54–8, 358.

67 Emile Durkheim and Marcel Mauss, *Primitive Classification*, 1903, tr. Rodney Needham, London, Routledge, 1970, pp. 7–8; Durkheim, 'The Dualism of Human Nature', 1914, tr. Charles Bland, in Kurt H. Wolff (ed.), *Essays on Sociology and Philosophy by Emile Durkheim et al*, New York, Harper, 1964, pp. 325–40; Durkheim, *The Elementary Forms of the Religious Life*, 1912, Paris, Presses Universitaires de France, 1968; tr. Joseph Ward Swain, London, Allen & Unwin, 1968, pp. 12–28, tr. pp. 9–20.

68 'The Dualism of Human Nature', pp. 334–5.

69 *The Elementary Forms of the Religious Life*, p. 20, tr. p. 14.

70 Durkheim, *Sociology and Philosophy*, 1898–1911, Paris, Presses Universitaires de France, 1979; tr. David Pocock, New York, The Free Press, 1974, pp. 58, 103–4, tr. pp. 41, 81.

71 *Ibid.*, pp. 73, 74, tr. pp. 54, 55.

72 *Ibid.*, 'Elle est, pour les consciences individuelles un objectif transcendent', p. 73. This is utterly mistranslated in the English, p. 54.

73 *Ibid.*, p. 70, tr. pp. 51–2.

74 *Critique of Practical Reason*, Pt I, Bk II Chs. IV–VI.

75 *The Elementary Forms of the Religious Life*, p. 20, tr. p. 14.

76 *Ibid.*, pp. 20–1, p. 15.

77 *Ibid.*

78 *Ibid.*, p. 25, tr. p. 18.

79 *Ibid.*, pp. 631–2, tr. p. 442.

80 *Ibid.*, p. 26, tr. p. 18.

81 *Ibid.*, p. 27, tr. p. 19.

82 *Ibid.*, pp. 23-4, 27, tr. pp. 17-18, 19.
83 *Sociology and Philosophy*, pp. 102-4, tr. pp. 80-1.
84 *Ibid.*, pp. 49-50, tr. p. 34.
85 *Ibid.*, pp. 94-5, tr. p. 73.
86 'Die Objektivität sozialwissenschaftlicher und sozial-politscher Erkenntnis', 1904, *Gesammelte Aufsätze zur Wissenschaftslehre*, Tübingen, J. C. B. Mohr, 1973; tr. 'Objectivity in Social Science and Social Policy', *Max Weber. The Methodology of the Social Sciences*, Edward A. Shils and Harry A. Finch, New York, The Free Press, 1949, p. 175, tr. p. 96 (G.R.).
87 *Ibid.*, p. 152, tr. p. 55, italics in the original.
88 *Ibid.*, p. 155, tr. p. 55 (G.R.), italics in the original.
89 *Ibid.*, p. 180, tr. p. 81 (G.R.).
90 *Ibid.*
91 *Ibid.*, p. 152, tr. p. 55.
92 *Ibid.*, p. 199, tr. p. 97, italics in the original.
93 *Ibid.*, p. 201, tr. p. 99, italics in the original.
94 *Ibid.*, p. 205, tr. p. 103.
95 *Ibid.*, p. 194, tr. p. 93.
96 'Kritische Studien auf dem Gebiet der Kulturwissenschaftlichen Logik', 1906, *Gesammelte Aufsätze zur Wissenschaftslehre*, tr. 'The Logic of the Cultural Sciences', *Methodology of the Social Sciences*, p. 275, tr. p. 173.
97 *Critique of Pure Reason*, B699.
98 Weber, *Economy and Society*, 1921, tr. Guenther Roth and Claus Widdith (eds), Berkeley, University of California Press, 1978, vol. 1, Pt 1, Ch. 1, secs 5–7.
99 *Ibid.*
100 *Ibid.*
101 Georg Simmel, *Soziologie Untersuchungen über die Formen der Vergesellschaftung*, Leipzig, Duncker & Humblot, 1908.
102 Leopold von Wiese, *Systematic Sociology on the Basis of the Beziehungslehre and Gebildelehre of Leopold von Wiese*, adapted and amplified by Howard Becker, New York, Wiley, 1932.
103 Parsons distinguishes his position from a Weberian methodological position by construing ideal-types as 'fictions'. He calls his own position by contrast 'analytical realism'. However, Parsons' view that the general concepts of science 'adequately grasp' aspects of the external world, and his persistent warnings against the 'reification' of abstract concepts, or the 'fallacy of mis-placed concreteness' are more accurately Weberian than his presentation of ideal-types as 'fictions', *The Structure of Social Action*, 1937, New York, The Free Press, 1968, vol. II, pp. 730, 476-7, 728, 757, 761, vol. I, 29.
104 On the metacritical argument, see Manfred Riedel, 'Einleitung', in Wilhelm Dilthey, *Der Aufbau der geschichtlichen Welt in den Geisteswissenschaften*, 1910, Frankfurt a.M., Suhrkamp, 1970, pp. 9–80; and Peter Krausser, *Kritik der endlichen Vernunft Dilthey's Revolution der allgemeinen Wissenschafts-und Handlungstheorie*, Frankfurt a.M., Suhrkamp, 1968.
105 The title of Hans-Georg Gadamer's major work 'Truth and Method' provides a caption for this argument, *Truth and Method*, Tübingen, J. C. B. Mohr,

1960; tr. London, Sheed & Ward, 1975. The first chapter of Walter Benjamin's *The Origin of German Tragic Drama*, 1928, is organized around the same
dichotomy, *Gesammelte Schriften*, Rolf Tiedemann and Hermann Schweppen-
häuser (eds), Frankfurt a.M., 1974, vol I. 1, tr. John Osborne, London, New
Left Books, 1977.

106 See n.104.

107 Mannheim's doctoral dissertation 'Structural Analysis of Epistemology',
1922, consisted of an attempt to do justice to both the question of validity and
the historical process, without reducing one to the other. He surveyed Lotze,
the Marburg and Heidelberg Schools on the problem of validity developed
as a critique of epistemology. By *Ideology and Utopia*, 1929, he had resolved
the question of validity and history by the development of a historical metacritique of validity. He preferred to characterize his 'non-evaluative conception of ideology' as 'ontological' in order to distinguish it from Weberian
sociology of values. Weber's view of cultural life as 'a conscious choice
between values' is contrasted with his own 'reference to the concrete situation
to which values have relevance and in which they are valid'. Mannheim refers
in the note to Lask's '*Hingelten*' in order to emphasize variation in the validity
of categories. See Paul Kesskemeti (ed.), *Essays on Sociology and Social Psychology*, London, Routledge, 1969, pp. 15–73, and *Ideology and Utopia*, London,
Routledge, 1966, pp. 72–3 and n., 74–8, 78–83.

108 These remarks refer to *Sein und Zeit*, 1927, where Heidegger criticizes the
neo-Kantian philosophy of validity for its ambiguity, and for debasing the
question of being. He points out how, since Lotze, 'validity' has been understood in three senses: as a form of actuality opposed to 'psychical' judgement;
as the meaning of the judgement in reference to its object; and as a norm for
everyone who judges rationally, *Sein und Zeit*, Tübingen, Niemeyer, 1972;
tr. *Being and Time*, John Macquarrie and Edward Robinson, Oxford, Basil
Blackwell, 1967, pp. 155–6, tr. p. 198.

109 Gadamer, *Truth and Method*, see n. 105, and 'Hermeneutics and Social
Science', *Cultural Hermeneutics*, IV (1975), 307–16.

110 See especially *Logical Investigations*, 1900, tr. J. N. Findlay, London, Routledge, 1970, vol. 1, pp. 214ff. and *passim*.

111 *Critique of Pure Reason*, B197, A111.

112 Compare Hegel, *Wissenschaft der Logic*, I, 70, tr. 72.

113 Jürgen Habermas, *Knowledge and Human Interests*, Frankfurt a.M.,
Suhrkamp, 1968, tr. Jeremy J. Shapiro, London, Heinemann, 1972, p. 202n.
tr. p. 340.

114 Alfred Schutz, *The Phenomenology of the Social World*, 1932, tr. George
Walsch and Frederick Lehnert, Evanston, North Western University Press,
1967.

115 Georg Simmel, *Die Probleme der Geschichtsphilosophie Eine Erkenntnistheoret-
ische Studie*, Leipzig, Duncker & Humblot, 1892, tr. *The Problems of the
Philosophy of History: an Epistemological essay*, 2nd edn 1905, Guy Oakes, New
York, The Free Press, 1977.

116 See n. 101.

117 Simmel, *Hauptprobleme der Philosophie*, 1910, Berlin, Walter de Gruyter,

1964, pp. 110-12. Plato's distinction between the Forms and empirical reality is usually known as the 'two-worlds theory'.

118 *Ibid.*, pp. 113-16.

119 See, for example, 'On the Concept and Tragedy of Culture', 1911, tr. K. P. Elzkorn, *Conflict in Modern Culture and Other Essays*, New York, Teachers College, 1968, pp. 27-46; and 'Wandel der Kulturformen' in *Brücke und Tür*, Michael Landmann (ed.), Stuttgart, K. F. Koehler, 1957, pp. 98-104.

120 See 'How is Society Possible?', the introductory chapter to *Soziologie* (1908), tr. Kurt M. Wolff, in *Georg Simmel 1858-1918: A Collection of Essays with Translations and a Bibliography*, K. H. Wolff (ed.), Athens Ohio University Press, 1959 pp. 337-56.

121 *Ibid.*, p. 338.

122 *Ibid.*

123 *Ibid.*

124 *Ibid.*, 340-2.

125 'On the Concept and Tragedy of Culture', p. 27.

126 Georg Simmel, *Philosophie des Geldes*, 1900, Berlin, Duncker & Humblot, 1958; tr. *The Philosophy of Money*, Tom Bottomore and David Frisby, London, Routledge, 1978, p. 7, tr. p. 62.

127 See Frisby's discussion of Simmel's critics, 'Introduction to the Translation', *ibid.*, pp. 1-49.

128 *Ibid.*, p. 15, tr. p. 69 (G.R.).

129 *Ibid.*, p. 16, tr. p. 69.

130 *Ibid.*, pp. 508-11, tr. pp. 451-3.

131 'Wandel der Kulturformen', p. 98.

132 *The Philosophy of Money*, p. 33, tr. p. 81.

133 See Hegel, *Vorlesungen über die Geschichte der Philosophie*, III, 329-86.

134 'Heidelberger Philosophie der Kunst (1912-1914)', and 'Heidelberger Ästhetik (1916-1918)', *Frühe Schriften zur Ästhetik*, vols I & II, *Georg Lukács Werke*, vols 16 & 17, Darmstadt, Luchterhand, 1979. Only one section of this was published in Lukács' lifetime, 'Die Subjekt-Objekt Beziehung in der Aesthetik', *Logos* (1918), 1-39; vol. 17, p. 11.

135 Kant, *Critique of Judgement*, Introduction, sec. IV.

136 Lukács, *Logos* (1918), 2-8.

137 'Phänomenologische Skizze des schöpferischen und receptiren Verhaltens', *Werke*, vol. 16, 43-150.

138 *Logos* (1918), 39.

139 Lukács, 'Emil Lask', *Kantstudien*, XXII (1913), 349-70, especially 354.

140 *History and Class Consciousness*, 1923, 'Fruhschriften', *Georg Lukács Werke*, vol. 2, pp. 298, 333-4, tr. Rodney Livingstone, London, Merlin, 1971, pp. 120, 150-1.

141 See Frisby, 'Introduction to the Translation', *The Philosophy of Money*, n. 126; also Gillian Rose, *The Melancholy Science. An Introduction to the Thought of Theodor W. Adorno*, London, Macmillan, 1978, pp. 34-6.

142 'The Old Culture and the New Culture', 1920, *Telos*, 5 (Spring 1970), 22.

143 'The Phenomenon of Reification', *History and Class Consciousness*, pp. 257-86, tr. pp. 83-110.

144 'Preface to the New Edition (1967)', *ibid.*, tr. pp. xxiii–xxiv, xxxvi.
145 *History and Class Consciousness*, p. 370, tr. p. 184, the translation does not render *Geltung* into English.
146 See Jürgen Habermas, 'Vorlesungen über Handlungsrationalität und gesell-schaftliche Rationalisierung', unpublished transcripts, University of Frank-furt, 1978–9.
147 See Andrew Arato and Paul Breines, *The Young Lukács and the Origins of Western Marxism*, New York, Seabury, 1979, chs 8 and 9.
148 'What is Orthodox Marxism?', *History and Class Consciousness*, pp. 171–98, tr. pp. 1–26.
149 Lukács, *The Young Hegel Studies in the Relations between Dialectics and Econo-mics*, 1948, tr. Rodney Livingstone, London, Merlin, 1975, *passim*.
150 *History and Class Consciousness*, p. 291, tr. p. 114 (G.R.).
151 *Ibid.*, p. 292, tr. p. 115.
152 *Ibid.*, p. 297, tr. p. 119, Lukács' italics; Fichte, *Die Wissenschaftslehre*, 1804, *Vortrag Werke* (Neue Ausgabe) ,IV, 288.
153 *History and Class Consciousness*, p. 371, tr. p. 185.
154 *Ibid.*, Lukács' brackets.
155 *Ibid.*, p. 385, tr. p. 197.
156 Fichte, *Wissenschaftslehre*, 1794, *Fichtes Werke*, I, 91–2, tr. 93.
157 Theodor W. Adorno, *Negative Dialectic*, 1966, *Gesammelte Schriften*, Frankfurt a.M., Suhrkamp, 1973, tr. E. B. Ashton, London, Routledge, 1973, pp. 190–1, tr. pp. 189–90.
158 *Ibid.*, p. 192, tr. p. 191.
159 *Ibid.*, pp. 191, 192, tr. pp. 190, 191.
160 *Ibid.*, p. 193, tr. p. 192.
161 *Ibid.*, p. 195, tr. p. 195.
162 *Ibid.*
163 *Ibid.*, p. 195, tr. pp. 195, 194.
164 *Ibid.*, p. 196, tr. p. 196.
165 *Ibid.*, p. 197, tr. p. 197.
166 See Hegel, 'Differenz der Fichteschen und Schellingschen Systems der Philosophie', 1801, *Jenaer Schriften 1801–1807* (tr.).
167 For this and the following six paragraphs, see G. Rose, *The Melancholy Science An Introduction to the Thought of Theodor W. Adorno*, chs 3, 5, 6, 7.
168 Adorno, 'Einleitung', *Der Positivismusstreit in der deutschen Soziologie*, Neu-wied, Luchterhand, 1969; tr. Introduction, *The Positivist Dispute in German Sociology*, Glyn Adey and David Frisby, London, Heinemann, 1976, pp. 7–79, tr. p. 167.
169 *Ibid.*, p. 9, tr. p. 3.
170 Adorno, *Minima Moralia*, Frankfurt a.M., Suhrkamp, 1951, tr. E. F. N. Jephcott, London, New Left Books, 1974, p. 89, tr. p. 73.
171 See *Friedrich Ueberwegs Grundriss der Geschichte der Philosophie* (n. 2), for an account which links Nietzsche's philosophy of values to Lotze via the work of Gustave Teichmüller, pp. 367, 371–2.
172 Nietzsche, *Beyond Good and Evil*, 1886, *Werke*, Karl Schlechta (ed.), Munich,

Ullstein, 1976, tr. Walter Kaufmann, New York, Vintage, 1966, sec. 36, p. 601, tr. p. 48.

173 See, for example, the account of Hugo Münsterberg, *Friedrich Ueberweg*, pp. 463-7.

174 See the Reification essay in *History and Class Consciousness, passim*; Adorno, *Drei Studien zu Hegel*, 1963, *Gesammelte Schriften*, 5, Frankfurt a.M., Suhrkamp, 1971, pp. 257-60, 265f., 273f.

175 Jürgen Habermas, *Knowledge and Human Interests* (n. 113), p. 11, tr. p. 3, my italics.

176 *Ibid.*, p. 14, tr. p. 5.

177 *Ibid.*, p. 9, tr. p. vii.

178 *Ibid.*, tr. p. 307.

179 *Ibid.*, tr. p. 308.

180 *Ibid.*, tr. pp. 307-8.

181 *Ibid.*, p. 240, tr. pp. 194-5, and, see the excellent discussion in Garbis Kortian, *Metacritique. The Philosophical Argument of Jürgen Habermas*, tr. John Raffan, Cambridge, Cambridge University Press, 1980, pp. 106-8.

182 Habermas, *Knowledge and Human Interests*, p. 240, tr. p. 194.

183 *Ibid.*, pp. 239-40, tr. p. 194.

184 *Ibid.*, p. 38, tr. p. 27.

185 *Ibid.*, p. 43, tr. p. 31.

186 *Ibid.*, p. 47, tr. p. 34.

187 *Ibid.*, pp. 52-7, tr. pp 37-41.

188 *Ibid.*, p. 86, tr. p. 63.

189 See Kortian, *Metacritique. The Philosophical Argument of Jürgen Habermas*, pp. 106-8, and Habermas, 'Vorbereitende Bemerkungen einer Theorie der Kommunikativen Kompetenz', in Habermas and Niklas Luhmann, *Theorie der Gesellschaft oder Sozialtechnologie Was leistet die Systemforschung?*, Frankfurt a.M., Suhrkamp, 1971, pp. 101-41.

190 Habermas, 'Urgeschichte der Subjektivität und verwilderte Selbstbehauptung', 1969, *Philosophische-politische Profile*, Frankfurt a.M., Suhrkamp, 1971, pp. 184-99.

191 For an excellent criticism of Habermas' interpretation of Hegel, see Michael Theunissen, 'Die Verwirklichung der Vernunft Zur Theorie-Praxis-Diskussion im Anschluss an Hegel', *Philosophische Rundschau*, Beiheft 6 (1970), 45-54.

192 For 'the cognitive paradigm', see Herminio Martins, 'Time and Theory in Sociology', in John Rex (ed.), *Approaches to Sociology. An Introduction to Major Trends in British Sociology*, London, Routledge, 1979.

193 Louis Althusser, *Reading Capital*, 1968, tr. Ben Brewster, London, New Left Books, 1970, p. 35. However, compare the different account of Hegel in Marx's Relation to Hegel', 1968, *Politics and History. Montesquieu, Rousseau, Hegel and Marx*, tr. Ben Brewster, London, New Left Books, 1972, pp. 163-86.

194 *Reading Capital*, pp. 35-6.

195 *Ibid.*, p. 34.

196 *Ibid.*, p. 24 and compare p. 41.

197 Compare p. 10, above.

198 Compare p. 13, above.
199 Louis Althusser, 'Ideology and Ideological State Apparatuses', 1968, *Lenin and Philosophy and Other Essays*, tr. Ben Brewster, London, New Left Books, 1971, p. 160.
200 *Ibid.*, p. 155.
201 *Ibid.*, p. 184.
202 *Ibid.*, pp. 168, 169.
203 Simmel, *Lebensanschauung Vier metaphysische Kapital*, 1918, Munich and Leipzig, Duncker & Humblot, 1922, p. 20.
204 Simmel, 'On the Concept and the Tragedy of Cultures', p. 29 (see n. 119 above).
205 Kant, *Critique of Pure Reason*, B824.
206 Kant, *Logik*, 1800, *Schriften zur Metaphysik und Logik*, 2, *Theorie-Werkausgabe*, VII, p. 437.
207 Kant, *Critique of Pure Reason*, B86. The neo-Kantians turned Kant's canon into an organon.
208 *Ibid.*, B828.
209 *Ibid.*, B824 and B831.
210 Hegel, *Die Wissenschaft der Logik, Enzyclopädie*, I, sec. 10.
211 *Ibid.*, sec. 60, Addition (2).
212 Hegel, *Differenzschrift, Jenaer Schriften 1801–1807*, 84, tr. 66.
213 See for example *Glauben und Wissen*, 1802, *ibid.*, especially Hegel's Introduction.
214 See the Introduction to *Phänomenologie des Geistes*, 3, (tr.).
215 *Ibid.*
216 Hegel uses this phrase in the Preface to the *Phenomenology, ibid.*, 31, tr. 16; and see the first page of the section, 'With what Must the Science begin?', *Wissenschaft der Logik*, 5, 65, tr. 67.

2. Politics in the Severe Style

1 *Philosophie der Religion*, 16, 236, tr. I 297 (G.R.).
2 *Phänomenologie des Geistes*, 3, 60, tr. sec. 64.
3 *Ibid.*, 59, tr. sec. 61.
4 *Ibid.*, 76–81, tr. sec. 82–89.
5 Karl Marx, *Critique of Hegel's 'Philosophy of Right'*, 1843, tr. Annette Jolin and Joseph O'Malley, Cambridge, Cambridge University Press, 1970, p. 11.
6 I do not intend to emphasize the difference between the works Hegel himself published and the various lecture series published posthumously by editors.
7 *Philosophie der Geschichte*, 12, 532, tr. 450.
8 Jürgen Habermas, 'Labor and Interaction: Remarks on Hegel's Jena *Philosophy of Mind*', 1963, *Theory and Practice*, tr. John Viertal, London, Heinemann, 1974, pp. 142–69.
9 *Enzyklopädie der philosophischen Wissenschaften*, 10, III, sec. 408 Zusatz; cf. *Rechtsphilosophie*, 7, sec. 32.
10 See Chapters 3 and 4 below.

11 *Vorlesungen über die Ästhetik*, 14, 247, tr. II, 616.

12 *Ibid.*, 249, tr. 617.

13 *Ibid.*, 250, tr. 618. The distinction between these styles is itself explicated in political terms. See Chapter 4 below.

14 First published in the *Kritisches Journal der Philosophie*, Bd II, Stück 2 (Nov-Dec), 1802 and Stück 3 (May-June) 1803. *Jenaer Schriften 1801–1807*, 2 434–530.

15 *Ibid.*, 439, tr. 59.

16 *Ibid.*, 444, tr. 63.

17 *Ibid.*, 445, tr. 63.

18 *Ibid.*, 448, tr. 66.

19 *Ibid.*, 445, tr. 64.

20 *Ibid.*, 506, tr. 114.

21 *Ibid.*, 448, tr. 66.

22 *Ibid.*, 442, tr. 61.

23 *Ibid.*, 454, tr. 70.

24 *Ibid.*, 454–5, tr. 71.

25 *Ibid.*, 454–8, tr. 71–4.

26 J. G. Fichte, *Grundlage des Naturrechts nach Principien der Wissenschaftslehre*, 1796, *Fichtes Werke* III, sec. 7, 85, tr. 126.

27 *Ibid.*, 458, tr. 74.

28 See Nicolai Hartmann, *Die Philosophie des deutschen Idealismus*, pp. 8–15. Hegel was very critical of Reinhold too, see *Differenzschrift*, *Jenaer Schriften, 1801–1807*, 2, 116–38, tr. pp. 174–95.

29 Karl Leonhard Reinhold, *Über die Möglichkeit der Philosophie als strenge Wissenschaft*, 1790, *Über das Fundament des philosophischen Wissens*, 1791, Hamburg, Felix Meiner, 1978.

30 Hartmann, *ibid.*, p. 15.

31 See Fichte, *Grundlage der gesammten Wissenschaftslehre*, 1794, *Fichtes Werke* I, 91, tr. 93.

32 *Jenaer Schriften, 1801–1807*, 2, 458–9, tr. 74.

33 *Ibid.*, 482, tr. 94.

34 *Ibid.*, 506, tr. 114.

35 *Ibid.*, 483–4, tr. 95.

36 *Ibid.*, 487, tr. 98.

37 *Ibid.*, 464, tr. 79.

38 *Ibid.*, 462, tr. 77.

39 *Ibid.*, 465–6, tr. 79–80.

40 *Ibid.*, 471, tr. 85.

41 *Ibid.*, 475–80, tr. 88–92.

42 *Ibid.*, 488–9, tr. 99.

43 *Ibid.*, 481–2, tr. 93.

44 *Ibid.*, 489–90, tr. 99–101.

45 *Ibid.*, 491, tr. 101.

46 *Ibid.*, 481, tr. 93.

47 *Ibid.*, 508, tr. 115–16.

48 *Ibid.*, 504f., tr. 112f.

49 *Ibid.*, 510, tr. 117.

50 One subsection is entitled *Die Sittlichkeit als System, ruhend* 56, tr. 146, and *'das Wahrhafte ist das System der Sittlichkeit'*, 62, tr. 157. All translations, except n. 98, are my own, but I have given the corresponding references to the English translation.

51 For example, Georg Lukács, *The Young Hegel Studies in the Relations between Dialectics and Economics*, 1948, tr. Rodney Livingstone, London, Merlin, 1975, p. 373; Schlomo Avineri, *Hegel's Theory of The Modern State*, Cambridge, Cambridge University Press, 1972, p. 87; Raymond Plant, *Hegel*, London, Allen & Unwin, 1973, p. 89.

52 Lukács, *ibid.*, pp. 371–2; Avineri, *ibid.*, pp. 87ff.; Plant, *ibid.*, pp. 92–6; Habermas, 'Labour and Interaction: Remarks on Hegel's Jena *Philosophy of Mind*', *Theory and Practice*, pp. 158–62.

53 *Vorlesungen über die Geschichte der Philosophie*, 20, 437–8, 441–3; see Peter Szondi, *Poetik und Geschichtsphilosophie* I, Frankfurt a.M., Suhrkamp, 1976, p. 222.

54 F. W. J. Schelling, *System des transzendentalen Idealismus*, 1800, Hamburg, Felix Meiner, 1957, *System of Transcendental Idealism*, tr. Peter Heath, Charlottesville, University of Vigrinia, 1978; and, see N. Hartmann, *Die Philosophie des deutschen Idealismus*, p. 112.

55 *System der Sittlichkeit*, 10, tr. 103.

56 *Ibid.*, 25, tr. 116–17.

57 *Ibid.*, 12–18, tr. 105–11.

58 *Ibid.*, 18, tr. 110–11.

59 *Ibid.*, 19, tr. 111.

60 *Ibid.*, 19, tr. 111–12.

61 *Ibid.*, 21, tr. 113.

62 *Ibid.*, 21–4, tr. 114–16.

63 *Ibid.*, 26, tr. 118.

64 *Ibid.*, 27, tr. 118.

65 *Ibid.*, 29, tr. 121.

66 *Ibid.*, 34, tr. 125.

67 *Ibid.*, 36–8, tr. 127–9.

68 *Ibid.*, 38–40, tr. 129–31.

69 *Ibid.*, 40, tr. 131.

70 *Ibid.*, 46–7, tr. 137.

71 *Ibid.*, 52, tr. 142.

72 *Ibid.*, 52, tr. 143.

73 *Ibid.*, 53, tr. 143.

74 *Ibid.*, 55, tr. 145.

75 *Ibid.*, 53, tr. 143.

76 *Ibid.*, 54, tr. 144.

77 *Ibid.*, 56–68, tr. 145–56.

78 Fichte, 'Erste Einleitung in die Wissenschaftslehre', 1797, *Fichtes Werke*, I, sec. 6, and 'Zweite Einleitung in die Wissenschaftslehre', 1797, *ibid.*, sec. 5.

79 Schelling, *System des transcendentalen Idealismus*, p. 94ff., tr. pp. 72ff.

80 *Differenzschrift, Jenaer Schriften, 1801–1807*, 2, 114–15, tr. 173–4.

81 *Phänomenologie des Geistes*, 3, 35, tr. sec. 31 (G.R.).
82 References are to the new edition of Hegel's *Gesammelte Werke*, ed. Rheinisch-Westfälischen Akademie der Wissenschaften, Hamburg, Felix Meiner, Bd 6, 1803–4 (1975) and Bd 8, 1805–6 (1976). Pt III of Bd 6 is tr. as 'First Philosophy of Spirit', in *Hegel's System of Ethical Life*.
83 Bd 6, 'Kampf um Anerkennung', 307–15, tr. 236–42; Bd 8 'Annerkanntseyn', 223f.
84 See Chapter 5.
85 *Jenaer Schriften, 1801–1807*, 2, 465, tr. 79.
86 Bd 6, 324–5, tr. 249.
87 Bd 8, 'Diese allgemeine Geist, oder der Geist der Gemeine', 283.
88 Bd 6, 325, tr. 249.
89 *Ibid.*, 325, tr. 249–50.
90 *Ibid.*, 325–6, tr. 250.
91 *Ibid.*, 330–1, tr. 251–3.
92 *Ibid.*, 330, tr. 251.
93 *Ibid.*, 330, tr. 252.
94 *Ibid.*, 330–1, tr. 252.
95 *Ibid.*, 331, tr. 252.
96 *Ibid.*
97 *Ibid.*, 331, tr. 252–3.
98 Bd 8, 277–87.
99 *Ibid.*, 278.
100 *Ibid.*, 278 and 279.
101 *Ibid.*, 279.
102 *Ibid.*
103 *Ibid.*, 280.
104 *Ibid.*, 279.
105 *Ibid.*, 281.
106 *Ibid.*
107 *Ibid.*, 284.
108 *Ibid.*
109 *Ibid.*
110 *Ibid.*, 285.
111 *Ibid.*, 283.
112 *Ibid.*, 286–7.
113 *Grundlinien der Philosophie des Rechts*, 7, 12, tr. 2.
114 *Ibid.*, sec. 7.
115 *Ibid.*
116 *Ibid.*, sec. 10.
117 *Ibid.*, sec. 270.
118 *Ibid.*, sec. 186 and Preface, 24, tr. 10.
119 See G. F. Hegel, *Vorlesungen über Rechtsphilosophie 1818–1831, Edition und Kommentar in sechs Bänden*, hrsg. von Karl-Heinz Ilting, Stuttgart, Friedrich Frommann, 1973, 'Einleitung', pp. 25–125.
120 Compare Herbert Schnädelbach, 'Zum Verhältnis von Logik und Gesell-

shaftstheorie bei Hegel', in Oskar Negt (ed.), *Aktualität und Folgen der Philosophie Hegels*, Frankfurt a.M., Suhrkamp, 1971, pp. 62–84.
121 *Rechtsphilosophie*, 7, 24, tr. 10.
122 *Ibid.*, 26, tr. 11.
123 *Ibid.*, 25, tr. 10.
124 Ilting discusses the matter in these terms, see n. 120 above.
125 *Rechtsphilosophie*, 26, tr. 11.
126 *Ibid.*, 26, tr. 12.
127 *Ibid.*, 26, tr. 11.
128 *Ibid.*, 27–8, tr. 12.
129 *Ibid.*, 28, tr. 12.
130 *Phänomenologie des Geistes*, 3, 20, tr. sec. 13.
131 *Ibid.*
132 *Rechtsphilosophie*, 28, tr. 13.
133 *Rechtsphilosophie*, sec. 11.
134 *Ibid.*, sec. 23.
135 See n. 6 above.
136 Kant, *Metaphysik der Sitten*, 1797, tr. of Introduction and Pt I, John Ladd, *The Metaphysical Elements of Justice*, New York, The Library of Liberal Arts, 1965.
137 *Ibid.*, tr. 52.
138 *Ibid.*
139 *Ibid.*, 70.
140 *Ibid.*, 71.
141 *Ibid.*, 77.
142 *Rechtsphilosophie*, secs 41 and 42.
143 *Ibid.*, secs 51 and 52.
144 *Ibid.*, sec. 57.
145 *Ibid.*, sec. 56.
146 *Ibid.*, sec. 108 (G.R.).
147 *Ibid.*, sec. 105 (G.R.).
148 *Ibid.*, secs 119f.
149 *Ibid.*, sec. 130.
150 *Ibid.*, sec. 124.
151 *Ibid.*, sec. 136.
152 *Ibid.*, sec. 182.
153 *Ibid.*
154 *Ibid.*, sec. 185.
155 *Ibid.*, secs 181 and 82 Zusatz.
156 *Ibid.*, sec. 211 (G.R.).
157 Compare *Enzyklopädie*, 10, sec. 529.
158 *Rechtsphilosophie*, secs 209 and 190.
159 *Ibid.*, sec. 157.
160 *Ibid.*, sec. 150.
161 *Ibid.*, sec. 150.
162 *Ibid.*, sec. 257 (G.R.).
163 *Ibid.*, secs 257 and 30.
164 See n. 6 above.

3. The Philosophy of History

1 See Chapter 1 above, p. 42.
2 *Philosophie der Religion*, I, 83, tr. I, 79.
3 *Ibid.*, I, 237, tr. I, 237.
4 *Vorlesungen über die Beweise vom Dasein Gottes, Philosophie der Religion*, II, 392, tr. III, 203.
5 *Ibid.*, II, 417–18, tr. III, 233–4.
6 *Enzyklopädie, I, Logik*, sec. 24 Zusatz (2).
7 *Ibid.* (G.R.).
8 *Ibid.*
9 *Philosophie der Religion*, II, 191, tr. II, 331.
10 *Philosophie der Geschichte*, 12, 26, tr. 14.
11 Kant, *Critique of Practical Reason*, tr. p. 31.
12 *Ibid.*, tr. p. 127.
13 *Ibid.*, tr. p. 129.
14 *Ibid.*, tr. p. 127.
15 Fichte, *Die Bestimmung des Menschen (1800), Fichtes Werke*, II, tr. *The Vocation of Man*, Roderick M. Chisholm (ed.), New York, The Library of Liberal Arts, 1956, 291, tr. 126.
16 *Ibid.*, 302, tr. 137 (G.R.).
17 *Ibid.*, 299, 300, tr. 135, 137.
18 Fichte was accused of atheism when the authorship of his *Attempt at a Critique of All Revelation*, 1792, was traced to him after at first being attributed to Kant, tr. Garrett Green, Cambridge, Cambridge University Press, 1978. Kant was accused of atheism when he published the second part of *Reason within the Bounds of Reason Alone*, 1793, tr. T. M. Green and H. H. Hudson, Chicago, The Open Court Publishing Company, 1934.
19 Kant, *Critique of Practical Reason*, tr. p. 130.
20 *Ibid.*, p. 130.
21 *Ibid.*, pp. 130–1.
22 *Ibid.*, pp. 124–6.
23 Fichte, *Die Bestimmung des Menschen, Fichtes Werke* II, 249, tr. 84.
24 *Ibid.*, 254, tr. 89.
25 *Ibid.*
26 *Ibid.*, 255, tr. 90.
27 *Ibid.*, 282, tr. 118.
28 *Ibid.*, 253–5, tr. 88–91.
29 *Ibid.*, 265, tr. 100.
30 *Ibid.*, 284–5, tr. 120.
31 *Ibid.*, 286, tr. 122.
32 *Ibid.*
33 *Glauben und Wissen*, first published in the *Kritisches Journal der Philosophie*, Bd II, Stück 1 (July) 1802, *Jenaer Schriften, 1801–1807*, 289–90, tr. 57.
34 *Ibid.*, 290, tr. 58.
35 *Ibid.*

36 Fichte, *Die Bestimmung des Menschen*, *Fichtes Werke* II, 255, tr. 90.
37 *Glauben und Wissen*, 291, tr. 59.
38 *Ibid.*, 293, tr. 60.
39 *Ibid.*, 293–4, tr. 60–1.
40 *Ibid.*, 294, tr. 61.
41 *Ibid.*, 295, tr. 61.
42 *Ibid.*, 299–300, tr. 65.
43 Kant, *Critique of Pure Reason*, B75.
44 *Glauben und Wissen*, 398, tr. 158.
45 *Ibid.*, 399–400, tr. 158–9.
46 *Ibid.*, 402, tr. 161.
47 Fichte, *Die Bestimmung des Menschen*, 304–5, tr. 140.
48 *Glauben und Wissen*, 402, tr. 161.
49 *Ibid.*, 404–5, tr. 163.
50 *Ibid.*, 406, tr. 164.
51 *Ibid.*, 406, tr. 165.
52 *Ibid.*, 409, tr. 168.
53 *Ibid.*, 413, tr. 171.
54 Fichte, *Die Bestimmung des Menschen*, 256, tr. 91.
55 *Glauben und Wissen*, 417, tr. 175.
56 *Ibid.*, 416, tr. 174.
57 *Ibid.*, 417, tr. 175.
58 This is discussed in *ibid.*, 'A. Kantian Philosophy'.
59 *Ibid.*, 422, tr. 180.
60 *Ibid.*, 429, tr. 187.
61 *Ibid.*, 425, tr. 183.
62 *Ibid.*, 424, tr. 182.
63 *Ibid.*, 424–5, tr. 182.
64 *Phänomenologie des Geistes*, 3, 23, tr. sec. 17.
65 Fichte, *Die Bestimmung des Menschen*, 304, tr. 140.
66 *Glauben und Wissen*, 431, tr. 190.
67 *Ibid.*
68 *Ibid.*, 931–2, tr. 190.
69 *Ibid.*, 432, tr. 190.
70 *Ibid.*
71 *Philosophie der Religion*, II, 203, tr. II, 347.
72 *Glauben und Wissen*, 430–1, tr. 190.
73 *Ibid.*, 432, tr. 190.
74 *Ibid.*
75 *Ibid.*, 432–3, tr. 191.
76 *Phänomenologie des Geistes*, 3, 23, tr. sec. 17.
77 *Philosophie der Religion*, II, 132, tr. II, 333.
78 *Philosophie der Geschichte*, 'der Geist in ihm selbst sich entgegen', 76, tr. 55.
79 *Philosophie der Religion*, II, 191, tr. II, 331 (G.R.).
80 *Ibid.*, II, 190, tr. II, 331 (G.R.).
81 *Ibid.*, I, 105, tr. I, 105 (G.R.).
82 *Ibid.*, I, 214, tr. III, 2, and I, 'Das religiöse Verhältnis', 101ff., tr. I, 101ff.

83 See n. 80.
84 *Ibid.*, I, 129, tr. I, 131.
85 *Ibid.*, I, 65, tr. I, 60.
86 *Ibid.*, I, 129, tr. I, 131
87 See n. 81.
88 *Ibid.*, I, 65, tr. I, 60.
89 *Ibid.*, II, 215, tr. III, 3.
90 *Ibid.*, I, 71, tr. I, 66.
91 *Ibid.*, I, 160, tr. I, 165.
92 *Ibid.*, I, 71, tr. I, 66 (G.R.).
93 *Ibid.*, I, 71–2, tr. I, 66–7.
94 *Ibid.*, I, 190, tr. I, 197.
95 *Ibid.*, I, 191, tr. I, 198.
96 *Ibid.*, I, 192, tr. I, 199.
97 *Ibid.*, this is the title of a subsection I, 186ff., tr. I, 193ff.
98 *Ibid.*, II, 256, tr. III, 51.
99 See the discussion in E. L. Fackenheim, *The Religious Dimension in Hegel's Thought*, Bloomington, Indiana University Press, 1967, chs 6 and 7.
100 *Philosophie der Religion*, II, 215, tr. III, 3.
101 *Ibid.*
102 *Ibid.*, II, 216, tr. III, 4.
103 *Ibid.*, 275, tr. III, 73.
104 *Ibid.*
105 *Ibid.*
106 *Ibid.*
107 *Ibid.*, II, 274, tr. III, 72.
108 *Ibid.*, II, 290, tr. III, 90.
109 *Ibid.*, II, 291, tr. III, 91.
110 *Ibid.*, II, 298, tr. III, 99.
111 *Ibid.*, II, 291, tr. III, 91.
112 *Ibid.*, II, 330, tr. III, 135.
113 See n. 81.
114 *Ibid.*, this is the title of a subsection, I, 114ff., tr. I, 115ff.
115 *Ibid.*, I, 57, tr. I, 51.
116 Ludwig Feuerbach, *The Essence of Christianity*, 1841, tr. George Eliot, New York, Harper & Row, 1957, esp. Pt I.
117 *Philosophie der Geschichte*, 12, 51, tr. 34.
118 See n. 80.
119 *Ibid.*, II, 175, tr. II, 312.
120 *Ibid.*, II, 158, tr. II, 293.
121 *Ibid.*, II, 175, tr. II, 312.
122 *Philosophie der Geschichte*, 12, 70, tr. 51.
123 *Ibid.*, 72–3, tr. 52–3.
124 *Philosophie der Religion*, II, 161, tr. II, 296.
125 *Ibid.*, II, 162, tr. II, 297.
126 *Ibid.*
127 *Philosophie der Geschichte*, 12, 391, tr. 323.

128 *Ibid.*, 403, tr. 334.
129 *Ibid.*, 398, tr. 329.
130 *Ibid.*, 396, tr. 327.
131 *Ibid.*, 396, tr. 328.
132 *Philosophie der Religion*, II, 303, tr. III, 105 (G.R.).
133 *Enzyklopädie, III*, sec. 552.
134 '*Der Geist des Christentums' Schriften 1796–1800*, 999, tr. 284.
135 *Ibid.*, 500, tr. 285.
136 *Enzyklopädie, III*, sec. 552.
137 *Ibid.*
138 *Philosophie der Geschichte*, 12.
139 *Ibid.*, 416–17, tr. 344.
140 *Ibid.*, 417, tr. 344–5 (G.R.).
141 *Ibid.*, 526, tr. 444.
142 See *Hegel's Political Writings*, M. Knox and Z. Pelczynski (eds), Oxford, Clarendon Press, 1964.
143 *Philosophie der Religion*, II, 342–3, tr. III, 150.
144 For Fichte's *Attempt at a Critique of all Revelation*, see n. 18. For 'depravity', see *Enzyklopädie III*, sec. 552; for 'abandonment', see *Philosophie der Religion*, II, 342–3, tr. III, 150.
145 *Ibid.*, II, 343, tr. III, 150 (G.R.).
146 *Ibid.*, II, 338, tr. III, 145 (G.R.).
147 *Enzyklopädie III*, sec. 552.
148 *Philosophie der Religion*, II, 343–4, tr. III, 151 (G.R.).
149 *Ibid.*, II, 343, tr. III, 150.

4. The Division of Labour and Illusion

1 *Ästhetik*, I, 405, tr. I, 312 (G.R.).
2 *Ibid.*, III, 339, tr. II, 1051 (G.R.).
3 *Ibid.*, I, 10, tr. I, 24 and 141, tr. 103.
4 See *ibid.*, end of Pt II and Pt III.
5 *Ibid.*, I, 107, tr. I, 75.
6 See n. 2 above.
7 See n. 1 above.
8 *Ibid.*, I, 104, tr. I, 73.
9 *Ibid.*, I, 123, tr. I, 89.
10 *Ibid.*, I, 141, tr. I, 102.
11 *Philosophie der Religion*, II, 119, tr. II, 249. In the English translation of the *Aesthetics*, *Darstellung* is translated as 'representation', thus obscuring the fundamental philosophical distinction between *Vorstellung* and *Darstellung*, representation and presentation, respectively, for example, see *Ästhetik* I, 9, tr. I, 22.
12 In the English translation of the *Aesthetics*, *Schein* is frequently translated as 'appearance', thus obscuring the two meanings of *Schein*, the connection with *Darstellung* and the contrast with *Vorstellung*, for example, *ibid.*, I, 9, tr. I, 22.

13 *Philosophie der Geschichte*, 12, 293, tr. 239 (G.R.).
14 *Ästhetik*, I, 151, tr. I, 111.
15 *Ibid.*, I, 236, tr. I, 179.
16 *Ibid.*, I, 145–50, tr. I, 106–10.
17 *Philosophie der Geschichte*, 12, 293, tr. 238.
18 *Ibid.*, 293–4, tr. 239.
19 *Ibid.*, 293, tr. 238.
20 *Ibid.*, 295, tr. 240.
21 *Ästhetik*, I, 297–9, tr. I, 229–30.
22 See the discussion of Socrates' life and death in *Geschichte der Philosophie*, I, 441–516. Søren Kierkegaard's M.A. dissertation was based on Hegel's discussion, *The Concept of Irony with constant reference to Socrates*, 1841, tr. Lee M. Capel, Bloomington, Indiana University Press, 1965.
23 *Philosophie der Geschichte*, 12, 31, tr. 18.
24 *Ibid.*, 59, tr. 41.
25 *Ibid.*, 58, tr. 40–1.
26 *Ästhetik*, III, 341, tr. II, 1053.
27 *Ibid.*, I, 337–8, tr. I, 260–1.
28 *Ibid.*, I, 338, tr. I, 261.
29 *Ibid.*, III, 342, tr. II, 1053.
30 *Ibid.*, III, 340, tr. II, 1052.
31 *Phänomenologie des Geistes*, 512, tr. sec. 700.
32 *Ästhetik*, I, 337, tr. I, 260.
33 *Rechtsphilosophie*, 7, sec. 4.
34 *Philosophie der Geschichte*, 12, 31, tr. 18.
35 *Phänomenologie des Geistes*, 3, 145–55, tr. secs 178–98, and see Alexandre Kojève's famous discussion, *Introduction to the Reading of Hegel*, 1933–9, tr. James H. Nichols Jr, New York, Basic Books, 1969. 'Therefore, the historical process, the historical becoming of the human being, is the product of the working Slave and not of the warlike Master.' p. 52f.
36 Compare n. 27 above.
37 Compare n. 27 above.
38 *Phänomenologie des Geistes*, 3, 155–6, tr. sec. 197.
39 *Ästhetik*, II, 25–6, tr. I, 437.
40 *Ibid.*, II, 13, tr. I, 427.
41 *Ibid.*, II, 18, tr. I, 431.
42 *Ibid.*, II, 24–5, tr. I, 436.
43 *Phänomenologie des Geistes*, 3, 353, tr. sec. 475.
44 *Ästhetik*, II, 33f., tr. I, 442f.
45 *Ibid.*, II, 52f., tr. I, 458f.
46 *Ibid.*, II, 54–7, tr. I, 460–2.
47 *Ibid.*, II, 56, tr. I, 461.
48 *Ibid.*, II, 58, tr. I, 463.
49 *Ibid.*, II, 58, tr. I, 462.
50 *Ibid.*, I, 301, tr. I, 232.
51 *Ibid.*
52 *Ibid.*, III, 522, tr. II, 1194.

53 *Ibid.*, I, 301, tr. I, 232.
54 *Ibid.*, III, 550, tr. II, 1218
55 *Ibid.*, III, 544, tr. II, 1213.
56 *Phänomenologie des Geistes*, 3, 348, tr. sec. 470.
57 *Ästhetik*, III, 522, tr. II, 1195.
58 *Ibid.*, III, 541, tr. II, 1210–11.
59 *Rechtsphilosophie*, 7, sec. 30.
60 *Ästhetik*, for example, III, 392–3, tr. II, 1092–3.
61 *Ibid.*, II, 111, tr. I, 505.
62 *Philosophie der Geschichte*, 12, 339, tr. 278.
63 *Ibid.*, 351, tr. 289.
64 *Ibid.*, 384, tr. 317.
65 *Ibid.*, 345–6, tr. 284.
66 *Ibid.*, 375, tr. 309.
67 *Ibid.*, 340, tr. 279.
68 *Ibid.*, 364, tr. 300.
69 *Ibid.*, 347, tr. 286.
70 *Ibid.*, 366, tr. 301.
71 *Ibid.*, 383–4, tr. 316–8.
72 *Ibid.*, 340, tr. 279.
73 *Ästhetik*, III, 341, tr. II, 1053.
74 *Ibid.*, I, 336–7, tr. I, 260 (G.R.).
75 *Ibid.*, III, 342, tr. II, 1053.
76 *Ibid.*, III, 260, tr. II, 988.
77 *Ibid.*, I, 197, tr. I, 149.
78 *Ibid.*, I, 198–9, tr. I, 150.
79 *Ibid.*, III, 240–1, tr. II, 973.
80 *Ibid.*, III, 243, tr. II, 976.
81 *Ibid.*, III, 250, tr. II, 981.
82 *Ibid.*, III, 242, tr. II, 974–5.
83 *Ibid.*
84 *Ibid.*, II, 128, tr. I, 518 and *Phänomenologie des Geistes*, 3, 158, tr. sec. 200 (G.R.).
85 *Ästhetik*, II, 132–3, tr. I, 521–2.
86 *Ibid.*, II, 137, tr. I, 524.
87 *Ibid.*, II, 138, tr. I, 525.
88 *Ibid.*, II, 139, tr. I, 527.
89 Compare the early Jena writings, Chapter 2 above, pp. 74–6.
90 Compare Chapter 3 above, p. 118–20.
91 *Ästhetik*, II, 221, tr. I, 595.
92 *Ibid.*, II, 223, tr. I, 595.
93 *Ibid.*, II, 249 and 253, tr. II, 616 and 620.
94 *Ibid.*, II, 249, tr. 616–17.
95 *Ibid.*, II, 249–50, tr. II, 617.
96 *Ibid.*, II, 250, tr. II, 617.
97 *Ibid.*, II, 250, tr. II, 618.
98 *Ibid.*, II, 251, tr. II, 618.
99 *Ibid.*

100 *Ibid.*, II, 252, tr. II, 619.
101 *Ibid.*, II, 253, tr. II, 619.
102 *Ibid.*, II, 210, tr. I, 585. '. . . this restrictedness of their subjectivity is itself only a fate . . .' (G.R.).
103 *Ibid.*, II, 214, tr. I, 588.
104 *Ibid.*, II, 219, tr. I, 592.
105 *Ibid.*, II, 219–20, tr. I, 592–3.
106 *Ibid.*, II, 215, tr. I, 589.
107 *Ibid.*, II, 239–40, tr. I, 609.
108 *Ibid.*, I, 93–99, tr. I, 64–9.
109 *Ibid.*, I, 93, tr. I, 65.
110 *Ibid.*, I, 95, tr. I, 66.
111 *Ibid.*, I, 96, tr. I, 67.
112 *Ibid.*, I, 97, tr. I, 67.
113 *Ibid.*, I, 408, tr. I, 315.
114 *Ibid.*, I, 409, tr. I, 316.
115 *Ibid.*
116 *Ibid.*, I, 391, tr. I, 301.
117 *Ibid.*, I, 397, tr. I, 306.
118 *Ibid.*, I, 401, tr. I, 309.
119 Compare *ibid.*, Pt II, sec. I, chs I and III.
120 *Ibid.*, I, 487, tr. I, 379, my italics.
121 See Hans-Georg Gadamer, 'Hegel und die Heidelberger Romantik', in *Hegels Dialektik Fünf hermeneutische Studien*, Tübingen, J. C. B. Mohr (Paul Siebeck), 1971, pp. 71–81. For a useful anthology of writings on universal poetry and irony, see *Romantik I Die deutsche literatur in Text und Darstellung*, Hans-Jürgen Schmitt (ed.), Stuttgart, Reclam, 1974.
122 *Ästhetik*, I, 487, tr. I, 379.
123 *Ibid.*
124 See Mann, *Doctor Faustus*, 1947, tr. H. T. Lowe-Porter, Harmondsworth, Penguin, 1968, ch. 22, p. 186. For discussion of Hegel and modernist aesthetics see *Die nicht-mehr schönen Künste, Poetik und Hermeneutik*, Hans-Robert Jauss (ed.), München, Wilhelm Fink, 1968.
125 *Ästhetik*, II, 221, tr. I, 595.

5. Work and Representation

1 *Phänomenologie*, 40, tr. sec. 39 (G.R.).
2 *Ibid.*, 35–6, tr. sec. 32 (G.R.).
3 *Ibid.*, 39, tr. sec. 37 (G.R.).
4 *Ibid.*, 40, tr. sec. 39.
5 For example, Lucio Colletti, 'Hegel and the "Dialectic of Matter" ', in *Marxism and Hegel*, tr. Lawrence Garner, London, Verso, 1973, pp. 8–27.
6 Marx, 'Critique of Hegel's Dialectic and General Philosophy', 'Economic and Philosophical Manuscripts (1844)', in *Marx Early Writings, The Pelican Marx Library*, Harmondsworth, Penguin, pp. 379–400.

7 *Phänomenologie*, 80, tr. sec. 88. See the excellent discussion in Werner Marx, *Hegel's Phenomenology of Spirit Its Point and Purpose—A Commentary on the Preface and Introduction*, tr. Peter Heath, New York, Harper & Row, 1975.
8 *Wissenschaft der Logik*, II, 256, tr. 586.
9 *Phänomenologie*, 28, tr. sec. 25.
10 *Ibid.*, 80, tr. sec. 87.
11 *Ibid.*, 72, tr. sec. 78.
12 *Ibid.*, 73–4, tr. sec. 79.
13 *Ibid.*, 75, tr. sec. 81 (G.R.).
14 *Ibid.*, 76, tr. sec. 84.
15 *Ibid.*, 37, 36, tr. sec. 33.
16 *Ibid.*, 37, tr. sec. 33.
17 *Ibid.*, 37, tr. sec. 33 (G.R.).
18 *Ibid.*, 37, tr. sec. 33 (G.R.).
19 *Ibid.*, 39, tr. sec. 37.
20 *Ibid.*, 72, tr. sec. 77.
21 *Ibid.*, 73, tr. sec. 78.
22 *Ibid.*, 72, tr. sec. 78.
23 *Ibid.*, 72, tr. sec. 78 (G.R.).
24 *Ibid.*, 72, tr. sec. 78. I owe this rendering – 'self-perficient scepticism' – to John Raffan.
25 *Ibid.*, 73, tr. sec. 78 (G.R.).
26 *Ibid.*, 73, tr. sec. 79.
27 *Ibid.*, 76, tr. sec. 84.
28 *Ibid.*, 77, tr. sec. 85.
29 *Ibid.*, 78–9, tr. sec. 86.
30 *Ibid.*, 79, tr. sec. 87 (G.R.).
31 *Ibid.*, 35, tr. sec. 31 (G.R.).
32 'Kausalität des Schichsals', see Jürgen Habermas, *Erkenntnis und Interesse*, 1968, Frankfurt a.M., Suhrkamp, 1971, pp. 312, 330; cf. 'das Schicksal und die Notwendigkeit des Geistes', *Phänomenologie*, 594, tr. sec. 801.
33 '*Der Geist des Christentums*' *Schriften 1796–1800*, 420–516.
34 *Phänomenologie*, 273, tr. sec. 363 (G.R.).
35 *Ibid.*, 274, tr. sec. 365.
36 *Der Geist des Christentums*, 442, tr. 229.
37 *Ibid.*
38 *Ibid.*, 443, tr. 230–1.
39 *Ibid.*, 448, tr. 236.
40 *Ibid.*, 509, tr. 294.
41 *Ibid.*, 499, tr. 284.
42 *Ibid.*, 501, tr. 287.
43 *Ibid.*, 500, tr. 286.
44 *Ibid.*, 500–1, tr. 286.
45 *Ibid.*, 510, tr. 295.
46 *Ibid.*
47 *Phänomenologie*, 266, tr. sec. 352–3.

48 *Ibid.*, 265, tr. sec. 351.
49 *Ibid.*, 268, tr. sec. 357.
50 *Ibid.*, 266, tr. sec. 353.
51 *Ibid.*, 267, tr. sec. 356.
52 Compare n. 17 above.
53 *Ibid.*, 169, tr. sec. 217.
54 *Ibid.*, 580, tr. sec. 796.
55 *Ibid.*, 572, tr. sec. 785.
56 *Ibid.*, 570–1, tr. secs. 784–5,
57 *Ibid.*, 571–2, tr. sec. 785.
58 *Ibid.*, 572, tr. sec. 785 (G.R.).
59 *Ibid.*, 164–5, tr. sec. 209.
60 *Ibid.*, 157, tr. sec. 199.
61 *Ibid.*, 159, tr. sec. 202 (G.R.).
62 *Ibid.*, 161–3, tr. sec. 205.
63 *Ibid.*, 163, tr. sec. 206.
64 *Ibid.*, 163, tr. sec. 206, 207.
65 *Ibid.*, 164, tr. sec. 209.
66 *Ibid.*, 164–5, tr. sec. 209.
67 *Ibid.*, 169, tr. sec. 217.
68 *Ibid.*, 169, tr. sec. 217 (G.R.).
69 *Ibid.*, 170–1, tr. sec. 219.
70 *Ibid.*, 170, tr. sec. 218.
71 *Ibid.*, 170, tr. sec. 219.
72 *Ibid.*, 171, tr. sec. 220.
73 *Ibid.*, 172, tr. sec. 222.
74 *Ibid.*, 170, tr. sec. 218.
75 *Ibid.*, 179, tr. sec. 225.
76 *Ibid.*, 173–4, tr. sec. 225.
77 *Ibid.*, 164–5, tr. sec. 209.
78 *Ibid.*, 175, tr. sec. 228.
79 'Die reine Bildung', *ibid.*, 385, tr. sec. 521; and cf. 'Die Barbarei der Kultur', *Jenaer Schriften, 1801–1807*, 271; and cf. Chapter 3 above, p. 119; n. 146.
80 *Philosophie der Geschichte*, 402–3, tr. 333.
81 *Ibid.*, 408, tr. 338.
82 *Ibid.*, 417–18, tr. 345.
83 *Ibid.*, 426, tr. 354.
84 *Ibid.*, 445, tr. 370.
85 *Ibid.*, 445, tr. 370.
86 *Ibid.*, 446, tr. 370.
87 *Ibid.*, 458, tr. 380–1.
88 *Ibid.*, 454–5, tr. 377–8.
89 *Ibid.*, 457, tr. 374.
90 *Ibid.*, 460, tr. 383.
91 *Ibid.*
92 See Chapter 2 above, p. 68.
93 *Phänomenologie*, 269, tr. sec. 359 (G.R.).

94 *Ibid.* (G.R.).
95 *Ibid.*, 271, tr. sec. 361.
96 *Ibid.*, 262-3, tr. sec. 363.
97 *Ibid.*, 273, tr. sec. 363.
98 *Ibid.*, 274, tr. sec. 365.
99 *Ibid.*, 275-6, tr. sec. 369.
100 *Ibid.*, 277-8, tr. sec. 372.
101 *Ibid.*, 278, tr. sec. 373.
102 *Ibid.*, 280-1, tr. sec. 377.
103 *Ibid.*, 281-2, tr. sec. 378.
104 *Ibid.*, 284-5, tr. sec. 382.
105 *Ibid.*, 285, tr. sec. 383.
106 *Ibid.*, 289, tr. sec. 389.
107 *Ibid.*, 359f., tr. sec. 484f.
108 *Ibid.*, 367, tr. sec. 494.
109 *Ibid.*, 368-9, tr. sec. 495.
110 *Ibid.*, 370, tr. sec. 497.
111 *Ibid.*, 372, tr. sec. 501.
112 *Ibid.*, 380, tr. sec. 513.
113 *Ibid.*, 385-6, tr. sec. 521.
114 *Ibid.*, 385, tr. sec. 521.
115 *Ibid.*, 423-4, tr. sec. 573 (G.R.).
116 *Ibid.*, 439, tr. sec. 594.
117 *Ibid.*, 426, tr. sec. 578.
118 Kant, *Critique of Practical Reason*, tr. p. 130.
119 *Phänomenologie*, 427, tr. sec. 578 (G.R.).
120 *Ibid.*, 423, tr. sec. 573.
121 *Ibid.*, 423-4, tr. sec. 573 (G.R.).
122 *Ibid.*, 577, tr. sec. 481 (G.R.).
123 *Ibid.*, 432, tr. sec. 584.
124 *Ibid.*, 433, tr. sec. 585.
125 *Ibid.*, 439-40, tr. sec. 594.
126 *Ibid.*, 440-1, tr. sec. 595.
127 *Ibid.*, 441, tr. sec. 595.
128 *Ibid.*, 439, tr. sec. 594.
129 *Ibid.*, 320, tr. sec. 434.
130 *Ibid.*, 293-4, tr. sec. 396.
131 *Ibid.*, 301, tr. sec. 405.
132 *Ibid.*, 303-4, tr. sec. 409.
133 *Ibid.*, 309-11, tr. sec. 417-18.
134 *Ibid.*, 311-12, tr. sec. 420.
135 Compare *ibid.*, 311-23, tr. secs 419-434 with Chapter 2 above, pp. 56-7.
136 *Ibid.*, 442, tr. sec. 598.
137 *Ibid.*
138 *Ibid.*, 443-4, tr. sec. 601.
139 *Ibid.*, 445, tr. sec. 602.
140 *Ibid.*, 445, tr. sec. 603.

141 *Ibid.*, 448, tr. sec. 606.
142 *Ibid.*, 453, tr. sec. 616.
143 *Ibid.*, 453, tr. sec. 617 (G.R.).
144 *Ibid.*, 454-5, tr. sec. 618.
145 *Ibid.*, 459-60, tr. sec. 625.
146 *Ibid.*, 461-2, tr. sec. 628.
147 *Ibid.*
148 *Ibid.*, 463, tr. sec. 630.
149 *Ibid.*, 463, tr. sec. 631.
150 *Ibid.*
151 *Ibid.*, 466, tr. sec. 633.
152 *Ibid.*, 467-8, tr. sec. 636.
153 *Ibid.*, 468, tr. sec. 637.
154 *Ibid.*, 469, tr. sec. 639.
155 *Ibid.*, 470, tr. sec. 640.
156 *Ibid.*, 472-4, tr. secs 643-9.
157 *Ibid.*, 475, tr. sec. 645.
158 *Ibid.*, 476, tr. sec. 646.
159 *Ibid.*, 477, tr. sec. 648.
160 *Ibid.*, 479, tr. sec. 653.
161 *Ibid.*, 481, tr. sec. 655.
162 *Ibid.*, 483-4, tr. sec. 658.
163 *Ibid.*, 484, tr. sec. 659.
164 *Ibid.*
165 *Ibid.*, 486, tr. sec. 662.
166 *Ibid.*, 493, tr. sec. 671.
167 *Ibid.*, 321-3, tr. sec. 436-7.
168 *Ibid.*, 579, tr. sec. 794.
169 *Ibid.*, 582, tr. sec. 797.
170 *Ibid.*, 581, tr. sec. 796.
171 *Ibid.*, 582, tr. sec. 798.
172 *Ibid.*, 584, tr. sec. 801.
173 *Ibid.*, 589, tr. sec. 806.
174 *Ibid.*, 589-90, tr. sec. 806 (G.R.).
175 *Enzyklopädie, III*, sec. 387 Zusatz.
176 *Ibid.*, 385 Zusatz (G.R.).
177 *Ibid.*
178 *Phänomenologie*, 321, tr. sec. 436.
179 *Ibid.*, 589-90, tr. sec. 806.

6. Rewriting the Logic

1 Compare Chapter 2, pp. 53-5.
2 Compare Chapter 3, p. 99 and n. 43.
3 Compare Chapter 3, p. 100 and n. 51.
4 *Wissenschaft der Logik*, 2, 541-8, tr. 818-23.

5 *Ibid.*, 555, tr. 829.
6 Compare Chapter 5, p. 184 and n. 178.
7 I have translated *Grenze* as boundary and *Schranke* as limit in Kant, Fichte and Hegel. The existing English translations of these terms do not coincide.
8 Kant, *Prolegomena*, sec. 57.
9 Compare Chapter 5, 'The End of Ethical Life', pp. 177–80.
10 Kant, *Prolegomena*, sec. 57.
11 *Ibid.*
12 Compare the *Phenomenology* VI C 6.
13 *Wissenschaft der Logik*, 1, 136, tr. 126.
14 *Ibid.* (G.R.).
15 *Ibid.*, 137, tr. 127 (G.R.).
16 *Ibid.*, 137–8, tr. 127.
17 *Ibid.*, 138, tr. 128.
18 *Ibid.*, 139, tr. 128.
19 *Ibid.*
20 *Ibid.*, 142, tr. 131.
21 *Ibid.*, 142, tr. 132.
22 *Ibid.*, 142–3, tr. 132.
23 Kant, *Prolegomena*, sec. 57.
24 *Logik*, 143, tr. 132.
25 *Ibid.*, 144, tr. 133.
26 *Ibid.*
27 *Ibid.*, 144–5, tr. 133 (G.R.).
28 *Ibid.*, 145, tr. 134.
29 *Ibid.*
30 *Ibid.*, 147, tr. 135.
31 *Ibid.*
32 *Ibid.*
33 *Ibid.*, 147, tr. 136.
34 *Ibid.*, 148, tr. 136 (G.R.).
35 Fichte, *Wissenschaftslehre, Fichtes Werke*, 1, 96, tr. 97 (G.R.).
36 *Ibid.*, 258, tr. 228 (G.R.).
37 Hegel, *Vorlesungen über die Geschichte der Philosophie*, III, 407.
38 Fichte, *Wissenschaftslehre*, 259, tr. 229 (G.R.).
39 Hegel, *Geschichte der Philosophie*, III, 404.
40 Fichte, *Wissenschaftslehre*, 260, tr. 229 (G.R.).
41 *Ibid.*, 260, tr. 230 (G.R.).
42 Hegel, *Geschichte der Philosophie*, III, 406.
43 Fichte, *Wissenschaftslehre*, 261 n., tr. 230 n., (G.R.).
44 *Ibid.* (G.R.).
45 *Ibid.* (G.R.).
46 Hegel, *Wissenschaft der Logik*, 1, 98, tr. 94.
47 *Ibid.*, 11, 16, tr. 391.
48 *Ibid.*, 11, 15, tr. 390.
49 *Ibid.*, 11, 19, tr. 395.

50 *Ibid.*, 11, 24, tr. 399.
51 Compare n. 38 above.
52 *Logik*, 11, 20, tr. 396.
53 *Ibid.*, 21–2, tr. 397.
54 *Ibid.*, 22, tr. 398.
55 *Ibid.*, 23, tr. 398.
56 *Ibid.*, 23–4, tr. 398–9.
57 *Ibid.*, 26, tr. 401.
58 *Ibid.*, 27, tr. 401.
59 *Ibid.*, 28, tr. 402.
60 *Ibid.*, 27, tr. 402.
61 *Ibid.*, 28, tr. 402.
62 *Ibid.*, 28–9, tr. 403.
63 *Ibid.*, 29, tr. 403.
64 *Ibid.*, 30, tr. 404.
65 *Ibid.*
66 *Ibid.*, 31, tr. 405.
67 *Ibid.*, 32, tr. 406.
68 *Ibid.*, 33, tr. 406.
69 *Ibid.*
70 *Ibid.*, 33–4, tr. 407.
71 *Ibid.*, 34, tr. 407.
72 *Ibid.*
73 *Ibid.*, 34, tr. 407–8.
74 *Ibid.*, 35, tr. 408.
75 *Ibid.*
76 *Ibid.*, 258, tr. 587.
77 *Ibid.*, 256, tr. 585.
78 *Ibid.*, 493–4, tr. 780.
79 *Ibid.*, 542, tr. 818.
80 *Ibid.*, 544, tr. 820.
81 *Ibid.*, 544–5, tr. 820.
82 *Ibid.*, 545, tr. 821 (G.R.).
83 *Ibid.*, second italics mine.
84 *Ibid.*
85 *Ibid.*, 546, tr. 821.
86 *Ibid.*, 547–8, tr. 823.
87 *Ibid.*, 548, tr. 823.
88 *Ibid.*
89 *Ibid.*, 548–9, tr. 824.
90 *Differenzschrift, Jenaer Schriften, 1801–1807*, 83, tr. 146.
91 *Ibid.*, 12–13, tr. 82.
92 *Ibid.*, 13, tr. 83.
93 *Ibid.*, 81, tr. 144 (G.R.).
94 *Ibid.*, 83, tr. 145–6.
95 *Ibid.*, 83, tr. 145.
96 *Ibid.*, 12–13, tr. 82.

97 *Ibid.*, 13–14, tr. 83.
98 *Ibid.*, 83, tr. 145.
99 *Ibid.*, 12, tr. 82.

7. With What Must the Science End?

1 Compare Chapter 1, p. 42, and Chapter 3, p. 92.
2 *Wissenschaft der Logik*, II, 186–240, tr. 529–71.
3 *Ibid.*, 273–301, tr. 601–22.
4 *Ibid.*, 436–60 and 461–87, tr. 734–54 and 761–79.
5 *Ibid.*, I, 258, tr. 587.
6 *Ibid.*, 548–9, tr. 824 and cf. Chapter 6, p. 199.
7 *Wissenschaft der Logik*, II, 208, tr. 546.
8 *Ibid.*, 208, tr. 546–7.
9 *Ibid.*, 202, tr. 542.
10 *Ibid.*, 209, tr. 547.
11 *Ibid.*
12 Fichte, *Erste Einleitung in die Wissenschaftslehre*, 1797, *Fichtes Werke*, I, 433, tr. 15 (G.R.).
13 *Wissenschaft der Logik*, II, 209, tr. 547 (G.R.).
14 *Ibid.*, 211, tr. 549.
15 *Ibid.*
16 *Ibid.*, 212, tr. 550.
17 *Ibid.*, 214, tr. 551.
18 *Ibid.*, 277, tr. 604.
19 *Ibid.*, 279, tr. 601.
20 *Ibid.*
21 *Ibid.*, 276, tr. 602 (G.R.).
22 *Ibid.*, 277, tr. 603.
23 *Ibid.* (G.R.).
24 *Ibid.*, 277, tr. 603–4.
25 *Ibid.*, 278, tr. 604.
26 *Ibid.* (G.B.).
27 Absolute necessity is 'blind', *ibid.*, 215–16, tr. 552.
28 *Ibid.*, 279, tr. 605.
29 *Ibid.*, 299, tr. 621.
30 *Ibid.*
31 *Ibid.*, 480–4, tr. 769–72.
32 *Ibid.*, 468, tr. 760.
33 *Ibid.*, 469, tr. 760.
34 For example, the famous last thesis on Feuerbach.
35 *History of Class Consciousness*, p. 297, tr. p. 119.
36 I refer to Chapter 1, p. 1.
37 Compare Chapter 1, p. 24.
38 For example, Talcott Parsons, *The Social System*, London, Routledge, 1951; and Anthony Giddens, 'Agency, Structure', *Central Problems in Social*

Theory Action, Structure and Contradiction in Social Analysis, London, Macmillan, 1979.

39 For example, Roy Bhaskar, *A Realist Theory of Science*, Brighton, Harvester, 1978.

40 Marx, 'Economic and Philosophical Manuscripts (1844)', in *Marx: Early Writings, The Pelican Marx Library*, pp. 379–400.

41 *Ibid.*, p. 391 (G.R.).

42 'Theses on Feuerbach', *ibid.*, p. 421. I have amended the translation from Lloyd D. Easton and Kurt M. Guddat (eds), *Writings of the Young Marx on Philosophy and Society*, New York, Anchor, 1967.

44 'Economic and Philosophical Manuscripts', *ibid.*, p. 390 (G.R.).

45 'A Contribution to the Critique of Hegel's "Philosophy of Right" ', (1844), Introduction, in *Critique of Hegel's 'Philosophy of Right'*, Joseph O'Malley (ed.), Cambridge, Cambridge University Press, 1970, p. 131. Compare the argument in Karl Korsch, *Marxism and Philosophy*, 1923, tr. Fred Halliday, London, New Left Books, 1970.

46 See, for the example, *Grundrisse* (1857–8), tr. Martin Nicolaus, Harmondsworth, Penguin, 1973, p. 111.

47 *Phänomenologie*, 73, tr. sec. 79.

48 'A Contribution to the Critique of Hegel's "Philosophy of Right" ', Introduction, *Critique of Hegel's 'Philosophy of Right'*, p. 138.

SELECT BIBLIOGRAPHY

1 Texts and translations

Hegel

'*Der Geist des Christentums*' *Schriften 1796–1800*, hrsg. Werner Hamacher, Frankfurt a.M., Ullstein, 1978, tr. Early Theological Writings, T. M. Knox, Philadelphia, University of Pennsylvania Press, 1971.

System der Sittlichkeit, Hamburg, Felix Meiner, 1967, tr. *Hegel's System of Ethical Life and his First Philosophy of Spirit*, H. S. Harris and T. M. Knox, Albany, State University of New York Press, 1979.

Jenaer Systementwürfe I, Gesammelte Werke 6, Hamburg, Felix Meiner, 1975; tr., Part III, as above tr. included in Harris and Knox;

Jenaer Systementwürfe III, Gesammelte Werke 8, Hamburg, Felix Meiner, 1976.

Theorie Werkausgabe, Frankfurt a.M., Suhrkamp

1 *Frühe Schriften*

'Über die neuesten inneren Verhältnisse Württembergs', tr. 'On the recent domestic affairs of Wurtemberg', T. M. Knox, *Hegel's Political Writings*, Oxford, Oxford University Press, 1964.

'Verfassung Deutschlands', tr. 'The German Constitution', ibid.

2 *Jenaer Schriften 1801–1807*

'Differenz des Fichteschen und Schellingschen System der Philosophie', (*Differenzschrift*), tr. *The Difference between Ficht's and Schelling's System of Philosophy*, H. S. Harris and Walter Cerf, Albany, State University of New York Press, 1977.

'Glauben und Wissen oder Reflexionsphilosophie der Subjektivität in der Vollständigkeit ihrer Formen als Kantische, Jacobische und Fichtesche Philosophie', tr. *Faith and Knowledge*, H. S. Harris and Walter Cerf, Albany, State University of New York Press, 1977.

'Über die wissenschaftlichen Behandlungsarten des Naturrechts, seine Stelle in der praktischen Philosophie und sein Verhältnis zu den Rechtswissenschaften', tr. *Natural Law. The Scientific Ways of Treating Natural Law, Its Place in Moral Philosophy, and Its Relation to the Positive Sciences of Law*, T. M. Knox, Philadelphia, University of Pennsylvania Press, 1975.

3 *Phänomenolgie des Geistes*, tr. *Hegel's Phenomenology of Spirit*, tr. A. V. Miller, Oxford, Clarendon Press, 1977.

4 *Nürnberger und Heidelberger Schriften 1808–1817*

'Beurteilung der Verhandlungen in der Versammlung der Landstände des Königreichs Württemberg im Jahre 1815 und 1816', tr. 'Proceedings of the

Estates Assembly in the Kingdom of Würtemberg 1815–1816' in *Hegel's Political Writings*, see *Band* 1 above.

5 *Wissenschaft der Logik I.*

6 *Wissenschaft der Logik II*, tr. Hegel's *Science of Logic*, A. V. Miller, London, Allen & Unwin, 1969.

7 *Grundlinien der Philosophie des Rechts*, tr. *Hegel's Philosophy of Right*, T. M. Knox, Oxford, Oxford University Press, 1967.

8 *Enzyklopädie der philosophischen Wissenschaften I, Die Wissenschaft der Logik*, tr. *Hegel's Logic*, William Wallace, Oxford, Clarendon Press, 1975.

9 *Enzyklopädie der philosophischen Wissenschaften II, Die Naturphilosophie*, tr. *Hegel's Philosophy of Nature*, A. V. Miller, Oxford, Clarendon Press, 1970.

10 *Enzyklopädie der philosophischen Wissenschaften III, Die Philosophie des Geistes*, tr. *Hegel's Philosophy of Mind*, William Wallace, Oxford, Clarendon Press, 1971.

11 *Berliner Schriften 1818–1831*. 'Über die englische Reformbill', tr. 'The English Reform Bill' in *Hegel's Political Writings*, see *Band* 1 above.

12 *Vorlesungen über die Philosophie der Geschichte*, tr. *The Philosophy of History*, J. Sibree, New York, Dover, 1956.

13 *Vorlesungen über die Ästhetik I*
14 *Vorlesungen über die Ästhetik II*
15 *Vorlesungen über die Ästhetik III*
   Tr. *Hegel's Aesthetics, I & II*, T. M. Knox, Oxford, Clarendon Press, 1975.

16 *Vorlesungen über die Philosophie der Religion I*
17 *Vorlesungen über die Philosophie der Religion II*
   Tr. *Lectures on the Philosophy of Religion, I, II, III*, E. B. Speirs and J. Burdon Sanderson, London, Routledge, 1962.

18 *Vorlesungen über die Geschichte der Philosophie I*
19 *Vorlesungen über die Geschichte der Philosophie II*
20 *Vorlesungen über die Geschichte der Philosophie III*
   (Tr. not used because of its inaccuracy.)

Register

Vorlesungen über Rechtsphilosophie 1818–1831, Edition und Kommentar in sechs Bänden, hrsg. von Karl-Heinz Ilting, Stuttgart, Friedrich Frommann, 1973.

Kant

Theorie Werkausgabe, Frankfurt a.M., Suhrkamp
Band III & IV. Kritik der reinen Vernunft, tr. *Critique of Pure Reason*, Norman Kemp Smith, New York, St Martin's Press, 1965.
Band V. Prolegomena, tr. *Prolegomena*, Peter G. Lucas, Manchester, Manchester University Press, 1953.

Band VII. Kritik der praktischen Vernunft, tr. *Critique of Practical Reason*, Lewis White Beck, New York, Bobbs-Merrill, 1956.

Grundlegung zur Metaphysik der Sitten, tr. *Groundwork of the Metaphysic of Morals*, H. J. Paton, New York, Harper & Row, 1964.

Band VIII. Die Metaphysik der Sitten, tr. Pt I, *The Metaphysical Elements of Justice*, John Ladd, New York, Bobbs-Merrill, 1965; Pt II, *The Doctrine of Virtue*, M. J. Gregor, New York, Harper & Row, 1964.

Die Religion innerhalb der Grenzen der blossen Vernunft, tr. *Religion within the Bounds of Reason alone*, T. M. Greene and H. H. Hudson, Chicago, Open Court Publishing Company, 1934.

Band X. Kritik der Urteilskraft, tr. *Critique of Judgement*, J. M. Bernard, New York, Hafner, 1972.

Fichte

Fichtes Werke, hrsg. Immanuel Hermann Fichte, Walter de Gruyter, Berlin.

Band I. Grundlage der gesamten Wissenschaftslehre (1794, 1802). *Erste Einleitung in die Wissenschaftslehre* (1797). *Zweite Einleitung in die Wissenschaftslehre* (1797).

Tr. *Science of Knowledge with the First and Second Introductions*, Peter Heath and John Lucas, New York, Appleton-Century-Crofts, 1970.

Band II. Die Bestimmung des Menschen (1800), tr. *The Vocation of Man*, Roderick M. Chisholm (ed.), New York, Bobbs-Merrill, 1956.

Band III. Grundlage des Naturrechts (1796), tr. *The Science of Rights*, A. E. Kroeger, London, Routledge, 1970.

Band IV. Das System der Sittenlehre (1798).

Band V. Versuch einer Kritik aller Offenbarung (1792), tr. *Attempt at a Critique of all Revelation*, Garrett Green, Cambridge, Cambridge University Press, 1978.

Band VI. Beitrag zur Berichtigung der Urteile des Publicum über die französische Revolution (1793).

Others

Ludwig Feuerbach, *The Essence of Christianity*, 1841, tr. George Eliot, New York, Harper & Row, 1957.

Søren Kierkegaard, *The Concept of Irony*, 1841, tr. Lee M. Capel, Bloomington, Indiana University Press, 1965.

Karl Leonhard Reinhold, *Über das Fundament des Philosophischen Wissens* (1791); *Über die Moglichkeit der Philosophie als strenge Wissenschaft* (1790), Hamburg, Felix Meiner, 1978.

F. W. J. Schelling, *System des transcendentalen Idealismus*, tr. *System of transcendental Idealism*, Peter Heath, Charlottesville, University Press of Virginia, 1978.

2 Hegel: Secondary Works

Schlomo Avineri, *Hegel's Theory of the Modern State*, Cambridge, Cambridge University Press, 1972.

Ernst Bloch, *Subjekt-Objekt Erläuterungen zu Hegel*, 1951, Frankfurt a.M., Suhrkamp, 1962.

William J. Brazill, *The Young Hegelians*, New Haven, Yale University Press, 1970.

Lucio Colletti, *Marxism and Hegel*, tr. Lawrence Garner, London, Verso, 1973.

Benedetto Croce, *What is Living and What is Dead in the Philosophy of Hegel?*, 1912, tr. Douglas Ainslie, New York, Russell & Russell, 1969.

Wilhelm Dilthey, *Die Jugendgeschichte Hegels und anderer Abhandlungen zur Geschichte des deutschen Idealismus*, *Gesammelte Schriften*, IV, Stuttgart, B. G. Teuchner, 1959.

Agnes Dürr, *Zum Problem der Hegelschen Dialektik und ihrer Formen*, Berlin, Verlag für Staatswissenschaften und Geschichte, 1938.

Lothar Eley, *Hegels Wissenschaft der Logik. Leitfaden und Kommentar*, Munich, Wilhelm Fink, 1976.

E. L. Fackenheim, *The Religious Dimension in Hegel's Thought*, Bloomington, Indiana University Press, 1967.

Iring Fetscher, *Hegels Lehre von Menschen*, Stuttgart, Frommann, 1970.

Hans Friedrich Fulda, *Das Problem einer Einleitung in Hegels Wissenschaft der Logik*, Frankfurt a.M., Klostermann, 1965.

—, *Das Recht der Philosophie in Hegels Philosophie des Rechts*, Frankfurt a.M., Klostermann, 1968.

Hans Friedrich Fulda, Dieter Henrich (eds), *Materialien zu Hegels 'Phänomenologie des Geistes'*, Frankfurt a.M., Suhrkamp, 1973.

Hans-Georg Gadamer, *Hegels Dialektik Funf hermeneutische Studien*, Tübingen, J. C. B. Mohr, 1971, tr. *Hegel's Dialectic, Five Hermeneutical Studies*, P. Christopher Smith, New Haven, Yale University Press, 1976.

H. S. Harris, *Hegel's Development Toward the Sunlight 1770-1801*, Oxford, Clarendon Press, 1972.

Nicolai Hartmann, *Die Philosophie des deutschen Idealismus*, 1923, 1929, Berlin, Walter de Gruyter, 1960.

Dieter Henrich, *Hegel im Kontext*, Frankfurt a.M., Suhrkamp, 1967.

Sidney Hook, *From Hegel to Marx. Studies in the Intellectual Development of Karl Marx*, 1936, Ann Arbor, University of Michigan Press, 1976.

Jean Hyppolite, *Structure et Genèse de la Phénoménologie de L'Esprit*, Paris, Aubier, 1947.

—, *Studies on Marx and Hegel*, tr. John O'Neill, London, Heinemann, 1969.

Hans Robert Jauss (ed.), *Die nicht-mehr schönen Künste, Poetik und Hermeneutik, 2*, Munich, Wilhelm Fink, 1968.

Walter Kaufmann (ed.), *Hegel's Political Philosophy*, New York, Atherton Press, 1970.

George Armstron Kelly, *Idealism, Politics and History*, Cambridge, Cambridge University Press, 1969.

—, *Hegel's Retreat from Eleusis Studies in Political Thought*, Princeton, Princeton University Press, 1978.

Alexandre Kojève, *Introduction to the Reading of Hegel Lectures on the Phenomenology of Spirit*, 1933–9, tr. James H. Nichols Jr, New York, Basic Books, 1969.

Richard Kroner, *Von Kant bis Hegel*, 1921, 1924, Tübingen, J. C. B. Mohr, 1961.

Henri Lefebvre, *Logique formelle logique dialectique*, 1947, Paris, Editions Anthropos, 1969.

V. I. Lenin, *Konspekt zu Hegels 'Wissenschaft der Logik'*, 1914, *Werke*, 38.

Karl Löwith, *From Hegel to Nietzsche, The Revolution in Nineteenth-Century Thought*, 1941, tr. David E. Green, New York, Anchor, 1967.

Karl Löwith (ed.), *Die Hegelsche Linke*, Stuttgart, Fromann-Holzboog, 1962.

Hermann Lübbe (ed.), *Die Hegelsche Rechte*, Stuttgart, Fromann-Holzboog, 1962.

Georg Lukács, *The Young Hegel Studies in the Relations between Dialectics and Economics*, 1948, tr. Rodney Livingstone, London, Merlin, 1975.

Alasdair MacIntyre (ed.), *Hegel. A Collection of Critical Essays*, New York, Anchor, 1972.

Herbert Marcuse, *Hegels Ontologie und die Theorie der Geschichtlichkeit*, 1932, Frankfurt a.M., Klostermann, 1975.

—, *Reason and Revolution. Hegel and the Rise of Social Theory*, 1941, London, Routledge, 1969.

Werner Marx, *Hegel's Phenomenology of Spirit. A Commentary on the Preface and Introduction*, tr. Peter Heath, New York, Harper & Row, 1975.

Willy Moog, *Hegel und die Hegelische Schule*, Munich, E. Reinhardt, 1930.

G. R. G. Mure, *A Study of Hegel's Logic*, Oxford, Clarendon Press, 1950.

Oskar Negt (ed.), *Aktualität und Folgen der Philosophie Hegels*, Frankfurt a.M., Suhrkamp, 1971.

Richard Norman, *Hegel's Phenomenology. A Philosophical Introduction*, Brighton, Harvester, 1976.

Z. A. Pelczynski (ed.), *Hegel's Political Philosophy: problems and perspectives*, Cambridge, Cambridge University Press, 1971.

Raymond Plant, *Hegel*, London, Allen & Unwin, 1973.

Otto Pöggeler, *Hegel's Kritik der Romantik*, Bonn, Rheinische Friedrich-Wilhelms-Universität, 1956.

Manfred Riedel, *Studien zu Hegels Rechtsphilosophie*, Frankfurt a.M., Suhrkamp, 1969.

Joachim Ritter, *Hegel und die französische Revolution*, Frankfurt a.M., Suhrkamp, 1965.

—, *Bürgerliche Gesellschaft und Staat bei Hegel*, Neuwied, Luchterhand, 1970.

—, *System und Geschichte Studien zum historischen Standort von Hegels Philosophie*, Frankfurt a.M., Suhrkamp, 1973.

—, *Materialien zu Hegels Rechtsphilosophie*, Frankfurt a.M., Suhrkamp, 1975.

Günter Rohrmoser, *Subjektivität und Verdinglichung. Theologie und Gesellschaft im Denken des jungen Hegels*, Güterslohe, Gerd Mohn, 1961.

Stanley Rosen, *G. W. F. Hegel: An Introduction to the Science of Wisdom*, New Haven, Yale University Press, 1974.

Wilhelm Seeberger, *Hegel oder die Entwicklung des Geistes zur Freiheit*, Stuttgart, Klett, 1961.

Judith N. Shklar, *Freedom and Independence. A Study of the political ideas of Hegel's Phenomenology of Mind*, Cambridge, Cambridge University Press, 1976.

Ivan Soll, *An Introduction to Hegel's Metaphysics*, Chicago, Chicago University Press, 1969.

W. T. Stace, *The Philosophy of Hegel*, 1924, New York, Dover, 1955.

Peter Szondi, *Poetik und Geschichtsphilosophie*, I, *Antike und Moderne in der Ästhetik der Goethezeit. Hegels Lehre von der Dichtung*, Frankfurt a.M., Suhrkamp, 1974.

Charles Taylor, *Hegel*, Cambridge, Cambridge University Press, 1975.

—, *Hegel and Modern Society*, Cambridge, Cambridge University Press, 1979.

M. Theunissen, *Hegels Lehre von Absoluten Geist als theologisch-politischer Traktat*, Berlin, Walter de Gruyter, 1970.

—, 'Die Verwirklichung der Vernunft. Zur Theorie–Praxis–Diskussion im Anschluss an Hegel', *Philosophische Rundschau*, Beiheft 6, 1970.

—, *Sein und Schein. Die Kritische Funktion der Hegelschen Logik*, Frankfurt a.M., Suhrkamp, 1980.

Ernst Topitsch, *Die Sozialphilosophie Hegels als Heilslehre und Herrschaftsideologie*, Neuwied, Luchterhand, 1967.

Jean Wahl, *La Logique de Hegel comme phénomenologie*, Paris, Documentation Universitaire, 1969.

W. H. Walsh, *Hegelian Ethics*, London, Macmillan, 1969.

Eric Weil, *Hegel et L'Etat Cinq Conférences*, Paris, Librairie Philosophique J. Vrin, 1970.

Franz Weidmann, *Hegel. An Illustrated Biography*, tr. Joachim Neugroschel, New York, Pegasus, 1968.

Burleigh Taylor Wilkins, *Hegel's Philosophy of History*, Ithaca, Cornell University Press, 1979.

3 Neo-Kantianism

Andrew Arato, 'The Neo-Idealist Defence of Subjectivity', *Telos*, 21 (Fall, 1974), 108–61.

Hermann Cohen, *System der Philosophie*, Pt 1, *Logik der reinen Erkenntnis*, Berlin, Bruno Cassirer, 1902.

Wilhelm Dilthey, *Der Aufbau der geschichtlichen Welt in den Geisteswissenschaften*, 1910, Frankfurt a.M., Suhrkamp, 1970.

Hans-Georg Gadamer, *Truth and Method*, 1960, tr. edited by Garrett Barden and John Cumming, London, Sheed and Ward, 1975.

—, 'Hermeneutics and Social Science', *Cultural Hermeneutics* IV (1975), 307–16.

Martin Heidegger, *Being and Time*, 1927, tr. John Macquerrie and Edward Robinson, Oxford, Basil Blackwell, 1967.

Edmund Husserl, *Logical Investigations*, 1900, tr. 2 vols, J. N. Findlay, London, Routledge, 1970.

Peter Krausser, *Kritik der endlichen Vernunft Diltheys Revolution der allgemeinen Wissenschafts-und Handlungstheorie*, Frankfurt a.M., Suhrkamp, 1968.

Rudolf Hermann Lotze, *Mikrokosmos. Ideen zur Naturgeschichte und Geschichte der Menschheit*, 3 vols, 1856–64, Leipzig, E. Hirzel, 1896; tr. *Microcosmos. An Essay Concerning Man and his Relation to the World*, 2 vols, Elizabeth Hamilton and E. E. Constance Jones, Edinburgh, T. & T. Clark, 1894.

—, *System der Philosophie*, I, *Logik. Drei Bücher vom Denken, vom Untersuchen und vom Erkennen*, 1874; II, *Metaphysik*, 1879. *Logik*: 1928, Georg Misch (ed.), Leipzig, Felix Meiner.Tr. *Lotze's System of Philosophy*, Pt I, *Logic in Three Books of Thought, of Investigation and of Knowledge*, 2 vols, Pt II, *Metaphysic in Three Books, Ontology, Cosmology and Psychology*, Oxford, Clarendon Press, 1888, 2nd ed, trans. ed. Bernard Bosanquet.

Willy Moog, *Die deutsche Philosophie des 20. Jahrhunderts in ihren Hauptrichttngen und ihren Grundproblemen*, Stuttgart, Ferdinand Encke, 1922.

Paul Natorp, *Die Logischen Grundlagen der exakten Wissenschaften*, Leipzig, B. G. Teuchner, 1910.

Traugott Konstantin Oestereich, *Die deutsche Philosophie des XIX. Jahrhunderts und der Gegenwart, Friedrich Ueberwegs Grundriss der Geschichte der Philosophie*, IV, Berlin, E. S. Mittler, 1923.

Heinrich Rickert, *Der Gegenstand der Erkenntnis. Einführung in die Transzendentalphilosophie*, 1892, Tübingen, J. C. B. Mohr, 1928.

Alois Riehl, *Der philosophische Kritizismus und seine Bedeutungen für die positive Wissenschaft*, 2 vols, Leipzig, Wilhelm Engelman, 1876.

George Santayana, *Lotze's System of Philosophy*, 1889, Paul Grimley Kuntz (ed.), Bloomington, Indiana University Press, 1971.

Raymund Schmidt (ed.), *Die Philosophie der Gegenwart in Selbstdarstellungen*, 4 vols, Leipzig, Felix Meiner, 1922–3.

4 Sociology

Roy Bhaskar, *A Realist Theory of Science*, Brighton, Harvester, 1978.

Emile Durkheim and Marcel Mauss, *Primitive Classification*, 1903, tr. Rodney Needham, London, Routledge, 1970.

Emile Durkheim, *Sociology and Philosophy*, 1898–1911, Paris, Presses Universitaire de France, 1979, tr. David Pocock, New York, The Free Press, 1974.

—, *The Elementary Forms of the Religious Life*, 1912, Paris, Presses Universitaires de France, 1968, tr. Joseph Ward Swain, London, Allen & Unwin, 1908.

Anthony Giddens, *Central Problems in Social Theory. Action, Structure and Contradiction in Social Analysis*, London, Macmillan, 1979.

Paul Honigsheim, *On Max Weber*, tr. Joan Tytina, New York, The Free Press, 1968.

Steven Lukes, *Emile Durkheim: His Life and Work. A Historical and Critical Study*, London, Allen Lane, 1973.

Karl Mannheim, *Essays on Sociology and Social Psychology*, 1922–1940, London, Routledge, 1969.

—, *Ideology and Utopia*, 1929, London, Routledge, 1966.

Talcott Parsons, *The Structure of Social Action*, 2 vols, 1937, New York, The Free Press, 1968.

—, *The Social System*, London, Routledge, 1951.

Georg Simmel, *Die Probleme der Geschichtsphilosophie. Eine Erkenntristheoretische Studie*, Leipzig, Duncker & Humblot, 1892; tr. *The Problems of the Philosophy of History: an Epistemological essay*, 2nd edn, 1905, Guy Oakes, New York, The Free Press, 1977.

—, *Philosophie des Geldes*, 1900, Berlin, Duncker & Humblot, 1958, tr. *The Philosophy of Money*, Tom Bottomore and David Frisby, London, Routledge, 1978.

—, *Soziologie Untersuchungen über die Formen der Vergellschaftung*, Leipzig, Duncker & Humblot, 1908;

—, *Hauptprobleme der Philosophie*, 1910, Berlin, Walter de Gruyter, 1969;

—, *Lebensanschauung. Vier metaphysische Kapitel*, 1918, Munich and Leipzig, Duncker & Humblot, 1922.

—, *Brücke und Tür*, Michael Landmann (ed.), Stuttgart, K. F. Koehler, 1957;

—, *Conflict in Modern Culture and Other Essays*, tr. K. P. Elzkorn, New York, Teachers College, 1968;

—, *Georg Simmel 1858–1918: A Collection of Essays with Translations and a Bibliography*, K. H. Wolff (ed.), Columbus, Ohio University Press, 1959.

Alfred Schutz, *The Phenomenology of the Social World*, 1932, tr. George Walsch and Frederick Lehnert, Evanston, North Western University Press, 1967.

Leopold von Wiese, *Systematic Sociology on the Basis of the Beziehungslehre and Gebildelehre of Leopold von Wiese*, Howard Becker (ed.), New York, Wiley, 1932.

Marianne Weber, *Max Weber: A Biography*, 1926, tr. Harry Zohn, New York, Wiley, 1975.

Max Weber, *Gesammelte Aufsätze zur Wissenschaftslehre*, Tübingen, J. C. B.

Mohr, 1973, tr. *Max Weber: Methodology of the Social Sciences*, Edward A. Shils and Harry A. Finch, New York, The Free Press, 1949.

—, *Economy and Society*, 1921, tr. Guenther Roth and Claus Widdith (eds), Berkeley, California University Press, 1978.

Kurt H. Wolff (ed.), *Essays on Sociology and Philosophy by Emile Durkheim et al.*, New York, Harper & Row, 1964.

5 Marx and Marxism

Karl Marx, *Critique of Hegel's 'Philosophy of Right'*, 1843, tr. Annette Jolin and Joseph O'Malley, Cambridge, Cambridge University Press, 1970.

—, *Early Writings*, tr. Rodney Livingstone and Gregory Benton, *The Pelican Marx Library*, Harmondsworth, Penguin, 1975.

—, *Grundisse*, 1857–8, tr. Martin Nicolaus, *The Pelican Marx Library*, Harmondsworth, Penguin, 1973.

Theodor W. Adorno, *Minima Moralia*, Frankfurt a.M., Suhrkamp, 1951, tr. E. F. N. Jephcott, London, New Left Books, 1974.

—, *Negative Dialectics*, 1966, *Gesammelte Schriften*, Frankfurt a.M., Suhrkamp, 1973, tr. E. B. Ashton, London, Routledge, 1973.

—, Theodor W. Adorno (ed.), *Der Positivismusstreit in der deutschen Soziologie*, Neuwied, Luchterhand, 1969, tr. *The Positivist Dispute in German Sociology*, Glyn Adey and David Frisby, London, Heinemann, 1976.

Louis Althusser, *Reading Capital*, 1968, tr. Ben Brewster, London, New Left Books, 1970.

—, *Lenin and Philosophy and Other Essays*, 1968, tr. Ben Brewster, London, New Left Books, 1971.

—, *Politics and History, Montesquieu, Rousseau, Hegel and Marx*, 1959, tr. Ben Brewster, London, New Left Books, 1972.

Andrew Arato and Paul Breines, *The Young Lukács and the Origins of Western Marxism*, New York, Seabury, 1979.

Walter Benjamin, *The Origin of German Tragic Drama*, 1928, tr. John Osborne, London, New Left Books, 1977.

Jürgen Habermas, *Knowledge and Human Interests*, 1968, tr. Jeremy J. Shapiro, London, Heinemann, 1972.

—, *Theory and Practice*, 1968, tr. John Viertal, London, Heinemann, 1974.

—, *Philosophische-politische Profile*, Frankfurt a.M., Suhrkamp, 1971.

Jürgen Habermas, Niklas Luhmann, *Theorie der Gesellschaft oder Sozialtechnologie. Was leistet die Systemforschung?*, Frankfurt a.M., Suhrkamp, 1971.

Garbis Kortian, *Metacritique. The Philosophical Argument of Jürgen Habermas*, tr. John Raffan, Cambridge, Cambridge University Press, 1980.

Georg Lukács, *Frühe Schriften zur Ästhetik*, 1912–1916, *Georg Lukács Werke*, vols 16 and 17, Darmstadt, Luchterhand, 1979.

—, 'Emil Lask', *Kantstudien*, XII (1913), 349–70.

—, 'The Old Culture and the New Culture', 1920, *Telos* 5 (Spring 1970).

—, *History and Class Consciousness*, 1923, *Georg Lukács Werke*, 2, tr. Rodney Livinstone, London, Merlin, 1971.

Gillian Rose, *The Melancholy Science: An Introduction to the Thought of Theodor W. Adorno*, London, Macmillan, 1978.

INDEX

Adorno, T.W., 27, 29, 31–3, 36
Aeschylus, 132
  Oresteia, 134
Althusser, Louis, 37–9, 41
Archiv für Sozialwissenschaft, 18

Baden School,
  see Heidelberg School
Benjamin, Walter, 22, 29
Bloch, Ernst, 29
Bolzano, Bernard, 5
Boutroux, Emile, 14
Bosanquet, Bernard, 6
Brunschwig, Leon, 14

Chronos, 132
Cohen, Hermann, 2, 10–11, 13, 14,
  17, 37

Darwin, Charles, 35
Dilthey, Wilhelm, 22, 23, 40, 41
Durkheim, Emile, 1, 13, 14–18, 20,
  21, 22, 24, 39, 212, 213

empiricism, 37
Enlightenment, 172–4
Euripedes, 125

Feuerbach, Ludwig, 111, 215, 216
Fichte, J. G., 5, 30, 31, 32, 35, 36, 42,
  212, 214, 215, 218
  Hegel's critique of, 51, 62, 63, 68,
    70, 78, 79, 82, 83, 106, 112, 127,
    145, 150–2, 154, 160, 162, 180,
    181, 182, 185, 186, 198, 199, 201–
    3, 204–6, 210, 211

on natural law, 52–8, 60
  Vocation of Man, 95–105, 111, 163
  Wissenschaftslehre, 149, 192–5
  see neo-Fichtean
Frankfurt School, 1, 36
French Revolution, 172–4, 219

Gadamer, Hans-Georg, 22, 23
Goethe, J.W., 125
Green, T. H., 6

Habermas, Jürgen, 24, 33–6, 41, 50
Hamelin, Octave, 14
Hegel, G. W. F., 1, 5, 6, 19, 24, 27, 29,
  32, 33, 34, 35, 36, 37, 40, 41, 42, 44,
  48, 209–11
  Aesthetics, 120, 121–48 passim
  Differenzchrift, 95, 188, 201–3
  Early Theological Writings, 116,
    155–7
  Faith and Knowledge, 95–105, 185
  Jena lectures, 71–2, 127
    1803–4, 74–5; 1805–6, 75–8
  early Jena writings, 51
  Logic, 45, 47, 79, 95, 185–201 passim,
    204–8
  and Marx, 214–20
  Essay on natural law, 51–9, 72, 188
  Phenomenology of Spirit, 45–6, 50,
    72, 82, 83, 86, 117, 120, 122–3,
    125, 129, 149–84 passim, 185, 188,
    200, 203, 215
  The Philosophy of History, 49, 106,
    112–18, 135, 137–8, 164–7
  The Philosophy of Religion, 92–4,
    105–12, 118–20

The Philosophy of Right, 50, 51, 79–91 *passim*, 152, 185
System der Sittlichkeit, 59–72, 83, 86, 99, 127, 159, 167, 185, 208, 215
see speculative proposition
Hegelian, 28
Right-wing, 184, 211
Left-wing, 184, 211
Heidelberg School, 2, 6, 9, 11, 12, 25, 211–12
Heidegger, Martin, 22, 23
Hölderlin, Friedrich, 5
Homer, 125, 128
Odysseus, 128
Agamemnon, 128
Horkheimer, Max, 29
Husserl, Edmund, 23

immanent principle, 3

Jacobi, F. H., 5

Kant, Immanuel, 2, 5, 6, 7, 8, 9, 10, 11, 13, 14, 15, 17, 19, 20, 22, 24, 26, 30, 31, 34, 35, 36, 37, 42, 44, 46, 48, 215
Critique of Judgement, 5, 27, 101
Critique of Pure Reason, 2, 5, 10, 16, 25, 32
Hegel's critique of, 51, 62, 63, 68, 70, 78, 83, 106, 127, 150–2, 154, 160, 185, 186, 192, 196, 198, 199, 203, 204, 210, 211
Metaphysic of Morals, 84
on natural law, 52–8, 60
Prolegomena, 2, 187–91
on religion, 95–105
Kojève, Alexandre, 37

Lask, Emil, 27, 28
Leibniz, 5, 8
Leibmann, Otto, 2

logic, 8, 9, 10, 11, 17, 21–2, 32
of validity (*Geltungslogik*), 9, 13, 27, 28–9, 36, 37, 211, 212
Lotze, Rudolf Hermann, 5, 7, 8, 9, 10, 11, 12, 25, 34
Logic, 6, 8
Microcosmos, 8
validity and values, 6, 9, 13, 14, 18, 21, 25, 28
Lukács, Georg, 27–31, 32, 36, 211, 218

Mainon, S., 5
Mann, Thomas, 147
Mannheim, Karl, 22, 23, 40, 41
Marburg School, 2, 6, 9, 10, 11, 12, 13, 23, 25, 37, 211
Marx, 1, 19, 27, 28, 29, 31, 32, 33, 34, 35, 36, 37, 39, 41, 49, 83, 91, 209, 210, 214–20 *passim*
Marxism, 1, 25, 32, 40, 184, 212, 218–19
Hegelian, 27
neo-Kantian, 27
sociological, 36, 39, 42
metacritique, 14, 22, 24, 34, 35, 36, 38, 39, 40, 41, 212
see quasi-transcendental argument

Natorp, Paul, 10
neo-Fichtean, 24, 33, 36
see Fichte, J. G.
neo-Friesianism, 2
neo-Kantianism, 2, 6, 13, 14, 17, 20, 22, 23, 24, 25, 27, 29, 31–2, 33, 34, 35, 36, 37, 39, 40, 211–12
neo-Kantian paradigm, 1, 6, 8, 21, 36
neo-Kantians, 2, 5
Nelson, Leonard, 1
Nietzsche, Friedrich, 33, 37

Parsons, Talcott, 22
phenomenology, 1, 32, 41
Plato, 5, 7, 10, 25, 80
Popper, Karl, 32
positivism, 32–3, 34
Prometheus, 132

quasi-transcendental argument, 14,
    24, 34–5, 38, 41
    see metacritique

Reformation, 172–4
Reinhold, K. L., 5, 55
Renouvier, Charles, 14
Revue de métaphysique et de morale, 14
Rickert, Heinrich, 2, 11–13, 14, 17, 18,
    20, 23, 24
Riehl, Alois, 2
Romantics, 5, 209
    romantic irony, 145
Royce, Josiah, 6

Santayana, George, 6
Sartre, Jean-Paul, 37
Schelling, F. W. J., 5, 60, 63, 70
Schlegel, Friedrich, 145
Schutz, Alfred, 24
Simmel, Georg, 22, 24–7, 28, 29, 40–1
sociology, 1, 5, 6, 14, 21–2, 38, 211–14
Socrates, 125
Sophocles, 132
    Antigone, 134, 180–1, 184, 200

South-West German School
    see Heidelberg School
speculative experience, 1, 49, 81–2,
    121
speculative proposition, 48–9, 93–5,
    112

transcendent, 3, 12
transcendental, 1, 2, 3, 4, 8, 9, 16, 22,
    24, 34

validity, (Gültigkeit),
    logical, 4, 5
    objective, 2, 3, 4, 6, 15, 17
    subjective, 17, 34
    validity (Geltung), 6, 7, 8, 9, 10, 11,
        13, 18–21, 22, 24, 25, 26, 27, 31, 34,
        38, 212
    see Lotze, R. H.
value(s), 7, 8, 9, 11, 13, 17, 18–21, 24,
    26
Volkelt, Johannes, 2
von Wiese, Leopold, 22

Weber, Max, 1, 13, 14, 18–21, 23, 24,
    29, 212, 213–14
Windelband, Wilhelm, 2, 11
Wundt, Wilhelm, 5

Zeus, 132